Indelible Ink

22 PROMINENT CHRISTIAN LEADERS DISCUSS THE BOOKS
THAT SHAPE THEIR FAITH

Scott Larsen, GENERAL EDITOR

WATERBROOK
PRESS

INDELIBLE INK
PUBLISHED BY WATERBROOK PRESS
2375 Telstar Drive, Suite 160
Colorado Springs, Colorado 80920
A division of Random House, Inc.

All Scripture quotations, unless otherwise indicated, are taken from the *Holy Bible, New International Version®*. NIV®. Copyright © 1973, 1978, 1984 by International Bible Society. Used by permission of Zondervan Publishing House. All rights reserved. Scripture quotations marked (ESV) are taken from *The Holy Bible, English Standard Version*, copyright © 2001 by Crossway Bibles, a division of Good News Publishers. Used by permission. All rights reserved. Scripture quotations marked (KJV) are taken from the *King James Version*. Scripture quotations marked (NASB) are taken from the *New American Standard Bible®* (NASB). © Copyright The Lockman Foundation 1960, 1962, 1963, 1968, 1971, 1972, 1973, 1975, 1977, 1995. Used by permission. (www.Lockman.org). Scripture quotations marked (PHILLIPS) are taken from *The New Testament in Modern English* © 1972 by J. B. Phillips.

Italics in Scripture quotations reflect the authors' added emphasis.

Other permissions and acknowledgments appear on pages 319–321.

ISBN 1-57856-554-5

WATERBROOK and its deer design logo are registered trademarks of WaterBrook Press, a division of Random House, Inc.

Library of Congress Cataloging-in-Publication Data
    Indelible Ink : twenty-two prominent Christian leaders discuss the books that shape their faith / Scott Larsen, general editor ; with a foreword by Philip Yancey.—1st ed.
        p. cm.
    ISBN 1-57856-554-5
    1. Christian biography. 2. Christians—Books and reading. I. Larsen, Scott, 1974–
BR1702 .I53 2003
230—dc21   2002156135

Printed in the United States of America
2003—First Edition

10 9 8 7 6 5 4 3 2 1

To my wife, Mary,
whose influence on me has been deep and profound,
and with whom I am falling more deeply in love
as our own story is written.

CONTENTS

ACKNOWLEDGMENTS

The underlying truth that serves as the foundation for every word in this book is that books exercise an incredible influence over us—they play a significant role in the process of our continual, lifelong creation. In a similar fashion, the final shape of a book is created and molded by people. Hundreds of people played a part in the making of this book—more than I could thank individually. There are some, however, whose guidance, wisdom, and aid cannot go unrecognized.

This book would not be a reality had it not been for the encouragement of the editorial team at WaterBrook Press. In the initial stages, Erin Healy helped me work through the editing process. Ron Lee picked up where Erin left off and guided me through to the final product. Both of their work was invaluable.

A warm and personal thank you goes to each of the 22 authors who agreed to write essays for this project. It has been a pleasure and an honor to work with each one. In many cases, much work was facilitated by those who surround these authors: Lois Avoian, Dave Bellis, Nancy Bevers, Jim Black, Rhea Briscoe, Mary Anne Bunker, Danielle DuRant, Barbara Emerson, Claudia Ingram, Alberta Miller, Jamie Puckett, John and Prisca Sandri, David Sanford, Kathy Sutherland, Jim Tonkowich, Corey Widmer. In the same breath it must be said how much I value the shorter capsules offered by 136 additional contributors in the first appendix.

Dave Veerman, Robert Wolgemuth, and Harold Smith showed me the ropes when I was trying to recruit the most highly sought after Christian spokespeople for this project. All of these men work with many of the leading authors, and they have humbly shared their professional wisdom with me.

My pastor, Kent Hughes, and I spent more than one conversation dreaming about what this book could be, and how to best go about it. I deeply value his wisdom, guidance, and friendship.

Niel Nielson and Gray Roberson both were gracious enough to read some of my editorial thoughts and provide me with rich feedback.

My family, friends, and coworkers have all been more than supportive. Your patience, encouragement, and love have been felt and appreciated.

I would be remiss not to thank my wife, Mary, for her role in this project. Her endurance throughout the past few years is greater than she would admit and is a testimony of the deep wellsprings of her selfless love.

FOREWORD

Richard Wright, the author of *Native Son,* could not check out books from the Memphis library during his youth because of his race. He got around this problem by persuading a cooperative white man to lend him his library card, then forging a note to present to the librarian: "Dear Madam: Will you please let this nigger boy have some books by H. L. Mencken?" Thus began the intellectual liberation of one African American man in the apartheid South.

Growing up a little later as a white person in a South still segregated, I experienced a very different form of intellectual liberation. I have written of my racist, fundamentalist heritage so often that I dare not repeat myself here. Like Richard Wright, though coming from an opposite direction, I discovered in books a window to a new world outside. They directed my journey, first away from cloistered fundamentalism and then, most surprisingly, back toward a faith based on love and grace, not on anger and law. "A book must be the axe for the frozen sea inside us," said Franz Kafka.[1] Books have been chipping away at frozen seas all my life.

When Scott Larsen approached me about contributing to this book, I told him I was currently working on a book that named not two or three favorite authors, but thirteen. That book became *Soul Survivor: How My Faith Survived the Church.*[2] (One minister wrote that he was tired of hearing me complain about the church and felt like writing a book, *How My Church Survived Your Faith.*) I found it invigorating to review the people whose writings have most influenced my own faith.

Reading similar accounts in the pages of this book, I envision a giant web crisscrossing the centuries, conveying something of God's truth to those with eyes to see. Strands of the web intersect. You'll see C. S. Lewis's name crop up in these pages more than any other, and with good reason. By focusing on "mere Christianity," the kernel of faith that transcends culture and denomination, he reminds us of the permanent things with a felicitous prose style that has never been duplicated.

To switch metaphors, I once heard a writer describe other writers as the earthworms of society. "We aerate the soil," she said. By tunneling through *humus,* the essentially human, writers let in air and light, at the same time creating spaces that readers can fill on their own. Books have a certain decorum about them, because the earthworms who have created the tunnel are not staring you in the face, intimidating you into agreeing with them. They have digested the dirt and moved on.

For years, whenever I attended a church or Christian meeting, I would put on defensive armor. I trusted Christian speakers about as much as most people trust the Jehovah's Witnesses who appear at the door. I knew their tricks all too well: their ability to play on emotions like stringed instruments, their backstage hypocrisy. Books, though, were another matter. I could read them at my own pace, letting my emotions respond in a more authentic, less manipulated way.

Books keep religious writers honest. You can't lock an auditorium door or browbeat your audience or go into a trance. You stick the naked word on a page and it speaks for itself. As a result, Liz Curtis Higgs gives *Mere Christianity* a one-page test, then reads another, and another, and before long she has read the entire book and begun a steady return to faith. Chuck Colson, in very different circumstances, picks up the same book and gets the uncanny feeling that Lewis has perfectly diagnosed his spiritual disease, pride.

I doubt seriously that C. S. Lewis, an Oxford don, had anyone resembling Liz Curtis Higgs or Chuck Colson in mind when he wrote the book. He was delivering radio addresses in order to bring hope and spiritual renewal to a Britain devastated by World War II. And I feel certain that Alexandre Dumas had no one like Michael Card in mind when he wrote *The Count of Monte Cristo.*[3] Writers, and I speak from humble experience here, have little inkling of who will respond to our books and what impact they will have.

It is a schizophrenic existence that we writers live. I spent last week holed up in the mountains of Colorado trying to get a new book under-way. I realized, at the end of the week, that the only person I had spoken to all week was the cashier with the ring in her nose who took my order at a nearby Starbucks. Yet I worked on, in hope that my words and thoughts will someday connect with people I have never met. Writers live paradoxical lives, spending much time alone in an attempt to connect to others.

On reflection, I consider the schizophrenia a kind of moral protection. I do not know how rock musicians and Christian celebrities handle the adulation and applause when they deliver a message onstage. How do they keep from believing they are as charming, or as holy, as people assume them to be? I find that writing about faith challenges me to put my words through a distilling process that my own life could never tolerate.

Søren Kierkegaard wrote in his journal that he sought, as an author, to strive for a purity he had never attained in life, in order that he might somehow relieve his guilty conscience and abate the debt he had accumulated before God by his miserable life.[4] W. H. Auden, in "Thanksgiving for a Habitat," was even more blunt, praying that his books would save him from hell.[5]

In pessimistic moments (usually after watching television), I wonder if Western civilization has moved into a new Dark Age in which we sit around all day in recliner chairs listening to rap music, watching game shows and *Survivor* reruns, and eating fast food. Perhaps the church will be called on again, as it was in the original Dark Ages, to preserve literature and learning.

According to *Publishers Weekly*, the best-selling books of the 1940s included books by Ernest Hemingway, John Steinbeck, William L. Shirer, Winston Churchill, Pearl S. Buck, Richard Wright, and W. Somerset Maugham. As late as the 1970s, these names made the best-sellers list: Ernest Hemingway, Graham Greene, John Updike, Aleksandr Solzhenitsyn, Chaim Potok, Saul Bellow, J. R. R. Tolkien, William Styron. In the 1990s, however, forty-one of the fifty best-selling books of the decade were written by these six authors: John Grisham, Stephen King, Danielle Steel, Michael Crichton, Tom Clancy, and Mary Higgins Clark.[6]

We can either cluck our tongues and shake our heads at such a trend or make a determined effort to counteract it. I can think of no better way to start than by reading this book and then moving on to encounter the life-changing books profiled here.

As I peruse the writers honored in these pages, I see men and women who have earned our trust and deserve our attention. Some, like Hudson Taylor, lived through great adventures. Others, like C. S. Lewis and his Oxford colleague J. R. R. Tolkien, rarely traveled and had most of their adventures in lively conversations at a local pub. Some found wild success: Tolkien's *The Lord of the Rings* has sold more than fifty million copies worldwide and was named by *London Times* readers as the best novel of the twentieth century. Some labored in obscurity: No volume of Kierkegaard's sold more than six hundred copies during his lifetime.

I recognize friends in these pages, people who have influenced my own journey. Or I make a mental note to order a book I don't know from my favorite Internet out-of-print-books site. You will find a menagerie of books in these pages, from illustrated children's books to dense theological tomes. In some cases, you will learn as much about the reader of these books as about the books themselves.

"Reading ought to be an act of homage to the God of all truth," wrote Thomas Merton. "We open our hearts to words that reflect the reality He has created or the greater Reality which He is. It is also an act of humility and reverence towards other men [and women] who are the instruments by which God communicated His truth to us."[7]

—PHILIP YANCEY

INTRODUCTION

The kind of food our minds devour will determine the kind of
person we become.

—JOHN R. W. STOTT, *Your Mind Matters*

On any given day, that which we give our focus and energy to invariably
plays an increasingly significant role in our personal and spiritual development. It grows in significance as individual actions and decisions lead to
patterns, which then progress into comfortable habits. One drop of red
paint in a bucket of white will make no perceptible difference; one drop
every day for fifty years will result in a bucket of red paint. We may not
realize the impact of our daily decisions until our bucket of paint has
already turned red, which only underscores the importance of every decision we make. As I once heard a professor teach concerning the matter of
spiritual development, it does not matter where you start, but where you
are now and where you end up. We fix our focus and make decisions to the
benefit—or to the detriment—of our spiritual development.[1]

Consider your own life and all of its various components—family,
friends, church, job, school, clubs, sports, your neighborhood, cultural influences, political slants, media, entertainment, and reading material, just to
name a few. Though some play larger roles than others, it is difficult to
escape the ways in which these influences shape us, for better or for worse.
And we aren't simply passive receptors; our free will remains central throughout the process.

F. W. Boreham said that once we make our decisions, our decisions
turn around and make us.[2] We can sometimes choose the influences that
will affect us more deeply, though not always. Some, such as the larger cultural sphere, imbue every aspect of life, despite all attempts to shelter ourselves from them. Neither do we choose the family into which we are born.

But our friends, our choice of job, and our reading material are areas where we practice autonomy. It is on the realm of reading that this book aims its focus, and is where we must consider Boreham's axiom. In this area we make decisions, and then our decisions, our choices, make us.

Books shape us, dynamically molding our minds and souls. You are never the same person when you finish a book—even one that is read purely for escape or entertainment. A conviction may take root or deepen, the imagination may be sparked, a new perspective may dawn. A. W. Tozer has aptly stated that "the things you read will fashion you by slowly conditioning your mind."[3]

The decisions we make about what we read are vital. Romans 12:2 instructs us to be transformed by the renewing of our minds.[4] As human beings, we are in a constant state of becoming; at no time are we static or stagnant in our growth. As Christians who are called to continuously chew on the wonders of God, our reading diet is nothing to take lightly. T. S. Eliot, with his writer's perspective, clearly understood the weight of this.

> The author of a work of imagination is trying to affect us wholly, as human beings, whether he knows it or not; and we are affected by it, as human beings, whether we intend to be or not. I suppose that everything we eat has some other effect upon us than merely the pleasure of taste and mastication; it affects us during the process of assimilation and digestion; and I believe that exactly the same is true of anything we read.[5]

This does not mean that we can never read "lighter" material or that reading selections must come solely from the religious or theological shelves. Much else is worth reading. What it means is that *what we read matters* and directly affects who we become. We are fortunate with the wealth of books at our fingertips. Our lives can be changed by the words of contemporary authors just as they can be transformed—maybe even more so—by the wisdom set down in print by believers from past eras.

Philip Yancey has said that "across time and generations books carry the thoughts and feelings, the essence, of the human spirit."[6] We share a commonality with those who have gone before us. The common voice of the church echoes through the years, declaring each age relevant to the others. The pouring out of a heart in devotion to God, the precisely systematized and articulated theology of God and the church, the novel that cuts to the very nature of our humanness and captures some glorious truth and shapes it into story, the poet who brilliantly observes the created order and composes lines that flood the heart, the telling of a saint's life well lived—these are capable of drawing us deeper in and higher up. These are means of personal transformation. Writers of old share with us our humanity and our foundation on Christ and the Scriptures. But how often do we sit at their feet and find ourselves absorbed in their stories and teaching?

We ignore the written works of the fathers and mothers of the church to our own spiritual impoverishment. We cannot limit ourselves to reading only contemporary writers, as great as some are, and truly plumb the depths of our Christian heritage. Contemporary writers understand this and often quote from older writings, including the wisdom of largely forgotten writers who span the gap of time to feed our souls. Unfortunately, these are the books that long ago lost their place on the shelves of most bookstores, the authors and saints and thinkers who aren't known to the average Christian today.

In every generation God raises up certain individuals to guide the believers in their own era. The contemporary authors contributing to this volume are many of these people for our own generation. Their books and insights have greatly shaped today's church, and they often point us to those from previous generations who have pondered the glory and richness of God along with the life well lived in the light of His love.

Leaders from earlier generations have likewise put their thoughts to paper, though only a select few of their works have survived the ebb and flow of popular interest. Michele Rapkin, former editor in chief of Crossings Book Club, has identified this trend: "There are good books that really get you, and they can still be found. But it's getting a lot harder."[7] One of my desires for this book is not just to bring to light older titles that have lost a place on the shelves of the average Christian bookstore, but to uncover those books that Ms. Rapkin is referring to—books that "really get you," whether old or new.[8]

The question posed to each author who contributed to this volume was this: Which books (limiting it to three, if possible), other than the Bible, have most influenced your life? No further parameters were given, even that the book or books had to reflect a Christian worldview. I wanted only for these authors to provide a glimpse of the books that have left "indelible ink" on their souls—the works that have most greatly shaped their faith, and their lives in general. As a supplement to the 22 authors who go into greater detail and length, the first appendix comprises 136 other Christian leaders who share more briefly about the books that have shaped them. Within this list are hundreds of outstanding titles to consider for further reading. In a sense, the spiritual transparency these men and women reveal is a legacy entrusted to us—a legacy of experience and time-tested wisdom.

These leaders of the church, through their unique gifts and through the guiding hand and wisdom of God, have made a marked difference in the lives of contemporary believers through their own books, which collectively number in excess of 710 volumes! They understand how instrumental the written word can be. Heed their words. The books they write about have the power to change you. They can make you wiser, better prepared for the life of faith, and hungrier for more.

Allow these testimonies to guide you as you navigate your way through the bookshelves. You may discover a few books that end up altering the trajectory of your life, though every book you read will contribute a subtle transformation, a drop or two of paint in the bucket. Considering this, the question becomes clear: *Which books will you choose?*

—SCOTT LARSEN

Understanding God's Sovereignty

Joni Eareckson Tada

History in all its details, even the most minute, is but the unfolding of the eternal purposes of God. His decrees are not successively formed as the emergency arises, but are all parts of one all-comprehending plan, and we should never think of Him suddenly evolving a plan or doing something which He had not thought of before.

—LORAINE BOETTNER, *The Reformed Doctrine of Predestination*

In the summer of 1967 I found myself trapped inside a numb, useless body. Me, the teenager who just days earlier had saddled my horse for a ride in the morning, showered, then changed for tennis in the afternoon, had no idea the horror that lurked around the corner. It began as a casual trip to the beach on Chesapeake Bay. A stretch and a yawn at the shoreline, a snapping of the shoulder straps on my swimsuit, a shielding of my eyes and spotting an inviting raft rocking on gentle swells just offshore. I swam out and hoisted myself up onto the raft. It was a simple, thoughtless dive, but it changed my life forever. My head crunched against a sandy bottom, twisting my neck and severing my spinal column. And less than forty-eight hours later, I was lying on a Stryker frame hooked up to tubes and machines in an intensive care unit.

A thousand thoughts swirled through my mind. *God, why didn't You prevent my dive? You're in charge of water currents, tides, and shifting sand-bars. You could have distracted me…kept me on the beach…or at least put the idea in my head to swim in a safer area. Where were You? If You're good and powerful, why weren't You good enough to send an angel to pull me away from that raft? Why weren't You powerful enough to stop it from happening?*

My idea of God was unraveling. He had always been the Corinthian column, the Roman pillar, the unshakeable, reliable God who loved me in a really neat and cool way. Didn't He promise not to withhold good from those who walk uprightly? Didn't He promise that angels would guard and protect me lest I dash my foot on a stone? Didn't He desire to give me the abundant Christian life with all its peace and joy?

It was the sovereignty of God that I was pummeling. All through my days in intensive care, I continued to rail against the idea of God's being in control. When my friends visited me, I would ask them to read all those underlined verses in my old high-school Bible. Romans 8:28, "And we know that in all things God works for the good of those who love him, who have been called according to his purpose." *I remember that verse,* I fumed inside. *And—yeah—maybe it served me well as I sweated out twenty-five laps on a hockey field, but this is different. This is quadriplegia, total and permanent!* The sovereignty of God frightened me to my core.

Funny how it never unnerved me when I was a young Christian in high school. God's sovereignty was a Band-Aid. I had used it many times, applying it to a disappointing Friday night without a date or to a blowup with a sister over a borrowed blouse, carefully applying it to the situation as though I were pressing a bandage onto a skinned knee. I did that hundreds of times with all sorts of verses, flipping through the Bible to find something, anything that resonated or spoke to my latest experience. The

Bible was less a story about God and more like an *Encyclopedia Britannica,* the ultimate how-to manual. Just dip into a chapter, read a few verses, pick out the information that benefited me, and then close it up. If something went askew, then quickly flip to the information that promised to solve the problem. Grab Romans 8:28 and pour it like alcohol on a wound. There was no better dressing for a wound than Romans 8:28. Slammed with a D in physics? It'll all work out for good. Backstabbed by a friend's gossip? It's part of God's pattern.

Wasn't that the way one grew as a Christian? I was big on plugging principles into my life, especially before the accident. And in a world that had not yet spun out of control, the sovereignty of God had been a pleasant but remote doctrine. I kept it handy in case anything went haywire. It was a pretty mechanistic way to approach the Bible, but it worked. At least up until the accident.

Two long years passed. And when I was released from the hospital— still a quadriplegic—I continued to feel the prickling and needling of Romans 8:28 and Ephesians 1:11-12: "In him we were also chosen, having been predestined according to the plan of him who works out everything in conformity with the purpose of his will, in order that we, who were the first to hope in Christ, might be for the praise of his glory."

Predestined? My life encased in a numb and near-dead body? There it was again: God is sovereign. The idea that God could have prevented my accident, but didn't, hurt me deeply. The idea that He planned it appalled me. That He planned it for my good and His glory horrified me. Was He using some other dictionary than the human race uses?

At some point during those long months, during the peaceful afternoons of sitting in my wheelchair by the pasture that bordered our farmhouse, during a soft summer afternoon when the honeysuckle was sweet and fragrant, my anxious thoughts subsided like a late-evening breeze. *My life hasn't stopped. I'm still here, and yes, I'm in a wheelchair, but I'm…still.* "Be still, and know that I am God."[1] Well, Lord, I'm pretty good at the "still" part;

help me know who You are as my God, my Lord. I stopped asking *why* through clenched teeth and started asking *why* out of a searching heart.

I asked a friend to help me understand God's sovereignty. Just how and to what extent *is* He in control? My friend was an energetic student of the Bible, and so, together, we dug deep into the Scriptures. He avoided giving me second-source material that was light and easy to read. Rather, he steered me next to the window of our farmhouse living room and plopped onto the music stand in front of me weighty books like Berkhof's *Systematic Theology* and Calvin's *Institutes*. Holding a mouth stick between my teeth I would turn the pages, absorbing everything I could. *Institutes* was too heavy, but I sensed I needed to grasp what Calvin was saying, so my friend replaced it with Loraine Boettner's *The Reformed Doctrine of Predestination*.[2] It teetered on the edge of being too theological for my one-ounce pea brain, but after the first few chapters, I was hooked.

Somewhere in its pages I realized I was reading something man-sized. Rather, God-sized. Perhaps it expressed the unspoken desire of my soul: to encounter towering biblical doctrine like the Himalayan peaks that rise to the breathtaking height of Mount Everest. To apprehend a God who was much, much bigger than I ever imagined when I was on my feet. To delve into mysteries that were so enigmatic that they completely captured me. Somewhere into the fourth or fifth chapter of Boettner's no-holds-barred look at the goodness and the power of God, I realized that my suffering was the key to unlocking the hieroglyphics of God's foreordained will. I was about to embark on the adventure of my life.

The Reformed Doctrine of Predestination is purposely unlike most contemporary treatments of the sovereignty of God. It is arduous and often laborious reading. However, as I tackled each granite-hard sentence with my pickax of faith and deliberate curiosity, nuggets of gold began to reveal themselves.

And the light and dazzling truth of God's sovereignty began to dawn. Perhaps the most profound concept I unearthed was the specific nature of the sovereignty of God. Through a grand cross-reference of complex verses, Boettner helped me appreciate that our God doesn't say, "Into each life a little rain must fall," and then aim a hose in earth's general direction to see who gets the wettest. Rather, He screens the trials that come to each of us—allowing only those that accomplish His good plan because He takes no joy in human agony. Nothing happens by accident...not even tragedy...not even sins committed against us. God is in control, not in a general way, but in a very specific way.

Now I was getting down to the rub of my questions. *So, does this mean, Lord, that You* caused *this accident?* I mused as I flipped the pages of my Bible with my mouth stick, and then turned back to Boettner's book. I discovered that although God's decrees allow for suffering, He doesn't "do" it. He is the stowaway on Satan's bus, erecting invisible fences around Satan's fury and bringing ultimate good out of the devil's wickedness. Even in the book of Job, God exploited the deliberate evil of some very bad characters and the impersonal evil of some very bad storms *without smothering anyone or anything*—He forced no one's hand, bypassed no one's will, and, to our knowledge, suspended no natural laws.

These are deep waters: God decreeing but not necessarily doing? God exploiting but not smothering? How does He pull it off? Suddenly I realized I was part of the world of finite humans trying to comprehend an infinite God. What's clear is that God permits all sorts of things He doesn't approve of. He allows others to do what He would never do—He didn't steal Job's camels or entice Sabeans and Chaldeans to wreak havoc, yet He did not take His hand off the wheel for thirty seconds. This fact often does not sit well with people—as it once did not sit well for me when I was languishing in the hospital. But Boettner forced me to think of the alternative: Imagine a God who *didn't* deliberately permit the smallest details of my particular sorrow. What if my trials *weren't* screened by any divine plan? What if God insisted on a hands-off policy toward the tragedies swimming my way? Think what this would mean.

The world would be worse, much worse, absolutely intolerable…for everyone…every second. Try to conceive of Lucifer unrestrained. Left to his own, the devil would make Jobs of us all. The Third Reich would have lasted forever. Your head would be mounted on Satan's wall above his fireplace. The only reason things aren't worse than they are is that God curbs evil. "Satan has *asked* to sift you as wheat," Jesus told Peter—we can be certain the old snake didn't check in with God out of politeness.[3] He *had* to get permission, which means that he operates under constraints. Evil can raise its head only where God deliberately backs away—always for reasons that are specific, wise, and good, but often hidden from us during this present life.

I cannot begin to express the relief and release I felt as I plunged deeper into this marvelous truth that my diving accident was really no accident at all. Finally, long after I put down *The Reformed Doctrine of Predestination*, I yielded. I submitted. I exhaled a long, slow, satisfied breath and relaxed into the sovereign arms of God. If He loved me enough to die for me, then trusting Him with quadriplegia should be a cinch.

Nearly thirty-five years later—and after a couple of rereadings of Boettner's book—I come across countless numbers of people who, like me in that hospital so long ago, rail against the sovereignty of God. Maybe it's my paralysis that, like a magnet, draws out such statements. They break my heart. Such bravado, no matter how well meaning, is a hopeless mixture of truth and error. It's sad that we deny God's own words about Himself in our efforts to defend Him. He's the One who says without blushing, "Is it not from the mouth of the Most High that both calamities and good things come?" (Lamentations 3:38).

If God didn't control evil, then evil would come hurtling at us, completely uncontrolled (read that one again!). I, for one, am relieved that God clearly claims to run the world—not "could" run it if He wanted to, or "can" step in when He has to—but *does* run it, all the time. Even when it sins. Even when we suffer. He claims that not the slightest thing touches us without first receiving His nod. All for the working out of His mysterious and wonderfully strange plan.

But still, when it comes right down to it, is the bleeding worth the benefit?

More than we realize. The sovereignty of God pushed me to embrace its supernatural outcome: the Day when the eyes of the blind will be opened, the ears of the deaf unstopped, and the lame shall leap like deer. God, through His overarching decrees, is moving the cosmos—us included—toward a grand finale, and "our light and momentary troubles are achieving for us an eternal glory that far outweighs them all" (2 Corinthians 4:17). As far as heaven is concerned, our troubles are "light" in comparison. It's another way of saying, "This is the way it will all turn out; this is the way it will be, you'll see!" It's like a scale. A pile of problems are on one side with heaven's glory on the other.

God is working everything out for our good and His glory. Are you convinced of that? Today, if the problem side of the scale seems heavy, then focus your faith on the glory side. When you do, you become a Rumpelstilt-skin weaving straw into gold. Like a divine spinning wheel, your affliction "*worketh*…a far more exceeding and eternal weight of glory" (2 Corinthians 4:17, KJV). Or as J. B. Phillips paraphrases it, "These little troubles (which are really so transitory) are winning for us a permanent, glorious and solid reward out of all proportion to our pain."

It's not merely that heaven will be wonderful *in spite of* your anguish; it will be wonderful *because of* it. Suffering serves you. A faithful response to affliction accrues a *weight* of glory. A bounteous reward. God has every intention of rewarding your endurance. Why else would He meticulously chronicle every one of our tears? "Record my lament; list my tears on your scroll—are they not in your record?" (Psalm 56:8).

Every tear you've cried—think of it—will be redeemed. God will give you indescribable glory for your grief. Not with a general wave of the hand, but in a considered and specific way. Each tear has been listed; each will be recompensed.

We know how valuable our tears are in His sight—when Mary anointed Jesus with the valuable perfume, it was her act of washing His feet with her tears that moved Him most powerfully. The worth of our weeping is underscored again in Revelation 21:4 where we read that "He will wipe every tear from their eyes." It won't be the duty of angels or others. It'll be God's.

"Weeping may endure for a night, but joy cometh in the morning" (Psalm 30:5, KJV). You will see your daughter unfettered from her cerebral palsy. You will know the freedom of a heart, pure and blameless. You will see your husband walk without a limp. You will know family members and friends as God intended them to be all along, their best attributes shining clearly, and their worst traits gone with the wind. No bruises on your daughter, free from the shackles of an abusive marriage. No confused thoughts, no mental illness, no Alzheimer's disease.

You will experience love like you never dared imagine. This is good news for people who have never been "the most important person" in anyone's life. But in heaven, as Jonathan Edwards once wrote, "All shall have as much love as they desire, and as great manifestations of love as they can bear.… Such will be the sweet and perfect harmony among the heavenly saints, and such the perfect love reigning in every heart toward every other, without limit or alloy, or interruption."[4] If you've never known love, don't worry: You'll be loved more than you can bear.

The suffering experienced by God's Son has an eternal perspective as well. In eternity, He will be honored not as the Lion, but as the Lamb. The sufferings of Jesus will never be forgotten. Unlike us, He will for eternity visibly bare His wounds to the universe, and for that, God the Father, Son, and Holy Spirit will enjoy a cacophony of praise and worship from the saints and the angels as never before. If any dark demon in any corner of the universe ever doubted the righteousness of God in stooping to rescue debased and defiled sinners, he'll be set straight. The sacrifice and suffering of Jesus was of such massive worth, such supreme value, that God's righteousness will shine even brighter. God was able to rescue sinners, redeem suffering, crush rebellion, restore all things, vindicate His holy name, provide restitution...and come out all the more glorious for it! Heaven will show this.

Finally, you step forward onto heaven's courts. You drop to your knees to express thanks and gratitude to your sovereign Lord. The Man of Sorrows steps from His throne and approaches you. He knows what you've suffered. He reaches toward you with His nail-scarred hands, and when you feel your hands in His, you are not embarrassed. Your own scars, your anguish, all those times you felt rejection and pain, have given you at least a tiny taste of what the Savior endured to purchase your redemption. Your suffering, like nothing else, has prepared you to meet God—for what proof could you have brought of your love and gratitude if this life left you totally unscarred?

You have something in common with Christ that is eternally precious: suffering! But to your amazement, the fellowship of sharing in His sufferings has faded like a half-forgotten dream. Now it is a fellowship of sharing in His joy and pleasure. Pleasure made more wonderful by suffering. *Oh, the pain of earth,* you half sigh. Then you smile, rising to your feet to live the life God has been preparing for you all along. Weeping may have endured for a night, but it is morning. And the joy has come.

This joy can begin even now. And it just might start with a dusty old theology book by a man named Boettner.

The Conversion of a Skeptic

Charles Colson

Now the whole offer which Christianity makes is this: that we can, if we let God have His way, come to share in the life of Christ. If we do, we shall then be sharing a life which was begotten, not made, which always has existed and always will exist. Christ is the Son of God. If we share in this kind of life we also shall be sons of God.

—C. S. LEWIS, *Mere Christianity*

The writings of C. S. Lewis have had such a profound impact on my life—and on my discovery of the Christian faith—that I tried to explain how it happened in my first book, *Born Again:*

I opened *Mere Christianity* and found myself...face-to-face with an intellect so disciplined, so lucid, so relentlessly logical that I could only be grateful I had never faced him in a court of law. Soon I had covered two pages of yellow paper with pros to my query, "Is there a God?"... The more I grappled with those words, the more they began to explode before my eyes, blowing into smithereens a lot of comfortable old notions I had floated through life with, without thinking much about them. Lewis puts it so bluntly that you can't slough it off: for Christ to have talked as He talked, lived as He lived, died as He died, He was either God or a raving lunatic.[1]

Such was the impact of my first encounters with the intellectual giant C. S. Lewis. As I revealed in *Born Again,* I was a natural-born skeptic, which was both my strength and my weakness. This attitude was indispensable to my success as a Washington lawyer and in challenging weak and faulty arguments. My studies at Brown, an Ivy League university, and especially later at George Washington University Law School only confirmed the trait in me.

Unfortunately, my habit of doubt and suspicion had kept me from seeing some very obvious truths along the way. Little did I know when my friend Tom Phillips put a copy of Lewis's *Mere Christianity* in my hands that this one book would have such a profound effect on me.

When Phillips, a top corporate executive who first introduced me to Christ in 1973, gave me that little book, I had never read anything by Lewis, but I felt as if I could actually hear his voice making the argument. It is appropriate that I would sense this, of course, because *Mere Christianity* was originally a collection of radio addresses. In slightly different form, the chapters were written as radio scripts, so the book is naturally a very oral presentation.

I could hear Lewis's arguments, as if I were sitting there in a courtroom, and it struck me that I had never come up against a more relentless, forceful defense attorney or a more powerful presentation of the facts of a case. Lewis was eloquent, logical, flawless, and sometimes maddening. At the very moment I thought I had spotted a weakness in his argument, Lewis would jump to that precise point and obliterate my quibbles.

That book eventually brought me to the point where I had to admit that Christianity was not just a set of ancient principles; it was a relationship with the Savior of mankind. I was forced to admit that Jesus was either who He said He was, or, as Lewis so brilliantly expressed it, He was a liar and a madman, on the order of a man who claimed to be a poached egg.[2] I could no longer pretend that Jesus was just another good man, as most skeptics would prefer.

By logic alone, Lewis drove me to the point where I had to admit, "Okay. Something in me is stirring. I can't control it. I am not even sure what it is. Something in me is desperately searching for God."

This was not easy for me. I had grown up with little Christian influence. While I never doubted that God was the Creator, basically I was a deist. I recognized that the complexity of the universe demands an intelligent Designer. Our well-ordered planet could never be as it is unless some supremely intelligent force had brought it into being. Even Einstein had gotten that far in his view of God.

I couldn't accept the idea that we are merely a chance collision of atoms, but I had never taken the claims of Christianity seriously either. I had grown up in a nominal Christian home and had occasionally gone to church, but I was skeptical about the Christian faith. Religion was for sissies. Nietzsche had famously said that Christianity is the morality for the "weak herd," and a doctrine that pales in comparison to the "natural aristocracy" of Nature's supermen.[3] Perhaps I believed that too, but one day I found myself in the presence of an Oxford professor who challenged me with such lucid arguments that, like it or not, I was absolutely captured by what he was saying.

The night that Tom Phillips told me about Jesus and gave me *Mere Christianity*, I sat in the driveway of his home unable to start my car, I was crying so hard. That was in the darkest days of Watergate, and I knew I needed what Tom told me about. I cried out to God for His help, and I just sat there in the car for a long time, an hour or longer. The next day my wife and I headed to the Maine coast for a holiday, and there I began reading *Mere Christianity*. I discovered that the God who had touched my heart that night in Tom's driveway was the same God Lewis was describing. It was then that I understood that Christ was in my life, and nothing has been the same since. Nothing could ever be the same again.

What happened thereafter was chronicled in my book *Born Again*. My conversion was first discovered when I attended a White House prayer breakfast in December 1973. No revelation of Watergate was greeted with more suspicion or more publicity. The improbable story of my conversion led the network news night after night. "The White House tough guy turns to God!" But in the midst of all the publicity, I realized that I could no longer fight the Watergate charges and that my Christian conversion was on trial as much as I was. So I pled guilty and was sentenced to one to three years in prison.

Later, after beginning my ministry to prison inmates, I began to read more of Lewis, including *The Abolition of Man*, which contains the great essay "Men Without Chests," and his equally profound essay "The Case Against Naturalism."[4] In time I read everything Lewis had written, and those writings have profoundly affected my life.

Lewis is arguably the single greatest apologist for the Christian faith of the last hundred years. So as I come to the question, "Which are the most influential books in my life?" I must begin with *Mere Christianity* because it is the book that pushed me over the edge. Lewis forced me, with his relentless persuasion, to come face-to-face with myself. He caused me to see for the first time who God is, who I am in relation to Him, and who Jesus Christ must then be. And while *Mere Christianity* holds a special place in my heart, I hasten to endorse all of Lewis's writings.

FORMING A CHRISTIAN WORLDVIEW

After Lewis, the writings of Augustine of Hippo, better known simply as St. Augustine, have had the most profound effect on my thinking. His

THE CONVERSION OF A SKEPTIC

writings give us a compelling apologetic for what it means to be a citizen of two kingdoms—the kingdom of man and the kingdom of God. So I would have to put Augustine's classic *The City of God* right behind C. S. Lewis on my list.[5]

I could identify with Augustine's conversion, which he described in detail in his book *Confessions*,[6] and that made it easier for me to grasp what he was saying in *The City of God*. His understanding of human nature and the Christian duty to serve the will of God reaches down through history. His definition of "just war" theory, for example, has never been more relevant than it is today. During the early days of America's war on terrorism, I was invited to the Pentagon to meet with Defense Secretary Donald Rumsfeld to talk about just-war theory and moral limits on the use of military force. Here was the second most powerful civilian military authority in the world turning to arguments advanced by a Christian scholar nearly sixteen hundred years ago because they have such powerful application to today's crises. At times like this you realize the enduring truth of the Christian faith and the tremendous power of ideas.

Augustine discussed as truth the concepts that the writers I had read during my college studies had presented merely as philosophy or as ideas about the nature of reality. Augustine wrote about reasoning applied to the Scriptures, the Word of God. That grabbed my attention. Whether he was writing about the nature of sin, the necessity of redemption, or the importance of unity in the body of Christ, he wasn't simply stating an opinion, but offering precious and well-honed insights into the very mind of God.

Augustine illustrates his arguments throughout *The City of God* by referring to the moral and political struggles of his day, between the fifth-century church and the Roman Empire, which already was tottering on the verge of collapse. But it was not a very big step to see that this warfare—between the City of God and the City of Man—was ongoing, even in the post-Watergate world I knew only too well. The City of Man held no promise for me. I had already discovered that the seat of earthly power offers nothing but disappointments and hardship if we allow that to become the sum total of our hopes and aspirations. Earthly power crumbles, ultimately, while the City of God is forever. And the truth it offers is greater than gold and more enduring. These things I learned from Augustine, who, second only to the apostle Paul, I believe, is the most influential theologian in the history of the church.

Third, after Lewis and Augustine, I would turn to the work of Francis Schaeffer. His clear exposition of what it means to be Christian in troubled times has taken many forms. Thousands of people—millions perhaps—have enjoyed the video series *How Should We Then Live?* which was used for decades in churches and Sunday schools around the world. That series was later capsulized in Schaeffer's book of the same name; and the book, in turn, helped many people come to grips with their faith and the importance of Christian cultural engagement.[7]

But I can't speak of the importance of Schaeffer's work without, at the same time, referring to the man who influenced Schaeffer (and who influenced me as well), Abraham Kuyper. A great theologian, a leader of the Christian Reformed movement in Europe, and a former prime minister of Holland, Kuyper gave us some of the finest arguments ever put forth for the all-encompassing importance of the Christian worldview. His Stone Lectures are a series of six academic presentations delivered at Princeton University in 1898 and have had a profound impact on Christian thought.[8]

Presented as a defense of the teachings of Swiss reformer John Calvin, the Stone Lectures covered religion, politics, science, art, and the future, all in the context of a comprehensive Christian life and worldview. Those lectures have influenced generations of teachers, pastors, and thinkers, and they had a particular impact on the writings of Francis Schaeffer.

During some of the most stressful days the church has endured, Schaeffer helped Christians, including me, to make sense of it all. The compelling arguments of books like *A Christian Manifesto, The God Who Is There,* and *He Is There and He Is Not Silent* are, in large part, a tribute to the thinking of Kuyper and his ideas on faith and culture.[9] And, further, they are a declaration of the necessity of Christian engagement in today's culture.

OUT OF THE DARKNESS

Before moving on, I must mention other writers without whom my thinking would be incomplete. First among these, the Russian novelists who helped frame my understanding of the great questions of life. Dostoyevsky's monumental works *Crime and Punishment* and *The Brothers Karamazov* should be essential reading for every believer.[10] And I give equally high marks to Tolstoy's *War and Peace* and *Anna Karenina*.[11] These two brilliant but deeply troubled writers spoke as few have ever done, with incredible insights into the human condition and mankind's intimate relationship with God.

You cannot read *The Brothers Karamazov*—and particularly the section titled "The Grand Inquisitor"—without coming to grips with the great drama of faith played out in our lives. During the years when the Stalinists were cracking down on dissidents and punishing every expression of free thought, the works of Dostoyevsky and Tolstoy were circulated throughout the Communist world as if for the first time. The works of authors like these kept Christian truth alive, even though reading such works could result in persecution.

More recently I have turned to the writings of another Russian, Aleksandr Solzhenitsyn, because of their remarkable power. They are some of the most compelling books of our time. First among these is *The Gulag Archipelago,* a massive three-volume series that contains Solzhenitsyn's own conversion story.[12] Solzhenitsyn's memoirs are powerful testimonies to the human spirit and to the power of Christ in overcoming the evil of this age. *The Gulag Archipelago* is documented with hundreds of personal letters and remembrances from witnesses who were there, making the whole book an indictment of the godless Soviet system. Solzhenitsyn's novel *Cancer Ward* makes a powerful case for the dignity of human life, and his short novel *One Day in the Life of Ivan Denisovich* is one of the most moving books I have ever read.[13]

I am also a fan of biographies, and a number of them have influenced my thinking. John Pollock's biography of William Wilberforce and Arnold Dallimore's classic biography of George Whitefield opened my eyes to the power of our commitment to Christian service.[14] In a similar vein, I have been greatly influenced by Wesley's *Journals,* Calvin's *Institutes of the Christian Religion,* and Bonhoeffer's remarkable book *The Cost of Discipleship.*[15] Talk about faith under fire! As a clergyman who refused to capitulate to the Nazis during World War II, Bonhoeffer was persecuted, imprisoned, and eventually killed for his courage. I have gone back to those writings again and again for encouragement in moments of weakness.

The books I have listed are noteworthy, but these works only became favorites after my conversion. I took literature courses in college, of course. I studied philosophy and read the works of John Locke, among others. I concentrated on political philosophy and the influences of the French Enlightenment on the American Founders. I studied Plato and Aristotle, and there are certainly great moments in all these writings. But what formed my thinking was not any of the things I read for academic purposes, but books like these that I read only after I became a Christian.

President Theodore Roosevelt observed that "to educate a person in mind and not in morals is to educate a menace to society,"[16] and I believe that is true. I had a good education and a grasp of my profession that brought me to the White House as special counsel to the president. But the best my earthbound wisdom could accomplish was to land me in prison, my name forever tarnished by scandal. But through the words of great writers and thinkers like those I've listed here, I discovered the truth that would change my life forever—a message of hope that I have shared through the ministry of Prison Fellowship for nearly three decades.

I warmly commend each of these books to you.

The Horizontal Gospel

Jay Kesler

> If the Christian works with all his might at some human
> project he is only a human being like others, and his effort
> is worth no more than that; but if he accepts his specific
> function as a Christian…this is decisive for human history.
>
> —JACQUES ELLUL, *The Presence of the Kingdom*

For Christians who want to grow to spiritual maturity and make a godly contribution in the modern world, I often find myself recommending Jacques Ellul's *The Presence of the Kingdom.*[1] At the time I first read it, I was deeply involved in attempting to reach high-school and college-age young people with the gospel. It was the late 1960s, and our nation was in the midst of a challenging time.

Things were happening within the youth culture that created a gap between the generations and also between youth and the church. The civil rights struggle, the drug culture, the sexual revolution, and demonstrations against the Vietnam War were all converging into what many felt was a youth revolution, if not the complete overturn of American society. College officials were being sequestered or assaulted, university administration buildings were being ransacked and burned, riots were erupting in the cities, student protestors were moving to Canada to avoid the draft, and a general unrest seemed to prevail at all levels of culture. As a Youth for Christ leader and an evangelist, I was struggling with the question, What is the role of the Christian in society? At Youth for Christ, we were focused on evangelism but sensed that social justice issues, national purpose, and public ethics were legitimately consuming the energies of youth. We believed that if the hearts of young people could be turned to Christ, it would affect these other agendas, but we questioned whether we could get a hearing for the salvation message without engaging these other issues.

Reading Ellul's short book (only 155 pages) brought a fresh and focused perspective to my life as a youth evangelist and as an evangelical believer. Ellul was a French professor of law and government who had served in the French Resistance during World War II and had been a critic of French military activities during the Algerian War. His book delivered needed wisdom and insight in the midst of a troubled world.

Ellul builds his argument around three New Testament ideas put forth by Jesus as the roles of the Christian in the world (he would argue that they are more than metaphors): (1) You are the salt of the earth; (2) you are the light of the world; and (3) I send you forth as sheep among wolves. These concepts, according to Ellul, define the Christian's role in the world as we are empowered by God through the presence of the Holy Spirit. Christians are citizens of the kingdom of God, Ellul stresses, while very much remaining citizens of the world. He disparages the idea that Christians can be separate from humanity in general because our world has become too intertwined, interdependent, and compromised. We indeed have all sinned and cannot escape as individuals from the judgment of all humanity. Christians admit their guilt and wholly rely on Jesus Christ for grace and atonement. Our very lives, redeemed by Christ, are a leavening power in a world bent on death. I had never given much thought to corporate sin until I read Ellul. Because of *The Presence of the Kingdom,* I was forced to join the human race. I could no longer pretend that, as a Christian, I was somehow exempt from the sins and struggles shared by all of humanity.

Legalists, after having "kept the law" as defined by their subculture, tend to see the world like a store checkout line with a sign that reads: "Only Seven Items or Less." They feel that because they aren't drunkards, adulterers, murderers, or thieves, they don't really need God's grace. Ellul helped me realize how shortsighted the dos and don'ts of evangelical subculture were. Evangelicals were preaching a truncated gospel by leaving out systemic and cultural sins in which everyone has direct or indirect involvement.

None of my conservative theology could extricate me from guilt or make me holy. I had to confess complicity in the sins of a fallen culture. I had to accept the tension that comes with living in a sinful world without becoming comfortable in the domain of the prince of this world. In Ellul's view, the world and all of its aspirations outside of Christ is a will toward death and suicide. As Christians, we must never give in to this death, but must constantly live and preach Christ, who alone is life.

In order to do this in the late 1960s, I found myself forming relationships with certain social activists on the left. However, as a Christian serving in an evangelical organization, I was often misunderstood by other evangelists. Some tried to tar Youth for Christ with the brush of liberalism or, even worse, Marxism. But others dubbed us "new evangelicals," recognizing that we had finally become aware of the horizontal dimension of the gospel as it applies to living as a kingdom citizen in a fallen world. Indeed, as new evangelicals, we were discovering the implications of the biblical synoptic that "our struggle is not against flesh and blood, but against the rulers, against the authorities, against the powers of this dark world and against the spiritual forces of evil in the heavenly realms" (Ephesians 6:12). The battle is not material only or spiritual only, but it is both at once.

Ellul insists that the "revolutionary spirit," wherever it is found—and I, of course, was dealing with the youth revolution in America—is a false Eden and can never bring about true change because human revolutions are built on false premises. In our day, revolution was almost always inter-preted in Marxist terms. These movements are not truly revolutionary but are based on man's greed and lust for power. History has shown that both Fascism and Communism are destined to fail, and it is because they are not revolutionary enough! Only Christ can truly revolutionize a human being.

These ideas were especially powerful because Ellul was speaking bibli-cal truth from a European perspective, uncluttered by American bias. *The Presence of the Kingdom* helped me realize that I dare not take sides and become an ally or ideologue of any human movement, but that I already had a position, a party, and an unwavering allegiance to Jesus Christ. I must live in a real world, though, and on a practical basis must choose, must care, must engage, must be involved.

This realization led those of us who were working in the Youth for Christ ministry to enter worlds previously unknown to us. We discovered the complex world of poverty, crime, drugs, and the institutionalized wel-fare system. We found ourselves seduced by the problems, and we were tempted to forget the role of the Fall at all levels of society. We became angry that Jesus didn't seem as outraged about a broken society as John the Baptist had been. And we wished we could do something to right the wrong. It was a revolutionary discovery for me that the poor and disad-vantaged could also be greedy, selfish, and without compassion. The con-fusion of this world refused to conform to neat categories. Neither the liberals nor the conservatives, neither the Republicans nor the Democrats had the answer. It became impossible to sort out the world short of Christ Himself, and I found myself to be imperfect in my attempts to follow Him. But rather than being immobilized by my weakness or using it as an excuse to retreat into the "interior life," I realized I must accept my sinful state. I must not simply dispense grace; I must above all receive it.

I will continue to make mistakes, to be deceived, and to be compro-mised. But that, after all, is why Christ died. All of us suffer the same frus-trating personal failings. To be a Christian means I must admit my sin and seek to rely only on Christ in every circumstance. The insight that came through Ellul's small book helped me escape a truncated faith that saw the world in a two-dimensional form. I was now free to live in a complex and nuanced world with a sense of who I am as a kingdom citizen, in a world that indeed is the enemy of grace.

This was a very freeing thing. I no longer struggled so much with my imperfection, nor did I need to solve all the world's problems. I relaxed with the realization that the battle belonged to the Lord and that I could see the humor in my failures and foibles and still feel a sense of accomplishment by His grace.

Those familiar with Jacques Ellul are aware that he accrued most of his acclaim through his writings on technological society, propaganda, and political illusion. His more detailed and complicated writings are captured in time to a greater degree than *The Presence of the Kingdom* and, as a result, feel more dated. Generally speaking, though, his observations about technology, media, and politics still hold true today. While his principles remain sound, the application of our faith to our specific lives must be made individually. I am most indebted to Ellul for his development of the idea that in God's intent humanity is an end, not a means to an end. In modern culture, people have become a means to serve economics or the state. In our world, almost all institutions are willing to sacrifice people for the accomplishment of their goals. Even in the field of higher education where I now work, I find that most education is expressed in utilitarian terms. It is considered useless unless it provides upward mobility, success, prestige, or power. Ellul's insights echo the sense of the Bible: We develop our mind in order to better worship God and serve Him in our world.

In recent years as a college president, I have continued to face the challenge of helping Christian parents understand that education in the Christian sense is not about gaining a preferred position in the marketplace. It is about giving of your best to the Master. We are not human *doings;* we are human *beings.* Who we are is far more important than what we do to make a living. The liberal arts are about the enrichment of the soul by the careful study of the work of God in history and by the careful observation of human experience—good and bad, noble and base—seeing the difference in light of God's revelation to us through His Son, His Word, and His creation. Most of us living in modern society have been so thoroughly infused by the philosophy of materialism that our lives tend to overlook the spiritual and the transcendent. We no longer appreciate or understand the complications of being created in the image of God.

The outline of history is God-infused: Creation, Fall, redemption, and eternity. However, I never understood that these are both the dividing truths and, at the same time, the uniting truths of history, until I studied Ellul. And they are not simply spiritual truths; they touch all of life. When applied to all of life and daily experience, they become transformational. To actually believe this stuff is what makes the difference.

I could point to other influential authors and books that I read at other times, but having recently reread *The Presence of the Kingdom*, I am convinced that it remains one of the most trustworthy prophetic books for a world still enamored by technology, yet confused about the purpose of it all.

If not for the insights of Jacques Ellul, there would have been in the 1960s and 1970s no "new evangelicals" whose eyes were opened to the horizontal as well as the vertical ramifications of the gospel. We would not have understood that the gospel *must* engage with the real world, and do so without compromising foundational biblical truth.

Certainly many other authors have amplified and developed these truths.[2] Many of the critics of evangelicalism, especially in the media, simply are not aware of the broad spectrum of evangelical works of practical charity, education, public health and policy that constitute the best expressions of responsible Christian citizenship. This pursuit of the horizontal dimension of the gospel can be traced to a philosophical shift influenced by Jacques Ellul's message: Citizens of the kingdom must also be biblically engaged citizens of the world.

FOUR

My Three Best Friends…Maybe

Calvin Miller

I count myself in nothing else so happy,
As in a soul remembering my good friends.

—SHAKESPEARE in *Richard II*

Books! They keep me up late. They sometimes wake me up, summoning me from my bed in the middle of the night. My best friends. My worst enemies. They are full of great ideas from great souls—ideas that stick to my fingers and chain my eyes to their old yellowed pages, daring me to try to let them go. They tease me with print too small for my bifocals and threaten me with their daunting poundage.

I beg them to look neat in my study. I try to pen them all up in shelved rows. But my books are escape artists. My shelves are always so gorged with them they cannot stand together neatly. So I pile them up—I lay them edgewise on top of their vertical brothers till they spill out in avalanches that force me to pick them up and jam them back on the peaks of their slippery stacks. They shove at my desk like rush-hour subway riders in Mexico City. There are always more of them. I secretly believe they breed in the darkness, and I have caught myself tiptoeing into my study, suddenly flipping on the light to try and catch them at their illicit conjugation. But alas, so far I have not.

I read as many as I can in bookstores to keep from bringing them home. But some of them forbid me to leave them standing stiffly on the store's prissy, much-neater shelves. They would rather crowd themselves into my skewed library and suffocate in the tumble-down piles of my study.

Why am I so narcolibric (a word of my contriving, meaning "print addicted")? Because every book I see says to me "come hither and I will make you wise." I have now read so many of them they cannot live up to their allurements. Yet all librophiliacs (book lovers, and I did not make this one up) are on the make for that one scintillating paragraph that hides in the deep interior of some book yet to be read. To put it more simply, I'm a sucker for a great read! I always feel the next book I pick up will be the one great book I dare not miss.

Books confront me and change me. At this point it is foolhardy to name only three and proclaim them to be the ones that have had the greatest impact on my life. It is like selecting at random three ancestors from my family tree and saying these are responsible for my entire DNA profile. This impossible, insane assignment is my publisher's idea, not mine. But let me set aside the thousands that have created my cerebrum and focus on the three books that have had the "most impact" upon me and offer this tiny trinity to you. I shall begin each one on the list with an epigraph to hint at the appreciable way these books have changed me forever. I have, of course, left out the Bible, since its impact has not only changed me forever, but it daily continues to change me. It is the one book I must read every day, since any day without it tends to be dingy and empty.

I. THE COLLECTED WORKS OF WILLIAM SHAKESPEARE

Life's…a tale told by an idiot…

Though this be madness, yet there is method in it.

—MACBETH in *Macbeth;*

POLONIUS in *Hamlet*

"O for a muse of fire…"[1] such a muse has ignited my imagination for a lifetime. I have seen nearly all the plays (nobody has ever seen all the Henrys). For years—every year, year by year—I read all thirty-seven plays along with the sonnets. My mind blazes with the artful characters that will always define for the West the essence of *all* characters. Was there ever a glutton like Falstaff, a patriot like Henry V, a sprite like Ariel, a scheming queen like Lady Macbeth, a shifty soul like Cassius, a fiend like Iago, a wounded prince like Hamlet, a more strutting patriarch than Capulet, a more off-the-wall shrew-tamer than Petruchio? I think not. I fancy sometimes when I approach my heavy volume of the collected works, I can hear the ogre's growl, the fairies' flutter, the neighing of war horses. And when I have five minutes, I open the book and peek in. Next to the Bible, the conversations and schemes of a thousand Shakespearean characters create my life and inform my philosophies.

I've rarely experienced a moment of trial or blessing than that the Bard does not shout his confirmation or warning or counsel.

When my children are less attentive than I would like, I hear Lear's lament: "How sharper than a serpent's tooth it is to have a thankless child!"[2]

When I have been betrayed by some friend, I have often answered his betrayal with "Et tu, Brute?" After my reply I bask in the simple wisdom of "When in disgrace with Fortune and men's eyes."[3] I know the whole sonnet by heart, and its counsel is steadfast. It turns my mind from the betrayals I so protest to my dear wife's consistent love.

When insecure in changing jobs, I remember Brutus's counsel: "There is a tide in the affairs of men, which taken at the flood, leads on to fortune; omitted, all the voyage of their life is bound in shallows and in miseries."[4]

When catching Christians fighting at a church business meeting, Puck flutters up before me and gigs me in the ribs and counsels me to pity pious immaturity: "Shall we their fond pageant see? / Lord, what fools these mortals be!"[5]

When tempted to let diplomacy blunt the edge of honesty, I hear

Henry's Hotspur remind me: "And I can teach thee, coz, to shame the devil by telling truth: tell truth and shame the devil."[6]

So, on and on go the days of our lives as poor players strutting on a stage, belting out tales told by idiots, full of sound and fury, signifying nothing. It is common for me to preach many times within the same week, but never do I do it but what I hear Hamlet counseling the players:

> Speak the speech, I pray you, as I pronounced it to you,
> trippingly on the tongue; but if you mouth it, as many of
> your players do, I had as lief the town-crier spoke my lines.
> Nor do not saw the air too much with your hand, thus; but
> use all gently: for in the very torrent, tempest, and—as I
> may say—whirlwind of passion, you must acquire and
> beget a temperance, that may give it smoothness. O! it
> offends me to the soul to hear a robustious periwig-pated
> fellow tear a passion to tatters, to very rags, to split the ears
> of the groundlings, who for the most part are capable of
> nothing but inexplicable dumb-shows and noise.[7]

I say—after reckoning with preachers who sweat up their homilies with melodrama—Shakespeare for homiletics!

Give me Desdemona as the ideal picture of trust in the face of jealousy!

Give me Cardinal Wolsey as the model for loyalty.

Give me Benedick as the most ardent and bumbling of suitors.

Give me the bumbling players of a *Midsummer's Night Dream* when I need to laugh, and Cordelia when I need a picture of grief and loyalty.

The Bard reminds me of the old truism: "There are no chaste minds: all minds copulate whenever they meet." So my life is ever informed by its swift union with other minds, the minds I keenly need to keep my own informed. "Let me not to the marriage of true minds admit impediments."[8] Now I am married to the wisdom of the Bard, and our union, I assure you, is for life.

II. THE COLLECTED WORKS OF T. S. ELIOT

> Against the Word, the unstill world still whirled
> About the center of the silent Word.
>
> —T. S. ELIOT, "ASH WEDNESDAY"

I never like poets who instantly make sense. Frost is too up front for me. Give me Eliot. I understand the enigma of growing older. I can expect with my advancing into senility I will become more cantankerous and fiercely libertarian: *"I grow old...I grow old...I shall wear the bottoms of my trousers rolled."*[9] But I like Eliot best when he advances past such obvious cynicism and gives me more. *Old Possum's Book of Practical Cats* is a nice kind of whim, but even that affords me no resting place from my fierce need to understand the mystery of existence.

Eliot is best when he paints in mauve and umber and lures me into the mystery of a line I cannot fathom. Yet even as I beg to be free, he chains me to his lines. God hangs out in his poetry, but he is not as accessible as he appears in denominational publications. Eliot is a prophet telling me that the world will end in a whimper, and when the world stands dead and silent, all that will tell a later civilization we existed is asphalt and lost golf balls. I have read all he wrote, and then read it again. His plays—acted out—never succeed with me. As Ibsen said of *Peer Gynt,* some plays should exist to be read, for to act them is to have too much flung at the mind at once. *Prufrock, Murder in the Cathedral,* even *Old Possum's Book of Practical Cats* must be read—and read aloud. To read them silently is to lose the mystery and forfeit the intrigue of their setting up camp in my soul. Such verses trick me. They bewitch me. They beckon my sluggish cerebrum to get a flashlight with brand-new cells before I dare enter to poke around in Eliot's great chasms of truth.

Now I must confess I have a quotable fondness for Sara Teasdale, "There will come soft rains and the smell of ground."[10] I am also wildly enthusiastic about Emily Dickenson. I have a friend who despises my fondness for the Belle of Amhurst. He disdains her work by saying that all her poems can be sung to the tune of "The Yellow Rose of Texas." I tried this late one night in the shower and found it to be largely true. Still I am addicted to Dickinson's succinct way of summing up my moods and feelings. But her poems are stacked with easy metaphors too easily understood to hold the mind in that suspended state by which I long to measure and ponder, doubt and believe.

But Eliot I have worked on for years. For he is truly "Shape without form, shade without colour, / Paralysed force, gesture without motion."[11] On Eliot's street there "is no beginning, no movement, no peace and no end / But noise without speech, food without taste."[12] I have pondered this one for quite some time: "The dove descending breaks the air / With flame of incandescent terror / Of which the tongues declare / The one discharge from sin an error."[13] Still our puzzlements are not to prevent our lives:

> We know of oppression and torture,
> We know of extortion and violence,
> Destitution, disease,
> The old without fire in winter,
> The child without milk in summer,
> Our labour taken away from us,
> Our sins made heavier upon us.
> We have seen the young man mutilated,
> The torn girl trembling by the mill-stream.
> And meanwhile we have gone on living,
> Living and partly living,

Picking together the pieces,

Gathering faggots at nightfall,

Building a partial shelter,

For sleeping and eating and drinking and laughter.[14]

There is nothing more intriguing or difficult than the attempt to get inside the mind of a truly brilliant man. This pilgrimage is unending, yet never boring nor barren. I feed on the sudden flaring of insight found in the dark chasm between two of Eliot's lines. He makes me rich as only a dead prophet can enrich me. Just when I despair that he is impenetrable, I am cast upon an insight, like Viola on the strands of some new exile. My own *Twelfth Night* is bright with some epiphany I could never have expected.

I never end up with anything less than Eliot's Magi who, having returned from seeking out the infant Christ, could only say, "There was a Birth, certainly, / We had evidence and no doubt."[15] So there is a birth. More than one birth. With Eliot, life comes like quintuplets from the fecund soul. So on I read, tripping over ideas too worthy, stumbling and falling into mysteries whose unraveling become a process of life.

Eliot is the way my world ends: It's all bangs and whimpers and seizures sometimes. I may understand; I may be heart-paralyzed. But whether you find me giddy at Prufrock's or sitting in the dark corner of Canterbury chewing my prayer book, you will know that my love affair with Eliot is terminal.

III. SILENCE

"Who is He?"

"He seems to be crazy. He's like a beggar;

but since yesterday he keeps saying that he's a Christian."

—SHUSAKU ENDO, *Silence*

Much of my reading across the years has been done in religious books. Any number of these books have instructed and, in many cases, transformed my life. When I was in junior high school, Jean Valjean taught me (in Hugo's *Les Misérables*) the value of a valorous life established on Christian character.[16] My second year of college was a year of insight on the nature of mission and witness informed by Elisabeth Elliot's *Through Gates of Splendor* and Helen Roseveare's *He Gave Us a Valley*.[17] Through books such as these I lived with an informed sense about difficulty in our Christian calling. Ian Thomas's *The Saving Life of Christ*, like Julian of Norwich's *Showings*, pointed me ever deeper into the ecstasy of Christian inwardness.[18] The same could be said for Richard Foster's *Celebration of Discipline* or Dallas Willard's *Spirit of the Disciplines*.[19] Eugene Peterson's *Run with the Horses* (like so many of Peterson's books) have all held place in my life—measuring and requiring ever more of my commitment to Christ.[20]

Some years ago I began reading ever deeper in the Christian life. I have, I am very much afraid, become highly addicted to the classic devotional writers. Now I am in love with the Christ of the mystics. It is not their mysticism that I hunger for. I hunger for the Christ who creates their passion to know him.

I have read many books that made me bleed for the joy of their mystery; but Shusaku Endo, who lived in my time, has written the single novel that has influenced me most.[21] I almost compel at gunpoint all future missionaries I know to read this book. I somehow feel that unless they do, they will live in a self-imposed naiveté that will keep them from measuring cross-cultural living in its fullest meaning. *Silence* is a story of martyrs in the Samurai era of Japan. The power of the Jesuit believers captured my soul as no other novel has ever done. I have read most of the Endo corpus. *The Samurai* touched my soul also as it examined the corrupted nature of institutions. But *Silence* I read in nearly one sitting of many hours. I was frozen to its narrative mystery and chained to its life-changing truth. I have not been the same since I read it. I never will be the same again.

I first read *Silence* while on a teaching mission to a seminary in the Philippines. It happened that in my classes I had some refugees from Indonesia who had fled their island homeland in retreat from Islamic terror. Their families had been reduced to starvation levels, their homes burned—their churches, too! Suddenly I was in the midst of a field of martyrs reading of the Jesuit martyrs of the seventeenth century. Endo's realism and depth led me to question the nature of missions and my own commitment to serving the Lord. I have found myself ever after in the most exhausting states of self-examination I have ever known.

My Three Best Friends?

With that, the three are named! But next month I shall no doubt wish I had named others. In fact, my list in any month would certainly be different than the one I composed just a month prior. Why? Because for fifty years I have read at least one hundred books a year. Sometimes two hundred. And every one was—in my estimation at the time of their purchase—worthy! For I have always made it a policy not to read worthless books. And I am addicted to reading. So there will always be more books vying for significance in my experience.

But I offer an apology to the wonderful writers I have not named: Yancey, Griffin, Wangerin. As for novelists, I have a similar list of mentors: Morrison, Walker, Allende, Irving, Buechner, Lewis, Tolkien, and others.

As for biographers and biographies—auto and less so—well you get the point! To list but three of the seven thousand books that have impacted me is a cheat. I am the product of so many more books than I could ever name.

And the best books I have read are yet to be read, perhaps even yet to be written. But when they are written, I'll be there waiting for light, upgrading my lens prescription, reading by day and ever being changed by the clamorous piles of books that call me from sleep to insomnia. Of the making of books there is no end. So it appears my love affair with my two concubines, Barnes and Noble, will go on forever.

I know I am old and my librophilia is terminal. But a ninety-two-year-old man once was asked, after he was caught studying Plato, "Why would you, at ninety-two, be reading *The Republic?*"

His reply is my reply: "To improve my mind, of course."

Hope in a Fallen World

Michael Card

> Live and be happy, beloved children of my heart, and never
> forget that, until the day comes when God will deign to reveal
> the future to man, all human wisdom is contained in these
> words: "Wait and hope!"
>
> Your friend,
>
> Edmond Dantès, Count of Monte Cristo
>
> —ALEXANDRE DUMAS, *The Count of Monte Cristo*

I still see, in my memory's eye, the exact place it stood on the shelf, lean-
ing against the other classics, in my parents' library. The cracked leather
cover and faded gold lettering whispered a wordless promise that I could
neither hear nor, at that time in my young life, understand. For almost as
important as the content of the book itself is the timing of the moment
when it first comes into your life.

It wasn't until some years later (I was fifteen) when *The Count of Monte
Cristo* reemerged.[1] It was in, of all the most unlikely places, a high-school
history class. Mrs. Zuccarello, a graceful Southern belle of a lady, handed
it to me, never guessing the momentous effect it would have on the rest of
my life.

I had known and loved the Bible for as long as I could remember and had grown up with parents who loved it as well. It received an honored place in our home. It was not allowed to be placed on the floor, no other book could be stacked on top of it, and it certainly would never be used as a coaster underneath a plate or glass!

Although I loved reading, I was said to be "slow" in my schoolwork. (People did not know about dyslexia in those days.) As I think back on it now, I believe I needed another book to provide a key to open up the rest of the world of books to me. Enter Dumas's amazing novel. It was the bridge from the world of the Bible into the rest of the literary world. There were so many points of contact between it and the stories of the Bible and, especially for me, the parable of my own life.

I will not presume the role of literary critic and try to explain what the symbols of this complex novel might mean for all time. I can only speak of my own experience and what it meant and still means to me.

First, *The Count of Monte Cristo* is a man's book that I, at fifteen, sorely needed. Yes it is full of romance, but shouldn't every man's life be filled with romance? After all, it was said of the author, Alexandre Dumas, that he was "as strong as Porthos, as adroit as d'Artagnan."[2] He lived in many ways as dashing a man's life as Edmond Dantès, the novel's principal character, and it is reflected on every page of the book.

It was, without a doubt, Alexandre Dumas's favorite work. He is believed to have written more than twelve hundred volumes, and yet *The Count of Monte Cristo* was woven into the fabric of his life more than any other. Like Dantès, he was educated by a priest. His huge Renaissance mansion, which bankrupted him in later life, was called *Monte Cristo*. Toward the end of his life, he published a weekly paper by the same title. André Maurois, literary scholar and critic, who likened the author to some of the other characters in his novels, maintained that Dumas was "as generous as Edmond Dantès."[3]

Second, Edmond Dantès, who later becomes the Count of Monte

Cristo, was the "coolest" figure in any book I had ever read. (Do not under-estimate the value of "coolness.") His bearing, his aloofness, the restraint he exercised over his considerable power and influence, even down to his appearance, tall and dark and dashing, raised the bar of "cool" to such height that every aspirer to coolness seemed pale and thin by comparison.

Finally, and most important, Dantès's experience of being mentored by the priest, Faria, established deep in me the desire to find a mentor of my own someday, not simply someone who would fill my head with informa-tion, but a man who would help me figure out my life and tell me who I might become. It has been said that our desires reveal our design. To expe-rience through the novel the secret process of receiving a genuine educa-tion, to see the almost fanatical dedication in both men, awakened in me the hunger for the labor of scholarship. To remain unfound and undefined would have been as tragic a fate for Dantès as remaining in the hell of the Château d'If. But he was discovered, fed, directed, and loved as a son. All of these things the abbé Faria did for Edmond.

If you are unfamiliar with this book, it might be helpful to know the basic plot. Edmond Dantès is a young sailor on a three-masted French ship called the *Pharaon*. Upon returning from a long voyage, he is promised, by the ship's owner, that he will become its new captain, the previous captain having died on the journey home. But even greater than the promise of a promotion is the hope Edmond has for sharing life with the beautiful Mercédès, his fiancée. The two lovers seem perched on the edge of the most perfect and promising life together.

But lurking in the shadows are three men who are bound together by their jealousy of Edmond. They devise his downfall by means of the false accusation that Dantès was in league with Napoleon, at this point banished to the isle of Elba. Without a trial Dantès is whisked away to the Château d'If, the darkest and most remote hole in France. He had lost his position as well as the love of his life. Eventually, he discovers that the conspirators even had a hand in the death of his own father, who died of starvation

while Edmund was in prison. This immense, crushing sense of hopelessness, injustice, and suffering is so powerfully painted by Dumas that we are
almost suffocated by the emotional world of Edmund Dantès. We can
almost taste his hunger for revenge.

In prison Dantès suffers every type of mental torment. At first, like Job,
he clings to his innocence. Next, he gives way to deep doubt, fleeing to the
arms of prayer. At last he gives way to despair and decides to end his life
by starvation. Then he hears a scratching sound behind the wall. Another
prisoner, the abbé Faria, has tunneled his way into Edmond's cell by mis-
take. What follows is one of the most inspiring exchanges of relationship
between two men in all of literature. Over the course of years, the abbé
teaches Edmond several languages, science, politics, mathematics, and more.
Simply by logic he unravels the plot of the three men that caused Dantès's
imprisonment. The two commit to escape together, but the elderly priest
suffers a cataleptic seizure. Though he encourages Dantès to escape without him, the young man refuses to leave the side of his mentor. The abbé,
in gratitude, reveals the location of an immense treasure on the isle of
Monte Cristo. When the priest finally dies, Dantès experiences a deep
aloneness; his only friend and mentor, his final source of hope is gone.
When he creeps back into the priest's cell, he discovers the body has been
sewn into a sack in preparation for a sea burial. Dantès tenderly removes
the body and sews himself into the shroud. He is cast into the icy sea in
one of the most well-known escapes in all literature. Dantès is symbolically
reborn in the process of the escape. Again, so masterful is Dumas's telling
of the tale that you and I feel as if we are reborn as well!

Dantès makes his way to the isle of Monte Cristo and discovers the
treasure. So massive is its value that he can do or buy anything he wants.
And what he wants most, of course, is revenge on the three who robbed
him of his life.

At this point Dantès takes on the guise of the Count of Monte Cristo.
At the same time he places himself in the role of God whom he calls

Providence. "I have substituted myself for Providence…" he says. His vengeance takes on a pseudobiblical quality. The notion of punishing the children for "the sins of the fathers," the concept of "an eye for an eye," all of these shape his desire to exact a slow and painful revenge on his enemies. The book becomes a commentary on vengeance. Dumas once again draws the reader so intimately into Dantès's experience that we feel the excitement of having discovered the treasure, of having become immeasurably rich and powerful. As we read the book, we, too, are tested. We look forward to the exacting of the revenge, which seems so justified. We almost approve of Dantès's blasphemy in assuming the role of God.

What follows is a series of convoluted story lines wherein each of his enemies is deliciously punished for his crimes against Dantès. The punishment is designed to destroy what is most important to each enemy. Fernand, who has stolen Mercédès, will lose her as well as his son. In his despair he commits suicide. Danglars, who loves money above all, is ruined financially. And finally, Villefort, perhaps the most wicked character in all of literature and who values position above all, is ruined socially and loses his mind. Only the last to be punished, Danglars, is given the chance to repent because by this time the Count himself has begun to experience a change of heart and sees his own need for repentance.

The final chapters deal with the romantic relationship between two young people, Maximilien, the son of Dantès's friend and former employer, and Valentine, the daughter of his archenemy, Villefort. In the lives of these young people, Dantès sees the hope he was violently robbed of. What melts the icy revenge in his veins is the renewed hope embodied in the love affair between the two young people. They become icons of hope, a reincarnation of the relationship he never had. Their union becomes the climax of the novel.

Of the many lessons contained in the book, a few in particular have most impacted my life. As I was drawn intimately into Dantès's experience of suffering and betrayal, I recognized that there is a plot at work in the world against all of us. The three enemies serve as personifications of evil, of Satan himself. They bring intense suffering to Dantès's life by means of false accusations (the word *diabolos* means "accuser"). In our own lives the devil works behind the scenes to deceive and, in effect, to throw us into dungeons of despair. The emotional turmoil of the imprisoned Dantès is a mirror to our own experience of life in a fallen world. His despair in the dungeon reflects darkly but magnificently our struggle here. As a young man, I became painfully aware of this struggle. Dumas gave me the emotional vocabulary to communicate this.

What is most liberating, however, is that, like Dantès, sometimes when we think we are about to lose our hopes and even our minds, we hear a scratching from beyond the walls and a voice whispering. Someone tunnels into our world to tell us who we are, to give us hope and a priceless treasure.

At a deeper level I felt drawn into the dark side of Dantès's experience of revenge. After all, these were genuinely wicked people who ruined his life. If anyone were ever justified in taking God's vengeance into his own hands, it was Edmond Dantès. He began by deluding himself, believing he was God's avenging angel; later he sought to take the place of God himself. And we are carried along irresistibly into his darkness. We all have the ability to convince ourselves we are doing things for God. But Dumas, by drawing us so deeply into Dantès's revenge, has wounded us from behind for our own edification. Each successive slice of revenge becomes more and more tasteless. Until finally, like the Count, we find ourselves asking for forgiveness from our own enemies. At the outset, we all believe revenge is sweet. We hope it will satisfy, only to discover when we get it that we are reduced to the level of the conspirators, of our enemies.

Mother Teresa said we should forgive our enemies in order not to become like them. The progression reminds us of Job, who moved from an experience of unjust suffering, to confusion, to accusation, and finally to repentance and restored relationship with God. Dumas adds to that sequence the exacting of revenge on one's enemies, an experience that ultimately leaves Dantès in despair and hopelessness. In the end, for both Dantès and Job, the only hope is in genuine relationship with God. Indeed it is *our* only hope as well. We must come to know God, who, after all, did not exact vengeance on us.

As I look at the full effect of *The Count of Monte Cristo,* I find that it is a book about hope, about the loss of hope, the substitution of vengeance for hope, and the renewal of hope through repentance and grace. It is, therefore, a story that reflects the gospel. Perhaps the greatest imprint *The Count of Monte Cristo* left on my life was the realization that if the gospel is indeed true, I would be able to see it reflected in innumerable ways all around me. If its truth were self-evident, it would be woven into great literature and art, even into the parable of my own experience. That first reading of *The Count of Monte Cristo* provided for me that luminous moment. I have come to recognize, with the help of this remarkable book, that I was granted the privilege of a mentor who found me and told me who I was. I did, by grace, escape the darkest of prisons by being reborn. And even now, when the plot that is at work against me seems about to succeed, by grace I hear a scratching sound behind the walls and a whispering, "Come this way and find freedom."

When God Moves In

Dallas Willard

I was crying all the time that God would fill me with His
Spirit. Well, one day, in the city of New York, oh, what a day!
I cannot describe it, I seldom refer to it; it is almost too sacred
an experience to name. Paul had an experience of which he
never spoke for fourteen years. I can only say that God revealed Himself to me, and I had such an experience of His
love that I had to ask Him to stay His hand. I went to preaching again. The sermons were not different; I did not present
any new truths; and yet hundreds were converted. I would not
now be placed back where I was before that blessed experience
if you should give me all the world.

—D. L. MOODY, quoted in James Gilchrist Lawson's
Deeper Experiences of Famous Christians

The one book other than the Bible that has most influenced me is a little-
known book by James Gilchrist Lawson called *Deeper Experiences of Famous
Christians*.[1] From a literary or scholarly point of view the book is of little
distinction, which perhaps explains why it is not widely known and seems
never to have been widely read. But, given to me in 1954 by a college

classmate, Billy Glenn Dudley, it entered my life at a very appropriate time; and, perhaps more importantly, it opened to me the inexhaustible riches of Christ and his people through the ages. This brought before me, in turn, a world of profound Christian literature of much greater significance for the understanding and practice of life in Christ than Lawson's book itself.

The author's peculiar doctrinal slant led him to interpret "deeper experiences" almost entirely in terms of the filling with, or baptism in, the Holy Spirit. That is an unfortunate grid to place upon the "deeper experiences" of famous or not-so-famous Christians, as becomes clear from the experiences of the individuals described in the book. But, fortunately, that peculiar slant did not hinder the author from going, in considerable detail, into what actually happened in the lives of a wide range of outstanding followers of Christ—few of whom would have shared anything close to his view of the relationship between filling or baptism and "deeper experiences" of God.

The book begins with discussions of biblical characters, from Enoch to the apostle Paul. Then, interestingly, it takes up certain "Gentile Sages" (Greek, Persian, and Roman), who also are described as under the influence of God's Holy Spirit. Then a section is devoted to outstanding Christians of the early centuries of the church, and finally, a section (very brief) devoted to "Reformed Churches" and the Reformation period.

The first individual to warrant his own chapter is Girolamo Savonarola (born in 1452), a major precursor of the Protestant Reformation. What most struck me about Savonarola—and I truly was smitten—was his drive toward holiness, toward a different and a supernatural kind of life, a life "from above," and his readiness to sacrifice all to achieve such a life. Indeed, this is what stood out in all of the people Lawson dealt with. And the "deeper experiences" that brought them forward on their way clearly were not all "fillings" or "baptisms" with the Holy Spirit, though no doubt the Spirit was always involved and genuine fillings and baptisms occurred.

The experiences did from time to time have the character of a filling or baptism, but more often than not, they were moments of realization, of extreme clarity of insight into profound truth, together with floods of feeling arising therefrom. These experiences often were what George Fox called "openings," and they went right to the bone and changed the life forever.

Thus, Lawson tells us:

> [John] Bunyan's complete deliverance from his dreadful
> doubts and despair came one day while he was passing
> through a field. Suddenly the sentence fell upon his soul,
> *"Thy righteousness is in heaven."* By the eye of faith he
> seemed to see Jesus, his righteousness, at God's right hand.
> He says, "Now did my chains fall off my legs indeed; I was
> loosed from my afflictions and irons; my temptations also
> fled away; so that, from that time, those dreadful Scriptures
> of God left off to trouble me! Now went I also home rejoic-
> ing, for the grace and love of God."[2]

The book's profound effect on me will be better understood if we consider the individuals singled out for chapter-length treatment. After Savonarola came Madame Guyon, François Fénelon, George Fox, John Bunyan, John Wesley, George Whitefield, John Fletcher, Christmas Evans, Lorenzo Dow, Peter Cartwright, Charles G. Finney, Billy Bray, Elder Jacob Knapp, George Müller, A. B. Earle, Frances Ridley Havergal, A. J. Gordon, D. L. Moody, General William Booth, and in the final chapter, "Other Famous Christians" (Thomas à Kempis, William Penn, Dr. Adam Clarke, William Bramwell, William Carvosso, David Brainerd, Edward Payson, Dorothea Trudel, Pastor John Christolph Blumhardt, Phoebe Palmer, and P. P. Bliss).

Clearly this is a selective and not well-balanced list of "famous Christians." But that did not bother me as I took up the book and studied it. In fact, that these were, by and large, quite ordinary people only impressed me all the more that the amazing life into which they were manifestly led could

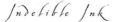

be mine. I had been raised in religious circles of very fine people where the emphasis had been exclusively on faithfulness to right beliefs, and upon bringing others to profess those beliefs. Now that, of course, is of central importance. But when that process alone is emphasized, the result is a dry and powerless religious life, no matter how sincere, and leaves a person constantly vulnerable to temptations of all kinds.

Therefore, to see actual invasions of human life by the presence and action of God, right up into the twentieth century, greatly encouraged me to believe that the life and promises given in the person of Christ and in Scripture were meant for us today. I saw that ordinary individuals who sought the Lord would find him real—actually, that he would come to them and convey his reality. It was clear that Lawson's "famous Christians" were not seeking experiences, not even the filling or baptism of the Holy Spirit. They were seeking the Lord, his kingdom, and his holiness.[3] Seeking was clearly, from the lives portrayed, a major part of life in Christ. The approach to Christianity that sought doctrinal correctness above all else was, in practice, one of nonseeking. It was basically a position of "having arrived," not of continuous seeking, and the next essential stop on its path was heaven after death. But in the light of these "famous Christians," it became clear that the path of constant seeking, as portrayed in the Bible, was the life of faith intended for us by God.[4] Salvation by grace through faith was a life, not just an outcome; and the earnest and unrelenting pursuit of God was not "works salvation," but the natural expression of the faith in Christ that saves. Constant discipleship, with its constant seeking for more grace and life, was the only sensible response to confidence in Jesus as the Messiah. And the natural (supernatural) accompaniment of that response would of course be intermittent but not infrequent "experiences" of God, some deeper and some not so deep.

Now "deeper" also meant "broader." Lawson was remarkably unbiased in his selection of the "famous Christians," and this taught me a lot. The individuals he selected ranged very broadly as to cultural and denominational connections. There were a lot of Baptists, which was my own denominational background. That helped me. But there were also Catholics, Anglicans, Methodists, Salvationists, and others.

Seeing that God does not respect sectarian boundaries in his call to holiness and power taught me that I should disregard a lot of the things that make for doctrinal insularity in others and place no weight upon them for myself. It taught me, in Paul's lovely image, to distinguish the treasure from the vessel and to attend to the treasure: Christ living in the individual life, and the individual living in obedience to Christ.[5] The blessing of God has a natural tendency among men to create denominations, but denominations have no tendency to uniquely foster the blessing of God on anyone. We can and often should honor a denomination or tradition because God has blessed those within it. But it, after all, is the vessel and not the treasure.

The hunger for holiness and for power to stand in holiness, resulting in the blessing of multitudes of people, also knows no social or economic boundaries. This, too, was made brilliantly clear in the lives of Lawson's "famous Christians," many of whom were either of no standing among humanity or had disowned their standing. Not only did that give me hope personally, but it opened afresh the events of Scripture for me and showed how "unlearned and ignorant men" (Acts 4:13, KJV) could bring the knowledge and reality of God to the world. It showed how God and one individual believer, no matter how insignificant that person is in the eyes of men, could make a great difference for good. I resolved that should anything come of my life and ministry, it would not be because of my efforts to make it happen.

As I moved on from Lawson's book to study the works of these and many other "famous Christians," it was first of all *The Imitation of Christ*, by Thomas à Kempis, that became my constant companion. Then it was the works of John Wesley, and especially his *Journal* and the standard set of his *Sermons*. Then William Law's *A Serious Call to a Devout and Holy Life*, and Jeremy Taylor's *Holy Living and Holy Dying*. Then the various writings of Charles Finney, especially his *Autobiography* and *Revival Lectures*.[6]

As my reading broadened, the writings of Luther and Calvin, along with the later Puritan writers, meant much to me, especially in filling out a theology that could support the spiritual life as one of discipleship and the quest for holiness and power in Christ, without the least touch of perfectionism or meritorious works. (Book III of Calvin's *Institutes* has been especially helpful in this regard.) I learned that the follies of "Christianity" that is free of discipleship, and the common pursuit of what Bonhoeffer called "cheap grace," could never be derived from Luther or Calvin.

These Christian writings meshed closely with the continuous reading of the great philosophers, from Plato on, which I began upon graduation from high school and continued through two years of life as a migrant agricultural worker. (I carried a volume of Plato in my duffle bag.)

The effect of all my reading has been constantly to bring me back to the Bible, especially the Gospels, and to find in Jesus and his teachings—in what Paul rightly called "the unsearchable riches of Christ" (Ephesians 3:8, KJV)—the wisdom and reality for which the human being vainly strives on its own.

Jesus answers the four great questions of life: (1) What is real? (God and his kingdom); (2) Who is well-off or "blessed"? (Anyone alive in the kingdom of God); (3) Who is a genuinely good person? (Anyone possessed and permeated with *agape,* God's kind of love); and (4) How can I become a genuinely good person? (By being a faithful apprentice of Jesus in kingdom living, learning from him how to live my life as he would live my life if he were I.) These are the questions that every human being must answer, because of the very nature of life, and which every great teacher must address. Jesus Christ answers them in the Gospels and, then, in his people, in a way that becomes increasingly understandable and experimentally verifiable, and as no other person on earth has ever answered them. He evades no question and ducks no issues. The present age is waiting for his disciples to do the same.

I never cease to be thankful for James Gilchrist Lawson and his little book. It came to me at the right time and helped me see the actual presence of Jesus Christ and his kingdom and Spirit in the real lives of real people. Thus it helped me know something of "what is the hope of his calling, what are the riches of the glory of his inheritance in the saints, and what is the surpassing greatness of his power toward us who believe, in accordance with the working of the strength of his might which he brought about in Christ, when he raised him from the dead and seated him at his right hand in the heavenlies" (Ephesians 1:18-20, author's paraphrase).

Readers should take from the reading of Lawson's book the simple but profound truth that they, too, can know by experience the truths of Christ and his kingdom that are set forth in the Bible: that if with all their heart they truly seek God, they will be found and claimed by him.[7] This is what human life is for.

SEVEN

Coming In out of the Wind

Jill Briscoe

If I find in myself a desire which no experience in this world can satisfy, the most probable explanation is that I was made for another world.

—C. S. LEWIS, *Mere Christianity*

It was Britain in the fifties after the Second World War, and I was training to be a teacher at a college in Cambridge. This august place of learning was exciting, heady, and very stretching. People believed all sorts of things about all sorts of things, and some had chosen to believe nothing at all about nothing at all! They debated the merits of such in the pubs, on the banks of the Cam River, in the ancient halls of learning, and in the dorms. I reveled in it all.

Some learned theologian in Germany had decided that God was dead, and we self-conscious, clever, and erudite students seriously considered this interesting possibility. I wondered who had acquired such complete knowledge to come to this stupendous conclusion. Surely only someone who knew everything there was to know could announce the death of the Almighty.

Then Christmas came, my first at Cambridge. Our noisy and rather arrogant group of girls obeyed tradition and went together to King's College chapel for the famous Christmas Eve service. We marveled at the building's spectacular architecture and the old-fashioned music. We observed what was (to us) the misplaced congregational reverence for all things holy in such a day and age. Sitting in an ancient pew and looking at the ancient vicar to match, we wondered how long the ancient service would last. I took note of the incredibly ancient Bible that was chained to the lectern for safety. "Quite right," I muttered to the equally skeptical friend at my side, "that's exactly where that book belongs, chained to the past!"

My mind wandered to stories I had heard growing up in the British school system when our Scripture teacher had taught us the Bible. It was a good Church of England curriculum, so I still remembered the rudiments of the dogmas of the Christian faith. I remembered the doctrines of Creation and the Fall, redemption and glory. The concepts of heaven and hell had seemed plausible back then. But that was in grade school. Hitler had dominated my life for years, and somehow hell was believable because of the concentration camps and the ghoulish things people were enduring on our broken globe. As C. S. Lewis would later write in *The Problem of Pain,*

> There is no doctrine which I would more willingly remove
> from Christianity than this [the doctrine of hell], if it lay in
> my power. But it has the full support of Scripture and,
> specially, of Our Lord's own words; it has always been held
> by Christendom; and it has the support of reason. If a game
> is played, it must be possible to lose it.[1]

I later learned that Lewis handled the doctrines of heaven and hell with great skill, sending both into the battle over the prevailing disbelief in the supernatural. Out of all his books, the powerful imagery in *The Great Divorce* later gave me an unforgettable picture of the ominous emptiness of the Grey Town. Totally self-centered folk departed after death to the

Grey Town, where they were haunted by the fear that the grey would someday turn into infinite night. There is no hope of escaping the Grey Town, which houses real personalities who have absolutely no meaning or significance.[2]

Just as Lewis brought hell into the war against unbelief, so he brought heaven to the front lines of the battle. It was *The Weight of Glory* that later made heaven believable for me. And not only believable, but also attainable through the Christ who was the love of Lewis's life after years spent as a formidable antagonist to all things Christian. He writes, "At present we are on the outside of the world, the wrong side of the door.... We cannot mingle with the splendours we see. But all the leaves of the New Testament are rustling with the rumour that it will not always be so. Some day, God willing, we shall get *in*." And again: "A cleft has opened in the pitiless walls of the world, and we are invited to follow our great Captain inside."[3] GLORY!

I read Lewis's brilliant perceptions of heaven and hell some time later. But in the meantime, it was not difficult for me to acknowledge the very real possibility of hell. The evidence of people behaving hellishly had become overwhelmingly evident as the Allies liberated the Nazi concentration camps. It was easy to conceive of another evil realm, a place where hellish things happened in an afterworld. Reason also dictated that there must be an opposite to this hellishness. So it was that I came to believe in the "reasonableness" of hell. As I tried to make sense of it all, I was amazed to find that heaven was the breathless hope of my heart! Surely there was a saving "opposite" of the atrocious living nightmare we had endured during the war. Glory was a distinct, obvious necessity for hope to be realized, or all was lost and life truly was meaningless.

If, at this time, I had read Lewis's famous words, "If I find in myself a desire which no experience in this world can satisfy, the most probable explanation is that I was made for another world,"[4] perhaps I would have sought a little more diligently to test his theory for myself. But other things crowded out my more introspective moments. Things I had believed in the past gave way to things I believed in the present.

The present was postwar Britain—a country decimated by the world-wide conflict that had been raging for too many years. A Britain that had gone to church before the war, but that did not return after the war. With the war a recent, horrible memory, I was a teenager, churchless and increasingly godless, fumbling around for a reason to be significant and staggering toward truth.

I had absolutely no concept of the size and scope of the saving grace of God. What could I say about the mercy of God that included me in the atonement—this merciful God who loved me so? How could a God who was real and holy, offended by my easy blasphemy, forgive my rejection of His truth, character, and even reality, and walk toward me in forgiveness? I was about to find out.

At Cambridge truth was up for grabs; ancient belief systems such as Christianity were dismantled. There were so many clever people who were apparently living complete lives and who seemed to do very well without any spiritual dimension to their thinking. It was only the dumber variety of student, I decided, who appeared to gravitate toward a form of Christianity that caused them to be obnoxious and insistent on being listened to. Or was it? I found myself taking a closer look.

I was meeting a new breed of Christian converts all over the place. Were they really nonthinkers? As I bumped into more and more of them, I began to notice that it was me, not them, who was rushing 'round the university speaking from the depths of my considerable ignorance! And it was the brightest and best of Cambridge who had joined the God Club, as we sarcastically called these people.

I was playing tennis for my college, and I discovered, to my chagrin, that the captain of the tennis team was "one of them." My debating captain (a bright and beautiful girl from Northern Ireland) was one of them too.

When it came time for college elections, I voted for the senior student who obviously stood head and shoulders above us "normally gifted" girls. Two days after Grace was elected to office, I was asked to take a message up to her room. I knocked on her door, and not waiting for an answer, I rudely burst in. I found Grace on her knees with her face to the Rising Son. I stood transfixed. I had voted into office a member—nay, a leader!—of the God Club. It was the fresh gracing on her face; the brush of beauty not her own that comes from intimacy with God that I witnessed. She did not jump up, embarrassed to be surprised at prayer. She just smiled at me and asked, "Yes, Jill? What is it?" I threw the note on her bed, and not trusting myself to speak, exited the room, slamming the door behind me.

I leaned against the wall outside her room, trying to figure out my reaction. Why was I so angry with her? Could it be that the hunger generated in my heart by the sight of a beautiful girl on her knees, saying, in effect, "Here I kneel, I can do no other," triggered a longing inside me that was so intense I had to find out what this God worship was all about? My soul had begun its long journey home.

At that time, in the world of the Cambridge elite, lived this man C. S. Lewis. He was professor of Medieval and Renaissance English, though just then I had no awareness of his burgeoning influence. If only I had known he would become one of the most important Christian thinkers and writers of our century! His famous book *The Screwtape Letters* was written during those years. I could not have known that this very book would be the first Christian book that I would read.[5]

Life at school continued on apace, and I enjoyed it all. Yet a nagging sense of unease persisted. Despite all my efforts, my thoughts would wander to the image of Grace on her knees with heaven's serenity painting her features. Or I would be irritated with the cheerful way our tennis captain lost a match! Her good sportsmanship rebuked my bad sportsmanship. I knew her attitude had something to do with her faith. And then one night I got really sick, and the school rushed me into hospital.

In the next few days as my condition worsened, I had nothing to do but revisit the stirrings of my soul and, without words, cry out to a God I wasn't even sure existed. He had, of course, everything lined up to answer that heart cry. In a ward of some twenty people, a Christian was in the bed next to mine. Janet was a nurse who herself was sick, but though in pain, she was alert enough to take me on as a project!

It didn't take her and God long. A few short glorious days of unpacking the truth and feeding it to me in bite-sized pieces convinced me. This was truth that I wonderingly believed. This was about Jesus. This was about what my sin did to Him. This was about His everlasting love demonstrated in a manger, on a cross, and in an empty tomb. Suddenly I was back in my bomb shelter as a little girl, no longer wondering about the validity of Creation, the Fall, redemption, and glory, but embracing it all.

It was done! I was reduced to size, and oh, so sorry I had hurt Him so! I was told that my sorry heart was being made whole, but all I knew was to hold my soul in my hands until it became totally contrite and broken. It didn't feel whole to me; it felt shattered. I cried bitter, sorry tears. For the first time in my thoroughly self-centered life, I cried for someone other than myself. I cried for Him. For the cross He had to endure to bring me home.

The next day, a copy of *The Screwtape Letters* appeared on my bedside table. "Read it," Janet advised me. "The devil is mad he has lost you, and you must not be ignorant of his devices." And so my spiritual education began with C. S. Lewis's startling images of the old devils and the young devils who desire to chew us up and spit us out to assuage their diabolical hunger. It began with images from this man's pen that I have never forgotten—images that have hugely influenced my journey of faith.

Those images not only influenced my thinking and believing, but my teaching and writing, too. I think, write, and teach using images and pictures, allegory and fantasy married to fact. As most disciples do, I try to emulate my Master Teacher as I seek to awaken my world to the cornerstone doctrines of the faith—Creation, Fall, redemption, and glory—doctrines I believe with all my heart, soul, mind, and strength. When I get to heaven I will most certainly ask to spend one of my first days off with C. S. Lewis!

I will thank him for his book that warned me the devil will attack my "holy habits" first, last, and always. In his book, Uncle Screwtape reproaches the apprentice demon, Wormwood, for permitting his "patient" to become a Christian.

> There is no need to despair; hundreds of these adult con-
> verts have been reclaimed after a brief sojourn in the
> Enemy's camp and are now with us. All the *habits* of the
> patient, both mental and bodily, are still in our favour.[6]

If a convert's habits remain the same, they will realize little of their life in Christ. I credit Lewis with "frightening" me into holy habits that have lasted a lifetime. He encourages the disciple of Jesus to keep "listening to that other voice."

> The real problem of the Christian life comes where people
> do not usually look for it. It comes the very moment you
> wake up each morning. All your wishes and hopes for the
> day rush at you like wild animals. And the first job each
> morning consists simply in shoveling them all back; in
> listening to that other voice, taking that other point of view,
> letting that other larger, stronger, quieter life come flowing
> in. And so on, all day. Standing back from all your natural
> fussings and frettings; coming in out of the wind.[7]

Wonderful passages such as this have helped me put myself intention-ally into God's sweet presence, and to hold my heart still until it is kissed by heaven itself in the person of Jesus! It was Lewis who alerted me to the absolute necessity of stretching the sides of my soul devotionally day by daily day, and Lewis who insisted that the friend of Christ not grow weary in well doing and in the work of God. As I have practiced what Lewis calls "coming in out of the wind," God has renewed and smoothed the frayed edges of my emotions until I am refreshed and ready to do battle again.

The writings of C. S. Lewis have helped me celebrate God through everyday experiences. To look for and bask in those patches of what he calls "Godlight."

As I travel the world in the autumn of my life, the wind blows hard in my face. In Russia this year, traveling across eleven time zones, teaching and training, evangelizing and arguing the gospel, I turned exhausted one night to *The Lion, the Witch and the Wardrobe,* a book I found on the bookshelf of a child in the missionary home in which we were staying. Stuart, my husband, and I were there just before Christmas, and I reread the description of the people who lived in the White Witch's domain. These were people who celebrated Wintermas, not Christmas. I read about Aslan again, and how the ice and snow melted in that frozen place when the Great Lion roared. I thought about the faces I was meeting all over Russia who, having been locked in a grim winter of Communism, were still frozen of soul in the aftermath of the Cold War.

I prayed long into the night for the Lion's roar to be heard in Russia, for a melting of this grim winter of their souls. There in Siberia I thanked God again not only for the images and ideas that have kept my holy habits fresh, but that have also fueled my urgent need to take the gospel the world over so that people can "come in out of the wind."

As I delighted once again in *The Lion, the Witch and the Wardrobe,* Lewis's White Witch, whose breath froze everything in sight, contrasted sharply with Aslan's "God roar" that melted the ice and brought the warmth of life and sunshine to bear on a frozen world. This stark contrast elicited a Christmas sermon of my own. Lewis's phrase "winter without Christmas" brought to my heart and mind the danger of many of my friends back in America who remain outside of Christ. How many people do you know who have had too many Wintermases and never experienced a Christmas of their own? When I have the opportunity, I will certainly thank Lewis for how he boiled deep and difficult things down to such believable truth in his delightful stories of Narnia, and we will talk about his use of symbols to point us to unseen realities.[8]

I will also thank him for his raw honesty and how he wrestled through his ministry with a broken heart. How hard it is for famous Christians to bear private grief publicly, and yet how wonderfully does this mighty literary giant invite us into his pain. He shares with the world his search for solid ground as he watched Joy Davidman, the love of his life, fight her death battles.

"How, C. S.," I will ask, "did you ever manage to allow your searing personal pain to drive you to God and not away from Him? It is hard when you are hurting so much emotionally you can hardly breathe to spare some special time to comfort others in similar predicaments by your honest wonderings and triumphant conclusions." I am grateful that he allowed us into those sacred places. And I will want him to know that he has helped so many of us when our own time of testing has come.

One of the things I discovered as I began to devour everything written by Lewis is how doctrine could be made so simple. Not simplistic, but rather without guile and completely believable. He brought big truths down to small digestible concepts with a picture or a homely illustration. This ability of his taught me to allow all that I was learning about Christ to turn my focus outward to a lost and dying world. I came to understand through his writings that I was blessed to be a blessing and not just to be blessed. I have been saved to serve, not to look for others to serve me; to worry about my friends' eternal destiny as much as I have worried about my own. Along these lines, one particular passage in *The Weight of Glory* found a place in my heart, and it has never been dislodged:

> It may be possible for each to think too much of his own
> potential glory hereafter; it is hardly possible for him to

think too often or too deeply about that of his neighbour. The load, or weight, or burden of my neighbour's glory should be laid on my back, a load so heavy that only humility can carry it, and the backs of the proud will be broken. It is a serious thing to live in a society of possible gods and goddesses, to remember that the dullest and most uninteresting person you can talk to may one day be a creature which, if you saw it now, you would be strongly tempted to worship, or else a horror and a corruption such as you now meet, if at all, only in a nightmare. All day long we are, in some degree, helping each other to one or other of these destinations [Glory or corruption].... There are no *ordinary* people. You have never talked to a mere mortal.... It is immortals whom we joke with, work with, marry, snub, and exploit—immortal horrors or everlasting splendours.[9]

Lewis also used illustrations that relate to my world as a woman, unlike some preachers who use male illustrations only. Today in church I am surprised too seldom by an illustration that belongs to my woman's world. In *The Four Loves,* Lewis uses images from a woman's world such as kitchen implements or homemade stories to draw us into his meanings of *agape, phileo,* and *eros* love.[10] I understand and relate to his pictures and parables because he took time to understand me—a woman. He listened, observed, and has felt my "womanness" enough to use it to instruct my spirit in its quest for godliness and selfless love.

C. S. Lewis was a critic, a satirist, a visionary, and an apologist. I believe that in the New Millennium we have now moved beyond the New Modernity, which among other things took us from "thinking to feeling," and that the horrendous events of September 11, 2001, shocked us into returning from feeling to thinking again! On the infamous 11th of September, I found myself in the air on the way from Moscow to Chicago. I ended up being diverted to Newfoundland, along with at least 10,500 other flyers in fifty-seven carriers. There I was stranded for six and one-half days in a Salvation Army hall. I was surprised to discover that these were some of the most wonderful days of my life!

Not only did I have a chance to check and see if my theology was in good shape, but I had the wonderful opportunity to spend "talk time" with the 250 people on my flight who had nothing else to do but think about the issues of life and death that had suddenly and rudely interrupted our lives. In conversations that week I discovered myself drawing on my Lewis memories, concepts, and quotes. Once more it was time to face people up with his challenges. Truth, of course, is true for all times and conditions of humanity, but the approach that Lewis took to explain it to the "man on the street" was exceptionally useful during that stressful time. It was a glorious week!

For this unprecedented opportunity, as people's minds have been shocked awake, we have C. S. Lewis, in all his depth and richness; a thinker who speaks clearly to our day and age, unscrewing the inscrutable and explaining the unexplainable. The time is right and the fields of the world are ripe for harvest. Lewis puts a sickle in our hands. We should use the tools that this master writer and thinker has left behind for us as weapons in our arsenal to make Screwtape and his devils sorry they started the whole mess in the first place!

Happy reading.

EIGHT

A Newsstand Bestseller and a Changed Life

D. James Kennedy

He came to show us how to live, not for a few years but eternally. He explained truths that would make our souls joyous and free.

—FULTON OURSLER, from the preface of
The Greatest Story Ever Told

It would not be possible for me to explain, or to justify, how I chanced upon the book that probably influenced my life more than any other, without first putting it into its proper perspective in terms of my personal experience and condition at the time. The reason for this is that the book itself was actually a sequel to a more life-changing impact, which had been made upon me in the preceding days.

At the age of twenty-three, I was a spiritual derelict. Worse than that, I was thoroughly satisfied with my secular lifestyle as a ballroom dance instructor in Tampa's Arthur Murray Studio. I was a college dropout, but making good money in a job that I immensely enjoyed. I was single, popular, and pretty well unhampered by moral restraints. Nor could I recall ever having heard the gospel or having been "witnessed to" by anyone. I was in every respect a smug, indifferent, freewheeling, and (I thought) happy man of the world.

That was before my clock radio, in my rented apartment on South Boulevard in Tampa, threw me a curve. I had come in from an all-night dance party and thought I had set the appliance to wake me at the proper time with appropriate music for a soothing return to consciousness. But what I heard that Sunday afternoon was definitely not Guy Lombardo's "sweetest music this side of heaven." It was the thundering voice of Dr. Donald Grey Barnhouse, pastor of Philadelphia's Tenth Presbyterian Church. I jumped out of bed to switch the dial but was stopped almost in midflight by a question I couldn't brush aside.

In the penetrating, stentorian tones for which he was famous, this great preacher and broadcast evangelist asked, "Suppose that you were to die today and stand before God, and He were to ask you, 'What right do you have to enter into my heaven?'—what would you say?" I was completely dumbfounded. I had never thought of such a thing as that, and my nonchalance suddenly evaporated into thin air.

I sat on the edge of my bed, as though transfixed, groping for an answer to this simple question. I had enough common sense to realize that, even though I had no background in the Bible, this was the most important question that had ever entered my mind.

And I had no answer whatsoever. What is more, I understood in that instant that I desperately needed to get the answer. The Holy Spirit was opening my ears to hear the gospel, and I was being born again right there in range of that radio message. The spoken testimony of a believer was moving upon the heart of an unbeliever who had previously evidenced not the slightest interest in religion.

While the remaining words of Dr. Barnhouse's sermon provided me with additional information I needed, what shocked me most was the overpowering sense of wonderment mixed with a strange joy that I had never before experienced. I felt overcome with a burgeoning curiosity, a demand-ing desire to learn all there was to know about this God who held my eter-nal destiny in His hands and who was, even now, drawing from the depths of my heart a confession of every sin I had committed. What was He really like? Why was He willing to forgive me and take me into His heaven because of what Jesus Christ did? Who was that wonderful Son of God who came to this planet to take away its sin at a place called Calvary? What is this Bible, which I had ignored all my life, really about? These questions occupied my mind through the days following what I later came to under-stand as my conversion. I had to get the whole truth about the gospel, which I knew was changing my life 180 degrees.

To be frank, I was a Bible illiterate—I didn't have the slightest idea where to start looking for an explanation of the fundamentals of Christian theology. All I knew was that I had had a heart transplant, no longer car-ing for loose talk, for an occasional cocktail, for the satisfaction of the unwholesome appetites of the past. In their place was a driving awareness that I was living a new life with a new purpose and new affections. And I had begun a search for new knowledge that would make clear to me exactly what it was all about.

This brings me to the crucial role played by a book, the one book out-side of the Bible that has had the greatest influence on my life. As I men-tioned earlier, the book would have had little or no impact on me if I hadn't first been captured by God through the words of Dr. Barnhouse's sermon. That memorable week of mental, moral, and spiritual renewal was pro-logue to my happening upon the then-popular volume *The Greatest Story Ever Told* by Fulton Oursler.[1]

Like any young person seeking information on subject matter in which he had no background, I stopped by a corner newsstand and asked ingen-uously, "Do you have any religious books?" The proprietor said he had just one and handed me a copy of Oursler's bestseller. I eagerly took the book home and began reading it, a few chapters at a time, until I had finished it.

From the moment I opened the book, I had the peculiar feeling that it had been written expressly for me. The very format of the volume seemed to have been arranged for my easy understanding, step by step, of the entire gospel message. Not only were the contents divided into *Book One* through *Book Six*—each labeling a significant phase of the life of Jesus—but each section was broken down into chapters that clearly outlined the movement of the narrative from an introduction of the parents-to-be right through to the postcrucifixion comments of the enemies of the Savior. Seventy-two chapter titles whetted my appetite to devour this simplified presentation of what is, indeed, the greatest story ever told.

I had no knowledge of the author's background until many years later. I did not know that Fulton Oursler had been editor of the widely popular *Liberty* magazine, and later an editor of *Reader's Digest*. I didn't know that he had come out of twenty-five years of what he termed "contented agnosticism" before writing his masterpiece, which appeared in 1949. By that time, the distinguished Baltimore journalist had already been expressing concern over what he considered the nation's greatest disgrace. As Oursler put it, "[T]he unspoken scandal of our times was the hidden fact that Bible-reading had been largely given up in America."[2] He complained that common "front-porch" conversation once included Bible verses that were now forgotten. I discovered in later years that a trip to Palestine proved to be the catalyst in the writing and publishing of *The Greatest Story Ever Told*. It was a pattern somewhat reminiscent of the life-changing effect the Holy Land had on General Lew Wallace, who reversed his planned literary attack on Christianity to write instead his masterpiece, *Ben-Hur*.[3] In the case of Fulton Oursler, the journalist was so deeply impressed with the Land of the Bible that he extended his sojourn to gather a working knowledge of the people of Palestine and the geography of the Middle East. That prolonged visit supplied him with the invaluable familiarity and detailed information he needed for the local color that he would weave into the pages of his manuscript.

Long before his novel was published, Oursler conceived the idea of radio-program material based on the stories he was writing. In the Golden Age of radio, he envisioned a series of dramatized episodes telling the story of the life and ministry of Jesus and narrating several of His parables. But several years were consumed in negotiating for airtime, casting the best actors, and lining up a satisfied sponsor.

Recently, as I researched the careful work that preceded the writing of this phenomenal book, I discovered that not one script for the radio series was broadcast without the prior approval of a distinguished advisory board. All of the material was previewed by the senior ministers of the three largest churches in New York City, plus Otto Frankfurter, brother of Justice Felix Frankfurter of the United States Supreme Court. This meant that Oursler's presentation of the gospel message was deemed by Protestant, Catholic, and Jewish authorities to be biblically accurate and universally appealing.

When the dramatizations of the New Testament began in 1947 as regular Sunday-evening radio entertainment, they proved to be so popular that the sponsor of the half-hour show, Goodyear, was surprised to see full-page newspaper ads purchased by its competitor, the General Tire and Rubber Company, urging the public to tune in and enjoy its rival's programs. Providence had decreed that these wonderful scripts would be rewoven into a full-fledged novel, and that the book would end up in my hands just one week after another radio broadcast, Dr. Barnhouse's powerful (albeit unsolicited) gospel message. One would have to be blind not to recognize God's hand at work.

From a literary critic's point of view, I am aware that *The Greatest Story Ever Told* would not receive a four-star rating. It was produced with an eye toward marketability and popular appeal, just as were its successors, *The Greatest Book Ever Written* and Oursler's final work, completed by his daughter after his death, *The Greatest Faith Ever Known*.[4] Clearly, here was a formula that would sell. Nor, of course, would I claim that no other books exerted significant influence over my thinking, my life, and my ministry.

There are many, the foremost of which are Calvin's *Institutes* and Augustine's *Confessions,* as well as a host of others.[5]

But this book, which I read as an excited young man in Tampa some forty-nine years ago, was not the product of a theologian's mind. That was fortunate, because a theological work would have been hopelessly over my head. Oursler had a single goal, which was to tell the story of Jesus as faithfully to the New Testament text as it could be told. When I picked up his book, I had a single request, which could be expressed in the words of an old hymn: "Tell me the story of Jesus, write on my heart every word."[6] It was the perfect book to address what I desperately needed at that moment of my spiritual awakening and development.

Three decades passed, and I was invited to write a foreword to a special edition of Oursler's classic, in which I concluded with the following observations:

> When I completed the book, it seemed as if the Cross of
> Christ had been erected right in my apartment and now I
> knew—for the first time—I knew why Christ was suffering
> there. I slipped out of my chair onto my knees and asked
> Christ to come into my heart and forgive me and cleanse
> me of my sins. From that day unto this, my life has never
> been the same. I shall be forever grateful for the radio
> broadcast of Donald Barnhouse and for this book by Fulton
> Oursler, both of which God used to bring me to a saving
> knowledge of His Son. It is, therefore, with great joy that
> I present to you this special edition of Fulton Oursler's
> classic, *The Greatest Story Ever Told.* May it bring to your
> life the joy unspeakable which it brought to mine.[7]

Calvin, the *Institutes,* and Me

J. I. Packer

Our wisdom, in so far as it ought to be deemed true and solid
wisdom, consists almost entirely of two parts: the knowledge
of God and of ourselves.

—JOHN CALVIN, *Institutes of the Christian Religion*

The two volumes lie before me as I write. Written on the flyleaf of the first
volume in my mother's hand are these words: "Christmas 1949. Jim, with
best wishes from Father and Mother." The second is similarly inscribed by
my sister. This was the gift I had asked them for: *Institutes of the Christian
Religion by John Calvin. A New Translation by Henry Beveridge.* (I quote the
title page exactly.) In reality, the *New Translation* was more than a century
old, but the work had been unobtainable for two generations, and this
reprint, only a few months old in December 1949, was quite an event.[1]

On the dust jacket of the first volume (ragged, but still in one piece on
my copy) is a blurb by Dr. D. Martyn Lloyd-Jones, at that time Britain's
evangelical leader, a theologically alert and gifted Welsh preacher and pastor for whom at that stage of my life (I was twenty-three) I had a huge
regard. Hailing the reprint as "the best news I have heard for some time,"
he declared:

The *Institutes* are in and of themselves a theological classic. No work has had a greater or more formative influence on Protestant theology. It is not always realised however that in addition to its massive and sublime thought it is written in a style that is most moving, and at times thrilling. Unlike most modern theology which claims to derive from it, it is deeply devotional....

It is in the *Institutes* that one finds the systematic and formulated statement of his [Calvin's] essential position....

The most urgent reason why all should read the *Institutes*, however, is to be found in the times in which we live. In a world which is shaking in its very foundations and which lacks any ultimate authority, nothing is so calculated to strengthen and stabilize one's soul as this magnificent exposition and outworking of the glorious doctrine of the Sovereignty of God.[2]

Wisdom? Truth? A word for today? Yes, more than half a century later, I think so. But I must move on.

Below the inscription from my parents, I see that I copied in a similarly enthusiastic assessment by William Cunningham, nineteenth-century Scotland's counterpart to Charles Hodge of Princeton, who thought Cunningham the greatest living Reformed theologian. (Cunningham, be it said, returned the compliment.) Of the *Institutes,* Cunningham wrote:

The *Institutio* of Calvin is the most important work in the history of theological science...and has exerted...the greatest and most beneficial influence upon the opinions of intelligent men on theological subjects. It may be said to occupy in the science of theology, the place which it requires both the "Novum Organum" of Bacon, and the

"Principia of Newton" to fill up, in physical science—at
once conveying…the finest idea of the way…in which the
truths of God's word ought to be classified and systema-
tised, and at the same time actually classifying and systema-
tising them, in a way that has not yet received any very
material or essential improvement.[3]

For three years prior to Christmas 1949, I had been reading the Puritans and moving in circles where Calvin was spoken of as if he had uttered
the last word in human wisdom, but I had not up to then read anything
by him. So what did I find when I began digging into my family present?
Once I adjusted to the odd way Calvin was made to sound like a mid-
nineteenth-century Scotsman (Beveridge was a mid-nineteenth-century
Scotsman), I realized that here was a literary work of distinction, a massive
treatise written by a Renaissance stylist with a steady, well-paced flow of
thought and a lively, resourceful rhetoric; a logically laid out composition
in which every sentence counted, and with a warmth of heart permeating
its clarity that I had not expected at all. I read Beveridge for the next eleven
years; when in 1960 the Ford Lewis Battles translation in Westminster
Press's Library of Christian Classics appeared, I read that.[4] (It is more exact
and better annotated and indexed than Beveridge, I found, though it is also
less brisk.) I read some of Calvin's Latin, which is elegant almost to the
point of dancing, and I dipped into the sixteenth-century rendering by
Thomas Norton (fourth printing, 1583, which, believe it or not, I found
in fair shape in a secondhand bookshop for two dollars), which caught the
elegance of the eloquence better, to my mind, than any later version has
done. Lately I have taught graduate seminars on the *Institutes,* which have
kept me rereading the text, and though it runs to well over a thousand
pages in all modern English versions, I think I may claim by now to know
it fairly well. For those as yet unacquainted with Calvin's masterwork, however, I need to describe it before going further.

The *Institutes* began as a pocket book for Protestants on biblical Christianity, about three-quarters the length of the New Testament. It grew into a *vade mecum* for students of theology and a technical polemic on Reformation questions for Christian leaders as well, so that by its fifth and final edition in 1559, twenty-three years after it first appeared, it was five times its original length, as long as the Old Testament and Gospels together, and was arranged on a different plan, with eighty chapters instead of six. As a second-generation Reformer, trained in classics and law, Calvin saw his task not as innovation, but as consolidation, that is, as conserving, confirming, and setting in order the insights and gains of his older contemporaries, Luther, Bucer, and their colleagues. His integrating category for this purpose unites in itself the whole of Christian doctrine, experience, and behavior— namely, knowledge of God, a biblical concept covering knowing about God, which is theology, plus knowing God relationally, which is religion.

Significantly, Calvin's title from the start was *Institutes* (Latin *institutio*, "instruction in the basics") *of Christian Religion* (Latin *religio*), which is more than theology. The first edition's title continued, in the long-winded promotional style of those pre-dust-jacket-blurb days, as follows: *"...containing almost the whole sum of piety (pietas) and all that it is necessary to know in the doctrine of salvation: a book very well worth reading by all persons zealous for piety."* One guesses that Calvin's publisher, who had to sell the book, had a hand in that rather fulsome wording, but the book's contents truly warrant it. *Pietas* meant for Calvin real godliness, the Christian ideal, and guidance in *pietas* remains central—indeed, is from time to time augmented—throughout the work's progressive bulking up. Calvin holds doctrine and devotion together, as is right, and blends them brilliantly. When some say that the theme of the *Institutes* is knowing God through Christ, and others say that its theme is sanctification in Christ, each estimate is one-sided, but both are correct as far as they go.

To the question, What does it mean to know God? the *Institutes* replies, in effect: Knowing God means acknowledging him as he has revealed himself in Scripture; worshiping him, adoring him, and thanking him for all he gives us; humbling ourselves before him as sinners, and centering our faith, trust, hope, and confidence upon the Christ whom God the Father sent to be our Savior; living by faith in the promises of perfect pardon and permanent protection that God through Christ has given us; loving the Father and the Son with a love that answers the love they have shown to every believer; walking with God steadily, praying regularly, obeying God's law constantly, and so progressing in our Christian pilgrimage; looking forward to a joyful resurrection into a final transcendent glory; and seeking God's honor in all human relationships and all commerce with created things. This view of the life of knowing God is expounded throughout the book.

To the parallel and, from one standpoint, prior question, What do we know about God? the *Institutes* replies by laying out the contents of biblical theology under four heads in four books, following the order suggested by the sequencing of themes in the Apostles' Creed. *Book One* deals with knowledge of God the Creator, the triune Lord of all; *Book Two* with knowledge of Christ the Mediator, the Savior of sinners; *Book Three* covers knowledge of the grace of God in human life, through the action of the Holy Spirit; *Book Four* covers knowledge of the nature, ministry, and sacraments of the church, as God-given helps to our faith, growth, and faithfulness, plus knowledge of how to honor God in our relation to the state (civil government, seen as a means of grace within its proper limits). The two complementary angles of exposition are that these are the truths that are there in the Bible, for Christians to learn, and that the Lord Jesus Christ is the Truth, the *scopus* (focal center, reference point one way or another) of all that the Bible contains, on whom we must ever rely and whom we must seek to please and glorify in all that we do.

Thus, the *Institutes* transcends any supposed dichotomy between the intellectual and moral aspects of Christianity, and stands as a classic of both orthodoxy (right faith) and orthopraxy (right living).

Having said that much about the *Institutes,* I can move to the real purpose of this essay, which is to declare what, over the years (fifty-three so far), Calvin's book has done for me. Looking back, it seems that the short answer is that the *Institutes* helped me to grow up in Christ and get beyond some stunting influences to which I was exposed. The modern way of saying this is to affirm that the *Institutes* contributed to my Christian formation. I make the first point in global and comprehensive terms, drawing on what others have been kind enough to say about me. Alister McGrath, at his own initiative, wrote my life. It was published in the United States as *J. I. Packer: A Biography* and in the United Kingdom as *To Know and Serve God.*[5] Reviewing it, Ward Gasque wrote:

> McGrath's analysis of Packer's life and ministry is right on target. McGrath argues that Packer's work has emphasized four major dimensions of the contemporary evangelical situation: (1) the importance of history, (2) the primacy of theology, (3) the coherence of theology, and (4) the possibility of collaboration without compromise....
>
> In spite of his commitment to a strongly "Reformed" Anglican theology, Packer's greater commitment is to the "great tradition" of Christianity that transcends narrow denominationalism. The early and medieval fathers, the Reformers and the Puritans, eastern Orthodoxy and western Catholicism, Calvinism and Pentecostalism—all belong to this great tradition.... Packer wishes us to recover and revel in our theological inheritance with all the saints rather than to rejoice in our narrow distinctives. Thus, he is unafraid to join hands with all who seek to defend the essence of the gospel and to promote true spirituality that is grounded in Christ.[6]

There you have a well-drawn profile of what at least I try to be, and if you thought my early Christian nurture and later life–circumstances led me that way, you would be wrong. Insofar as any human mentor got me to this mind-set, it was Calvin, as I shall now attempt to make plain.

First, Calvin showed me *how to think to the glory of God.* Having come to faith in my first term at Oxford, in 1944, I was nurtured in a fellowship where zeal for Christ and evangelism, and fortitude in face of criticism, were magnificently present, but where the operative theology was limited to a few Bible-based, surface-level ideas about God, Christ, the Holy Spirit, and personal faith and faithfulness. The accepted view of theological inquiry was that it was an unspiritual and dangerous distraction from the real demands of discipleship, unfruitfully muddling the mind and hardening the heart. In my foreword to Bruce Milne's fine little handbook of theology, *Know the Truth,* I recounted what a fool I made of myself by explaining to my college chaplain that theology (not bad theology, but theology as such) is poison to the soul.[7] I was at that time a very young convert, naively regurgitating what those teaching me to love and serve my Lord had told me. Though I soon saw the stupidity of thus rubbishing theology and started profiting from the Puritans, who were theologians to their fingertips, I never realized how theologizing can sanctify the mind and heart and deepen one's doctrine, devotion, and doxology all together till I read the *Institutes* and found it happening to me as I followed Calvin's argumentation.

From that point, thank God, I have never looked back. Here, I saw, was the appropriate larger frame in which to set both the wisdom the Puritans were teaching me about Christian living and the insights across the biblical board that study for my theology degree was unfolding to me. My goal became, and remains, to think, speak, and write if I can to the same effect as did Calvin, ever making God look greater and more wonderful and man smaller and less significant than either had seemed before the theological thought process began. Two centuries ago the British evangelical patriarch Charles Simeon said that his preaching had three aims: to humble the sinner, to exalt the Savior, and to promote holiness. Half a century ago

I discerned these three aims in the *Institutes* and, with Calvin, made them central to my own attempts to glorify God and build up his people. What success I have had in this, others must judge; here I simply affirm that it was Calvin in the *Institutes,* more than anyone else, who set me going on this wavelength.

Second, Calvin confirmed me in *my view of Holy Scripture.* Despite my preconversion certainty that no educated person could treat the Bible as God's true and trustworthy Word, soon after my new birth I found myself unable to doubt that it was precisely that. But not till I read Calvin's *Institutes,* five years later, did I know what to make of this rather startling change. External influences during those years pressured me to revert to my preconversion view. But in my Beveridge translation of Calvin I found this: "Scripture bears upon the face of it as clear evidence of its truth, as white and black do of their colour, sweet and bitter of their taste" (I.vii.2). In other words, the immediacy of the Bible's impact authenticates it as God's truth; and more fully:

> Scripture, carrying its own evidence along with it…owes
> the full conviction with which we ought to receive it to the
> testimony of the Spirit. Enlightened by him, we…feel per-
> fectly assured—as much so as if we beheld the divine image
> visibly impressed on it—that it came to us, by the instru-
> mentality of men, from the very mouth of God…we feel
> a divine energy living and breathing in it…I say nothing
> more than every believer experiences in himself, though my
> words fall far short of the reality. (I.vii.5)

When first I read this, I remember, I laughed out loud for joy, for I knew, and knew that I knew, exactly what Calvin was talking about. Here he was telling me that, so far from being eccentric in my conviction, I was now in the Christian mainstream. His paragraph ended thus: "If at any time, then, we are troubled at the small number of those who believe, let us…call to mind, that none comprehend the mysteries of God save those to whom it is given"—and that sustained me, too, as indeed it still does.

Third, Calvin changed me *from a sectarian into a churchman.* If you had accused my Christian fellow students of sectarianism, they would have denied it indignantly, and I do not press the accusation. But certainly the mental attitude I developed as they taught me evangelical truth and the way of life that went with it were sectarian. Sectarianism has four unlovely features: (1) its elitism (we are the superior people, the only ones who really count); (2) its standoffishness (we will not cooperate in anything with any who will not march consistently to our tune); (3) its narrowness (we are only interested in people, past and present, of our own stripe, and take notice of others only to prove them wrong); and (4) its hidden arrogance, which regularly masquerades as faithfulness. It was Calvin more than anyone else who made me realize that my sectarianism, like so much else about me in those days, was the juvenile immaturity of a half-baked student, and that as part of my growing-up process I must exchange it for the responsible adult churchmanship that he himself modeled. Evangelical pietists for three centuries have so concentrated on personal faith and experience, and so habitually individualized New Testament teaching on the calling of the church, as to be chronically weak in their churchliness, and I was no exception. Sectarianism was part of the image of evangelicalism in my youth, and behind the image there was, I fear, a good deal of reality.

But Calvin devoted one-third of the *Institutes* to the church (all of *Book Four*) and made it evident from the start that the book was meant, among its other purposes, to disciple people for life in the church. He was observably formulating his Bible-led theology in conversation with the intellectual heritage of the early patristic and medieval Western church, and setting standards and limits and focusing ideals for the church of the future. Moreover, he saw that the church, the worldwide worshiping, witnessing, working fellowship of believers, embracing all gatherings where Word and sacrament were biblically ministered, is central to God's whole plan of redemption, from eternal election to the perfecting of New Jerusalem. None of us may think of ourselves as the only pebbles on God's beach. As we are saved to serve in a benighted world, so we are saved to share in a corporate life. I took Calvin's point; my belief that honest, humble holiness and godliness must ever come first did not waver or wither in the least. But being the church and building the church became central concerns, alongside my other concern (his, too) never to let the centrality to the gospel of justification by faith be obscured.

I, too, began to draw on the entire wealth of the Christian theological tradition to help me grasp the depth and breadth of Bible teaching, and joint ventures with Christians who would not call themselves evangelical but who loved the Bible, its Christ, and his church became part of my life. With present-day liberal Protestantism I have no common ground and can only see it (as Calvin would have done) as hugely mistaken. But other Christian conservatives who love Jesus my Lord—Pentecostal, Roman Catholic, Anglo-Catholic, and Orthodox for starters—are my fellow believers, sometimes despite their official doctrine. They are, as well, my cobelligerents in the war against the demonic misbelief and misbehavior that disfigure mainline churches today. I value their fellowship as I seek to bring together all biblical insights in formulations that are small-c catholic, that is, truly comprehensive and universal—the very job that the *Institutes* sought to do four and a half centuries ago! My biblical churchliness and convictional ecumenism, such as they are, owe more, I think, to Calvin as a model than to any other of my teachers—though the Puritan Richard Baxter in some respects runs him close. (But that is another story.)

Fourth, Calvin formed me as *a Bible-led rather than a system-driven systematist.* Calvin, a systematic thinker if ever there was one, is often viewed as a deductive theologian whose alleged fixation on predestination led him to follow speculative inferences about God beyond what Scripture says. But this is precisely what he was not and did not do. His method in theology is pictured in Psalm 119:105: "Your word is a lamp to my feet and a light to my path" (ESV). The picture is of having to travel cross-country in the dark, and so needing the equivalent of a flashlight to see where you are going and to walk in safety. A flashlight illuminates a few yards in front of you, but beyond that all stays dark. (Shining a flashlight is not like sunrise!) So, too, when we reach the outer limits of biblical teaching we face the darkness of the mystery of God, so much of whose being, mind, plans, and providential activity are unrevealed and thus unknowable to us. Calvin regularly went to the limit of what Scripture says, arguing that nothing in the Bible is superfluous, but he would not go to one step beyond that limit, insisting that the right course now was not to try to fill gaps in our understanding by guesswork, but rather to move into adoration and praise for all that God has told us. Observing speculative streaks in systems of thought around me—supralapsarian, Amyraldean, Arminian, classic Wesleyan, classic Pentecostal, universalist in various forms, and so on—I have tried throughout to stay within the limits, working with the Bible exegetically and canonically, observing the analogy of faith (Scripture's inner consistency) as Calvin did before me, and never losing sight of the mystery of God. And I have ended up a Bible-Calvinist, if I may put it so, rather than a system-Calvinist—that is, a man wielding his flashlight rather than wearing a ready-made straitjacket. Well, so be it; when all is said and done, Calvin's theological method seems to me right, just as most of his findings seem to me convincing. I do not think I am off track when, like King Wenceslaus's page, I tread boldly in the master's steps—though I would rather not be called a Calvinist as I do so. (What, then? A mere theologian, please; or a theologizer, as Alister McGrath prefers to label me.)

Fifth and last, Calvin set me *claiming, and reclaiming, all life for God in Jesus Christ, and valuing all goodness and beauty as his gift.* My early pietist instructors taught me cultural dualism, listing pleasures and activities to be eschewed as worldly and talking as if the only worthwhile jobs were pastor, missionary, physician, and schoolmaster. I briefly believed them, during which time I remember flooring my parents by telling them I could no longer listen to Beethoven because he did not write Christian music, but soon I was sure that these ideas were wrong. Not, however, till I read the *Institutes* on God's common grace (II.ii.12-17) and on grateful appreciation and enjoyment of pleasant things in moderation (III.x) did I clearly see how to respond to this well-meant and self-denying but false and impoverishing asceticism. Beyond this, it was Kuyper rather than Calvin who showed me how to acknowledge God's sovereignty and honor his grace in the many spheres and departments of our everyday life. (But that, again, is another story, though one that came to me very much as a footnote, or appendix, to this that I have now told.)

So I celebrate Calvin as my mentor, and his *Institutes* as the primary text through which, half a century ago and four hundred years after he wrote it, he pulled together Puritan insights I already had and, adding much wisdom of his own, got me into what is essentially my present theological and spiritual shape. Nor is he only a piece of my past; I still find as I read him that over and over again he anticipates and resolves today's problems, as he has been doing for me since 1949. His was a mind for the ages, not just for the sixteenth century, and his teaching is still out ahead of us to a most amazing extent.

In 1991 in *Christianity Today*, I wrote a whimsy piece under the title "Fan Mail to Calvin."[8] I round off this essay by reproducing it.

Dear John,

This is a fan letter, naked and unashamed, one that I have long wanted to write, even though for obvious reasons I cannot mail it to you. But public acknowledgment of one's debts is good for the soul, and when one is a teacher of theology it is good for the church, too. I don't know why, but Christians I meet seem to think that theologians who

teach spring fully formed from the womb and work in
isolation from one another—hence the "I am of Calvin"/
"I am of Finney"/"I am of Pannenberg," which Paul would
surely have nailed as pure Corinthianism. I hope that by
declaring my debt I can reduce the possibility of the world
or church ever being bothered by "I am of Packer" people.

I wish people grasped that theologians, like other Christians, learn with the saints in the multigenerational fellowship that is the church, where mentors, pastors, and peers
help us to see things we hadn't seen before. Augustine had
Ambrose, and you had Augustine, Luther, and Bucer, and
I had Owen, Warfield, and you. We get to where we are
by standing on others' shoulders and benefiting from their
brainwork. You were clear on that—much clearer than
some of the hero-worshipers who have written books about
you! No true theologian works as a one-man band.

One thing you helped me see is where theologians
really fit in. The church lives through the potency of
preaching—the mystery of God's Spirit applying God's
Word to God's people through God's spokesman. So the
primary function of theologians is to ensure, so far as
human beings can, that the Bible is explained right and
applied properly. I think I only give the film version of your
thought when I tell people that theologians are the church's
plumbers, water engineers, and sewage-disposal experts—
back-room boys whose crucial though unspectacular job is
to secure for the pulpits a flow of pure and unpolluted Bible
truth. You, of course, had a larger role; you were a preaching pastor, and you educated other preaching pastors in the
academy. How you managed to get through it all, especially
in those grisly last years when you were dying by inches, I

shall never know. But it is for your clear grasp of the theologian's task that I admire you now.

Another thing I learned from you was the true nature and ideal shape of what we nowadays call systematic theology. Your *Institutes* is a marvelous tapestry of evangelical wisdom that modeled for me the apostolic way of tying together the many strands of revealed truth about God's grace to a sinful world. You put the sovereignty of God, the mediation of Christ, and the ministration of the Spirit right at the center; you set up the life of faith and praise as the goal; and you did not write a speculative sentence from start to finish of your 700,000 words! I would like you to know that I have had the *Institutes* by me for 40 years, that I keep finding fresh wisdom in its pages to a degree that is positively uncanny, and that I am very grateful.

The way you dealt with predestination, in particular, strikes me as an all-time brilliancy. Like Paul in Romans, you separated it from the doctrine of providence and postponed it till you had spelled out the gospel, with its *bona fide,* whosoever-will promises; then you brought in the truth of election and reprobation, just as in Romans 8 and 9, not to frighten anyone, but to give believers reassurance, hope, and strength. It's a beautifully biblical and powerfully pastoral treatment.

The irony is, as I expect you know, that in the...[nineteenth] century the idea spread that all serious theologians arrange everything round a single focal thought, and yours was predestination, so they lost sight of your biblical breadth and balance and pictured you as a speculative monomaniac who pulled Scripture out of shape to make it fit a scheme of your own devising. That's still your public image, and biblicists like you are still called Calvinists in a way that implies they have lost their biblical footing. Such is life! I expect you're glad to be out of it.

With deepest respect and gratitude,

J. I. Packer

Heart of a Rebel

Liz Curtis Higgs

Fallen man is not simply an imperfect creature who needs
improvement: he is a rebel who must lay down his arms.

—C. S. LEWIS, *Mere Christianity*

FEBRUARY 1982

The ceilings were high, the windows drafty, and the heat in my century-
old apartment house was little more than a rumor. Curled up in a sagging
club chair, intently reading, I hardly noticed the midwinter cold, warmed
as I was by the words before me and the late-afternoon sun pouring
through the long, narrow windows of my study.

"Read this book," two friends had urged me. Because I'd grown to love
and respect them, and because the title intrigued me, I purchased *Mere
Christianity* and began, as all serious readers do, with the preface: "The contents of this book were first given on the air…"[1] Well, now. Hooked from
the very start. Hadn't I spent the last five years working as a radio broad-
caster? I burrowed deeper into my faded chintz cushions and kept reading,
intrigued by the writer's strong sense of who he was and who he was not. "I
am a very ordinary layman of the Church of England, not especially 'high,'

nor especially 'low,' nor especially anything else."[2] Odd. My friends had insisted he was a genius. Three pages into the book, *humble* seemed a much better fit.

I knew nothing of Lewis's work or reputation. A title like *The Chronicles of Narnia* left me shaking my head. Kurt Vonnegut Jr. lived on my bookshelf, along with Robert A. Heinlein and Ray Bradbury. Not J. R. R. Tolkien. And not C. S. Lewis. Perhaps that was for the best. I came to Lewis without my defensive shield at the ready. Even had I been prepared, the honesty of his words would have disarmed me: "There are questions at issue between Christians to which I do not think I have the answer."[3] Uh-oh. I had nothing *but* questions—questions about the existence of God, the validity of faith, the necessity of church. Such things mattered a great deal to my two friends, which bewildered me. Intelligent, talented, well-read, much-traveled people, yet they were genuinely enthusiastic about going to *church*. How was that possible?

"Read this..."

And so I kept reading, all through the wintry afternoon. There was no denying this Lewis guy had me pegged: a disillusioned young woman of twenty-seven who'd gotten turned off by denominational infighting and hypocritical churchgoers. At least that's what I told people. *Fear* was the real reason: fear that I'd gone too far, done too much. Fear that, if God *was* real, I'd blown it, big time. Enter Lewis, a middle-aged British male, a scholar and a soldier, who put into words the deepest longings of my soul: "There is something, or a Someone, who against all divergences of belief, all differences of temperament, all memories of mutual persecution, speaks with the same voice."[4]

I'd heard that voice as a child. When I sang, "Jesus loves me, this I know," I really *did* know. I'd sensed Jesus nodding in agreement. Heard him say, "Yes, child."

When had I stopped listening? And would that voice still speak to me, after all I'd done? All the men, all the drugs, all the booze, all the lies—after all that, would the Someone I once called God the Father care about his long-lost daughter?

I kept reading, pulled from one paragraph to the next by Lewis's clarity of thought and ironclad logic. Within five pages he'd not only convinced me that Right and Wrong existed—me, the queen of loosey-goosey, do-what-feels-good relativism!—he'd also assured me that none of us was any good at keeping that sacred law. Ouch. Even worse, Lewis stated that when we stumbled we invariably shifted the responsibility for our failures elsewhere and conjured up flimsy excuses. "It is only our bad temper that we put down to being tired or worried or hungry; we put our good temper down to ourselves."[5] Ouch again.

Tempted as I might have been to toss the book against the wall at such bold claims, I couldn't bring myself to do so because his arguments were irrefutable: I *did* know Right from Wrong. Although I'd spent ten years convincing myself that I enjoyed being a bad girl, the ugly truth was, I hated it. Living at the bottom of a dark pit had grown lonelier with each passing year. Shocking people with my edgy lifestyle had lost its appeal. The term paper from my sophomore year of college—"Why I Don't Believe in God"—suddenly felt like blasphemy.

Chastised, I continued reading, certain that after he built a strong case against my moral failures, Lewis would offer a ray of hope. He seemed genuinely concerned that I understood what was at stake. Nothing short of eternity; nothing less than everything. Surely he wouldn't quit before giving me some good news, some way of escape. He was leading up to a critical conclusion, that much was clear. Something monumental. Undeniable. Change was in the air, tangible as the dust motes in my study.

True confession: I'm the sort who chafes at persuasion, bolts the room at manipulation. There was none of that in his writing, nothing unkind or judgmental about his tone. Nor did I need to know a single verse of Scripture to grasp what he was talking about. *Mere Christianity* depends very little on quoting the Bible by chapter and verse to prove what is false and what is true. Lewis realized that humans, made by our Creator, have the capacity to recognize truth when it is presented as such. Hadn't my friends lived out that truth in my presence for five months? "We are imperfect people loving a perfect God," they'd said, welcoming me into their home and into their church to experience the fellowship of the saints. When I began asking probing questions, they'd pointed me toward a bookstore. "Read this..."

Rather than quoting Scripture, Lewis paraphrased it. Romans 7:15 states, "For what I am doing, I do not understand; for I am not practicing what I would like to do, but I am doing the very thing I hate" (NASB). Lewis simply wrote, "[T]he Law of Human Nature tells you what human beings ought to do and do not."[6] Clever man, to use a phrase like *Human Nature,* capitalizing it as though it were important, as though our own opinion mattered above all others. It made me trust him. Feel safe around him. He wasn't going to take me anywhere I didn't want to go. At one stage, as if sensing his readers' potential withdrawal, he cautions, "Do not think I am going faster than I really am. I am not yet within a hundred miles of the God of Christian theology. All I have got to is a Something which is directing the universe."[7]

Oh, is that all? Never mind that he'd escorted me—and a few million other readers over the last sixty years—a *thousand* miles, from not believing in God to agreeing that God exists. Right there in my armchair, within easy reach of a toasted-cheese sandwich and a cold beer, I'd been guided by a benevolent stranger over the dividing wall between belief in nothing to belief in Something. He'd done it with nothing but words on a page, spilling nary a drop of blood on my study floor.

How does a writer like C. S. Lewis manage such a feat? With great care and by the power of the Holy Spirit. He invites us to examine our own lives and see if we agree with his assessments. He asks questions that beg answers: "Is the Life-Force the greatest achievement of wishful thinking the world has yet seen?"[8] *"Yes,"* we whisper, only too aware of our propensity to buy into such faulty logic a week earlier. He woos his readers, appealing to our common sense, our day-to-day lives, and our very Human Nature. He spins simple scenarios about letter carriers and clocks and insists he has no intention of preaching, even as he presents the gospel with a foundation more solid than the ground beneath any mahogany pulpit. "Shrewd as a serpent, innocent as a dove," that one.

I'm reminded of Susan in Lewis's novel *The Lion, the Witch and the Wardrobe,* and her question about the great Aslan, "Is he—quite safe?" To which Mr. Beaver wisely answers, "Who said anything about safe?... But he's good."[9]

Lewis is not safe. But he's definitely good.

Lewis is also not for the casual reader, nor is *Mere Christianity* meant to be read in a single sitting. That February long ago I allowed his dangerous words to sink in, first one evening, then the next, reading with a mix of dread and anticipation as he described "the thing we most need and the thing we most want to hide from."[10] I'd been hiding from God for a decade. Was it too late for this bad girl? Was redemption no longer an option, and goodness beyond my grasp? Lewis came to my rescue on that question: "Badness is only spoiled goodness."[11] Ah. Hope, then.

We spent a week together—Lewis on the printed page, I in my armchair—wrestling demons of doubt and despair. More than once, he made me laugh: "When you are arguing against Him you are arguing against the very power that makes you able to argue at all: it is like cutting off the branch you are sitting on."[12] Ha, ha, ha. Chain saw, please.

He didn't mince words, stating in no uncertain terms that God did "not come to torment your natural self, but to kill it."[13] I was a product of the self-indulgent '60s, honed by the feminism of the '70s. Kill my natural self? Humph. This God of his was expecting a lot. And yet...each time my temper notched up a degree, Lewis would touch a cool drop of water to my lips: "When you come to knowing God, the initiative lies on His side."[14] Oh. I wasn't expected to manage things on my own, then.

Assuaged once again, I kept reading.

Well-crafted phrases like "asinine fatuity" demonstrate his mastery of the English language, yet it was the profoundly simple ones that I underlined. "Mere improvement is not redemption";[15] "Good and evil both increase at compound interest";[16] and one aptly describing Lewis himself as he explains what our God wants from us: "a child's heart, but a grown-up's head."[17]

In the dead of that distant winter, I had just the opposite of what was called for: the hardened heart of a wayward adult and an infantile knowledge of God's Word. But I was willing to listen, and Lewis was more than willing to teach. I did not agree with every word then, nor do I now. He seems to approve of capital punishment, insisting it's "perfectly right for a Christian judge to sentence a man to death."[18] From my own viewpoint, the story of the woman caught in adultery gives us a different answer (see John 8:1-11). That decidedly guilty woman, sentenced to death for her crime, was set free by Jesus, who said to her, "Neither do I condemn you" (John 8:11). She was not required to "pay" for her obvious sins because Jesus would pay the death penalty for her soon enough, even as he paid for all our sins. Elsewhere Lewis himself declares, "by dying He disabled death itself."[19] Indeed.

In another instance, Lewis describes a child *in utero* using terms that suggest we aren't fully human from conception forward: "We were once rather like vegetables, and once rather like fish; it was only at a later stage that we became like human babies."[20] My only concern with such a statement is that it might be used to further the efforts of the proabortion movement—"it's not a baby, it's a cauliflower." I don't think for a minute Lewis was making any such case; I only fear that others might.

Why draw attention to such tiny sticking points in an otherwise glorious work? Because (1) Lewis wisely taught me, at the very dawn of my Christian walk, to think seriously about God and the creatures he made in his image; and (2) based on Lewis's own summation, the author would have welcomed such dialogue: "How gloriously different are the saints."[21] The fact that Lewis invites, even applauds, differences of opinion says a great deal about his confidence in his beliefs and his focus on the central issue of Christianity, the *Mere* of the book's title. How simply that core truth is stated: "Now, today, this moment, is our chance to choose the right side."[22] And how cunningly we avoid such surrender, to which Lewis warns, "If you are contented with simply being nice, you are still a rebel."[23]

That was me back then, rebellious to the core. On many days, that still *is* me. Chafing against God's will for me, preferring my own carefully plotted calendar. Daily I have to lay down my rebel's weaponry and embrace the eternal truth, eloquently stated by Lewis in the final pages: "The more we get what we now call 'ourselves' out of the way and let Him take us over, the more truly ourselves we become."[24]

And are you wondering what became of that young rebel, reading C. S. Lewis in her drafty apartment many Februarys ago? On a Sabbath evening, I closed Lewis's book in stunned silence, only one thought left banging around in my head: If a man that brilliant, that educated, that seasoned by love and war, believed with all his heart and mind that "there is one God and that Jesus Christ is His only Son,"[25] then who was I to argue with such a man?

So I did not argue. Nor did I stop with Lewis, turning instead to a more seminal work. Seated at an old maple table rescued from my mother's attic, I opened my Bible to the book of Romans (also recommended reading from my helpful friends) and soon found Romans 5:8: "But God demonstrates His own love toward us, in that while we were yet sinners, Christ died for us" (NASB).

This rebel's heart was finally and completely undone. My forehead fell onto the Bible's pages, and I drenched them with my tears. Sorrow and joy flowed, mingled down. Deep inside me, the truth beat like a drum: I was a sinner. I was loved. And I was forgiven.

ELEVEN

Prayer, Mysticism, Faith, and Reason

Donald G. Bloesch

The object of Faith is not the teaching but the teacher.

—SØREN KIERKEGAARD, *Philosophical Fragments*

The course of my spiritual pilgrimage has been shaped by a number of outstanding books, not the least of which are Søren Kierkegaard, *Philosophical Fragments;* Anders Nygren, *Agape and Eros;* and Friedrich Heiler, *Prayer.*[1] I was already a believing Christian when I read these books, but they have all expanded my spiritual and intellectual horizons. They have helped me recognize that the way to reach outsiders for the faith is not by apologetic argument, but by sharing the gospel and demonstrating its truth in daily life. They have also enabled me to see that we come to know God not by the mastery of spiritual techniques, but by persevering in faith as we take up our cross and follow Christ in lowly discipleship.[2]

SØREN KIERKEGAARD ON FAITH AND REASON

Søren Kierkegaard, a nineteenth-century Danish thinker and author, wrote a plethora of books that have established him as a pivotal figure in religious existentialism. I was introduced to Kierkegaard in a class on the history of Christian thought at the University of Chicago Divinity School in 1950. His *Philosophical Fragments,* which contains his ruminations on faith and reason, gave me the intellectual tools to withstand the onslaught of evolutionary naturalism that permeated the Chicago Schools of Theology at the time.

Kierkegaard showed me that human reason cannot establish the credibility of faith. Faith is neither a form of conceptual knowledge nor simply an act of the will, but a gift of grace that opens our inward eyes to the truth of what God has done for us in Jesus Christ. The case for Christianity is founded not on rational speculation nor on evidential corroboration, but on divine revelation, personified and exemplified in Jesus Christ, who is a paradox to human reason. Revelation, in contrast to all forms of mysticism, signifies not an immediate sense of God's presence, but a communication of God's will through the event of the Incarnation. In contrast to rationalistic orthodoxy, Kierkegaard maintained that what is revealed is not propositional knowledge, but the meaning of an event in history that can be appropriated only in the form of paradox. He called God "The Absolutely Different"—the One who stands over against human reason rather than being congruous with it. Faith does not overthrow reason but transcends the parameters of reason. Revelation is something external rather than integral to humanity. It is not an inner discovery but a divine intervention in past history. We have access to the significance of this event in the Moment of decision, which involves human willing, but only on the basis of the prior gift of grace.

For Kierkegaard the main problem in theology was the penetration of philosophical idealism into theological discourse. He respected the sagacity of thinkers like Plato and Hegel, but he was insistent that Christianity is corrupted when it is united with any philosophical system. Philosophy can prepare the way for theology, but it cannot furnish the foundation for theology. Plato, Hegel, and other idealists postulated an identity between the known object and the knowing subject. For Kierkegaard, to the contrary, there is a distance between the two that can never be bridged. Idealism is fueled by an illusion that human beings already possess the truth and need only to become conscious of it. In contrast, Kierkegaard established that we can never possess the truth, but we can become poignantly aware of the truth through an encounter with the God-Man, Jesus Christ, whom he called "the Absolute Paradox." Christianity is not knowing the truth conceptually; it is being in the truth. This has profound implications for how one lives in the world. Love is not looking upward to the perfect object, but outward to our neighbor, the one whom we meet in daily experience.

Kierkegaard wrote as a Lutheran, and Luther's emphasis on faith over reason is reflected in *Philosophical Fragments* as well as in his other books. Yet Kierkegaard viewed Lutheranism as only a corrective to Catholicism, and when Lutherans and other Protestants try to ignore or downplay their Catholic heritage, they end up with a faith divorced from the demands of discipleship under the cross. As a representative of evangelical Pietism, Kierkegaard was adamant that while we cannot contribute to our salvation, we can manifest and demonstrate it by a Christian life. Kierkegaard had one foot in mysticism, but basically he was a relentless critic of both mysticism and rationalism. We find God neither in an ecstatic experience nor in metaphysical inquiry, but only in a meeting with God when his Spirit reaches out to us and claims us for his kingdom. In Kierkegaard's thinking we become united with God not by climbing a mystical ladder to heaven, but by God's descending to our level and claiming us for his own.

Kierkegaard is often treated as a philosopher of religion, but in reality he was a theologian in the guise of a philosopher. This is to say, he dialogued with philosophers not as a dispassionate inquirer after truth, but as one firmly committed to the truth revealed in Jesus Christ. In contrast to all philosophers, Kierkegaard conceived of truth not as a teaching, but as a person. The key to knowing this truth is neither logical deduction nor mystical rapture, but inward conversion by the Spirit of God.

Drawing upon both Kierkegaard and Luther, I have found in my own theological reflection that the truth of God is not accessible to me unless I am in a right relationship with Jesus Christ. But paradoxically I cannot be rightly related to Christ unless I see myself as a sinner saved only by grace. As a forgiven sinner and as one who has the assurance of salvation through Christ, I can then begin to understand the mystery of God's becoming incarnate in Christ. I can do theology through the illumination of the Spirit as he draws me closer to Christ. But even when I have partial knowledge of the mystery of God in Christ, I must still confess that I am totally dependent on his grace. I cannot think rightly or act rightly unless I acknowledge my need for continual conversion by the Spirit of God.

ANDERS NYGREN ON LOVE

Anders Nygren was for many years professor of systematic theology at the University of Lund and then served as Bishop of the Diocese of Lund in the Church of Sweden. His *Agape and Eros,* published in two volumes in English in 1938 and 1939, made an indelible imprint on my thought and on my Christian walk. With Nygren I hold that love is at the center of spirituality. How one loves determines how one matures in the spiritual life. What makes Nygren's book distinctive and even revolutionary is that it draws a sharp contrast between two types of love: *eros* and *agape.* Eros in its spiritual form as championed by the Greek philosophic tradition is the love that seeks the perfection of the self through union with God. Eros is basically egocentric and acquisitive. It is driven by a need to satisfy the deepest yearnings of the self for beatitude and interior peace. Eros is not mentioned in the New Testament, but it was widely employed in the patristic and Catholic traditions as indicative of a higher kind of love, a love that brings salvation by igniting in the soul a mystical quest. Eros spirituality was already ascendant in the emerging Gnosticism of the second century.

Agape is a word for love used in the New Testament to indicate the sacrifice of the self for the good of the other. It is basically oriented toward meeting the needs of our neighbor and thereby giving glory to God. Agape is spontaneous and other-regarding as opposed to self-regarding (as in the case of eros). Agape is also unmotivated, in the sense that it does not depend on any worthiness or merit in the object of love. It is indifferent to value, going out freely to sinner and saint alike. Its opposite is not selfhood but self-centeredness. It takes a person out of the self into the trials and heartaches of one's neighbor. Agape is the initiator of fellowship with God. We do not find God through a mystical quest, but God finds us in the gift of his Spirit—the awakening to faith.

In the Latin West, agape and eros were united in *caritas* (charity), but eros emerged triumphant in this synthesis. Augustine, who pondered deeply over the nature and implications of love, retained the note of agape in his concept of grace; yet in our response to God's grace, he saw eros as much more significant. It is through our love for God that we gain the satisfaction and fulfillment of the self. Nygren makes a credible case that the egocentric motif is predominant in Augustine's doctrine of the spiritual life.

According to Nygren, agape in its biblical sense was rediscovered by the Reformers, particularly Martin Luther, in the sixteenth century. In Luther's view we do not climb our way to heaven on some spiritual ladder, but heaven comes down to us in the person of Jesus Christ. Agape confers worth on the person loved, whereas eros finds worth in the object of love. Luther made this insightful observation: "Sinners are loved not because they are beautiful, but they are beautiful because they are loved."[3] Eros is an ascending love that directs us to realities beyond this world; agape is a descending love that takes us into the midst of the world's tribulation with the message of redemption.

A pivotal question that arises in this area of theology is whether biblical faith sanctions or nullifies self-love. From Nygren's perspective faith negates self-love and replaces it with other-love. I prefer to say that faith subordinates self-love to other-love. Eros can be purified or sanctified by agape and thereby brought into the service of agape. Married love, for example, will ideally contain a strong measure of eros, for it involves the uniting of both wills and bodies; yet it is redeemed and fulfilled only by agape, which transforms natural desire into a desire for the well-being of the other. My wife and I find that the more we try to serve each other in love (agape), the greater our affection for each other. The passion for autonomy, which dominates the contemporary scene, is highly detrimental to the marriage relationship.

Agape and Eros must not be accepted uncritically, but its basic thesis is unassailable: Christianity introduces a new motif into spirituality—the paradoxical love of the cross, the love that does not raise us to a perfection beyond this world but makes us channels of redemption to the lost and needy around us. Such love contradicts the spirituality that pervades our culture—that which is centered in the fulfillment of the self through the satisfaction of spiritual need. The love of the cross is, as Luther said, a "lost love,"[4] for it goes out to the undeserving sinner without any expectation that it will be returned.

Nygren's book taught me to see that there is a marked contrast between the mystical tradition of the church, which bids us look inward, and the biblical ethos, which compels us to look outward to the needs of others. The Christian vocation does not lead us to withdraw from the world into a utopian or monastic community but sends us into the depths of the world's poverty with a message that heals and transforms. This fact does not rule out, however, the possibility of communal or paraparochial fellowships that provide for a time a needed refuge from the storms of life and that function as training centers for Christian mission. I have visited fellowships of Christian renewal in this country and in Europe and have personally experienced inward peace and joy through coming to know people whose faith is visible through works of love. Such persons can also be found in most of our congregations, though when faith subsides in our churches, visible sanctity becomes much more rare. Worldliness can also infiltrate monasteries and other religious communities, as Luther saw so poignantly, and such institutions then stand in need of radical reform in the light of the Word of God.

FRIEDRICH HEILER ON PRAYER

A third book that has made a lasting imprint on my thought and life is Friedrich Heiler's *Prayer*. Heiler, who died in 1967, was a convert from Roman Catholicism to Lutheranism. His critique of mysticism is especially significant for my theology, since it hinges on the contradiction between biblical personalism and mystical idealism.

Heiler's typology of prayer is extremely helpful in understanding the diversity in the life of prayer. First is primitive prayer—the attempt to bend the will of God for personal gain and benefit to the self. Second is ritual prayer—the reduction of prayer to prescribed acts and words that are thought to release divine power on behalf of the suppliant. Third is the religion of ancient Greece in which we entreat the gods for assistance in living the moral life. Fourth is philosophical prayer, consisting of surrender and resignation to a god or gods who are distant from the travails of humanity.

Finally, Heiler introduces us to what he deems the two highest modes of prayer: the mystical and the prophetic. Mystical prayer is the heroic attempt to reach God by disciplines of devotion and ecstatic experience. The goal of prayer becomes the union of the soul with God. Prophetic prayer, which appears in Judaism and Islam as well as in biblical Christianity, is bringing before God our innermost needs and petitions, seeking his pardon and deliverance. In contradistinction to ritual prayer, prophetic prayer is a spontaneous outburst of emotion. It contains both a revolutionary and an intolerant thrust in that it posits only one way to salvation—God coming to humanity in a particular event or events in history. Mystical prayer, in contrast to prophetic prayer, is inclusive and syncretic. Mysticism rises above religious provincialism and credalism and exults in the union of the individual soul with God.

In Heiler's view, mysticism and prophetic religion both repel and attract each other. They repel each other because they present two irreconcilably different pictures of God—one as a loving heavenly Father who hears our cries for deliverance and acts to save us (as in prophetic religion), and the other as a suprapersonal ground or depth of being that lures us to himself by the sheer magnetism of his beauty (as in mysticism). Mysticism and prophetic religion attract each other because they both see prayer as the key to a creative and meaningful life in relationship to God.

Heiler can possibly be criticized for leaving out prayer in the new spirituality emerging in Romanticism and modern skepticism. The new spirituality is postmodern rather than modern, for it celebrates particularity and diversity over universal laws. Secular or political prayer, the kind espoused by Nikos Kazantzakis, Teilhard de Chardin, and J. A. T. Robinson, among many others, teaches not withdrawal from the world, but penetration through the world to God.

Heiler insightfully reminds us that whenever ritualism and formalism gain the upper hand, the intimacy of personal communion with a living God is placed in jeopardy. Yet it is well to recognize that worship and prayer need outward forms in order to maintain continuity with a religious tradition. Heiler acknowledges the inevitability of ritual prayer, but he sees it as something deleterious rather than beneficial to the prayer life.

Where Heiler has helped me personally is in his firm insistence that prophetic religion transcends and negates all other types of religion. Too many of today's manuals on prayer are oriented around the stages of the mystical life, beginning with purgation and proceeding to illumination and then contemplation. They seem to take for granted that human beings are free to prepare the way for the coming of grace into their lives. What is missing is a realistic portrayal of the human condition in the light of God's self-revelation in Jesus Christ. This would involve an admission that through sin the human will is bound to the power of sin and death and needs to be liberated by the Spirit of the living God. This liberation, moreover, takes place when we are united with Christ in faith as a free gift of his bounteous mercy. Worship and prayer cannot be renewed in our churches until we break free from the philosophical and spiritual traditions of ancient Greece and Rome and recover an evangelical understanding of human redemption and deliverance.

EPILOGUE

It should be obvious that these three books have far-reaching ecumenical implications. Whereas evangelical Protestantism highlights the agape motif (à la Nygren), Roman Catholicism and Eastern Orthodoxy make a prominent place for the eros motif. While the evangelical ethos is shaped by prophetic prayer, the Catholic tradition elevates mystical prayer (as Heiler correctly observes). The danger in the evangelical understanding is a logocentric theology in which experience is overshadowed by Scripture and in some cases by creeds as well. Mysticism, on the other hand, too quickly devolves into a pneumatocentric theology in which the Spirit or the inner light is the final court of appeal. We must transcend the cleavage between mysticism and rationalism, subjectivism and objectivism. We can do this in a theology of Word and Spirit in which an emphasis on the spiritual life is combined with a theology that holds together the objective and the subjective, the cerebral and the mystical. Instead of either a logocentric or a pneumatocentric theology, I favor a Trinitarian theology that unites Father, Son, and Spirit as coequal agents in both revelation and salvation.

The theology that I have endorsed is not novel, for Word and Spirit has been a salient theme in mainstream Catholicism and Eastern Orthodoxy as well as in Reformation and revivalistic Protestantism. At times, though, an imbalance has occurred: Spirit is unduly elevated above Word or vice versa. This imbalance has been especially noticeable in heterodoxical movements.

Rationalism has been pronounced in both Catholic and Protestant forms of scholasticism. Spiritualism has been evident in both Catholic mysticism and radical Pietism. We can learn from the mystics and pietists not to neglect the decisive role of experience in coming to faith and in the life of faith. But we must also be alert to the fact that the truth of biblical revelation transcends religious experience just as it constitutes a paradox to reason (as Kierkegaard reminds us). Faith that is vital will seek understanding; yet the mysteries to which it directs us are in the final analysis incomprehensible. A faith that will renew the church is one that respects mystery even while trying to find meaning within mystery.

The threat facing the church today is a religious syncretism that elevates the mystical quest over fidelity to a particular revelation in world history. We see this both in the New Age movement and in religious existentialism. Christianity has indeed an irrevocable existential dimension (as Kierkegaard acutely perceived) as well as a perduring mystical tinge (as the church fathers readily acknowledged). But Christianity must never be reduced to the passion of inwardness or to rational assent to propositional truths (though it surely includes these elements). Faith will most assuredly contain an existential passion, the significance of which is given in the biblical testimony.[5] Likewise, faith will include knowledge; yet it is not dispassionate knowledge, but the unswerving conviction of realities not seen. Faith is inexplicable apart from love, for faith works through love (see Galatians 5:6). This is not, however, the love that seeks possession of the highest good (eros), but the love that reaches out to help those in need (agape). Faith summons us to a life of prayer; yet it is not the prayer that lays hold of a divine energy or that sinks itself in a cosmic consciousness, but the prayer that throws itself upon the mercy of a sovereign and holy God. It is not the prayer that devotes itself to the transfiguration of the self, but the prayer that strives for the redemption of one's neighbor, and it is precisely in sacrificial service to our neighbor that we gain a glimpse of the glory of God.

Christianity does not call us to cultivate an interior piety that insulates us from the hardships and tumults of the world. Instead, it summons us to a holy worldliness in which we bring the message of redemption to lost and despairing sinners. General William Booth, founder of the Salvation Army, gave this advice to his coworkers: "Go for souls, and go for the worst."[6] Many of the biblically oriented mystics would respond positively to this challenge, but those who are more radical or consistent in their mysticism would enjoin their hearers to detach themselves from the daily pressures of life and create a holy enclave where the life of the spirit might prosper.

It is well to note that all three books in this discussion draw a sharp distinction between biblical or evangelical piety and the mystical heritage of the church. Mysticism as a philosophy of life must be distrusted, but this should not prevent earnest evangelical Christians from reading the works of the mystics with critical appreciation. We can learn from those who conceptualize the faith differently and whose style of life may be in conflict with the ethos of the Reformers, but this is because not a few of the mystics are at the same time believing Christians and appeal to the same source of authority as the Reformers—namely, Holy Scripture illumined by the Holy Spirit.

Borden of Yale '09

Kenneth N. Taylor

I cannot understand it! There is no accounting for such a life.

—comment of a militant unbeliever

who read *Borden of Yale '09*

Borden of Yale '09 fell into my hands when I was a college student, and it helped set my life goals in a God-ward direction from which I have never changed course.[1] It is the story of William Borden, born into a wealthy Chicago family and a Christian home, who gave away many millions of dollars bequeathed to him by his father.[2] At the age of twenty-five, Borden sat on many boards of directors of Christian enterprises, not only because of his financial contributions to them but also because of his wisdom and open-heartedness to God and man alike.[3]

One Sunday afternoon when William was only six, his mother gathered the children around her for a Scripture lesson. Several young cousins were with them. Apropos of something in the lesson, Mrs. Borden suggested the children should each take a slip of paper and write down what they would most like to be when they grew up. The slips of paper were put inside a sealed envelope and forgotten. When found ten years later, it was discovered that William had written, "I want to be an honest man when I grow up, a true and loving and kind and faithful man."[4]

His biographer, Mrs. Howard Taylor, reports, "To his last day, by the grace of God, the man could have looked into the eyes of the child without shame."[5]

William was a fun-loving child and was devoted to active and even dangerous games. His cousin, John Whiting, was his chief ally in escapades of all sorts. In the biography, Whiting recalls the following incident when the boys were seven years old:

> Late one Saturday afternoon we decided that we wanted to play in the gymnasium of the school.... That the building was locked up for the weekend made no difference. We found the cover of a coalhole loose and dropped in through that. We fooled around the gym until tired, then took a leisurely shower and dressed, not realizing how late it was. We got out by a window which we had to leave unfastened. I was visiting William at the time and when we reached home, about seven-thirty p.m., we were met by Mr. and Mrs. Borden, worried and almost alarmed over our non-appearance. When the cause of our tardiness was discovered, we were promptly sent to bed with bread and milk for supper. It was meant for punishment, but nothing could have suited us better. We were tired and hungry, and while it was only bread and milk, the supply was unlimited.[6]

One day William and his cousin, looking out from his home onto the expanse of Lake Michigan after a terrible storm, saw a ship loaded with lumber that had gone to pieces. The great timbers were lying at all angles along the shore. Seeing the work that had to be done, the boys of seven or eight were soon outside gathering the lumber and putting it in orderly piles. A group of laborers appeared before long, but William and John kept on working, and at the end of the day lined up with the others and received their pay.

One of the deepest things in Borden's life was devotion to his mother. During his college years, after his father's death, he made time to write to her every day. His mother had passed on to him many of his grandfather's lovable qualities.

But there was something more important that she passed on to this child. When William was about seven years old, his mother entered a life-changing spiritual experience. Always a devoted mother, she now became an earnest, rejoicing Christian. She joined the Moody Church in Chicago. It was there, one Sunday afternoon, that the pastor, Dr. R. A. Torrey, gave everyone present an opportunity to dedicate their lives to the service of God. William quietly rose—a little fellow in a blue sailor suit. It was consecration from which he never drew back.

He graduated from high school at age sixteen, and his parents felt that a year spent traveling around the world would be worthwhile before he entered college. William's traveling companion was Dr. William Erdman, scholarly, brilliant, full of humor, and a recent graduate from Princeton University and Seminary. His chief recommendation in Mr. and Mrs. Borden's eyes lay in his Christian character.

Their first stop was Japan, which only fifty years previously had been visited by Commodore Perry to force the Island Kingdom into the family of nations. At Kyoto, they visited the Temple of the 33,333 Gods. It was at Kyoto that William wrote to his mother:

> Your request that I pray to God for His very best plan for
> my life is not a hard thing to do, for I have been praying
> that very thing for a long time. Although I have never
> thought very seriously about being a missionary until lately,
> I was somewhat interested in that line as you know. I think

this trip is going to be a great help in showing things to me in a new light. I can't explain what my views were, but I met such pleasant young people on the steamer who were going out as missionaries, and meeting them influenced me.... I realize things as I never did before. When I look ahead a few years it seems as though the only thing to do is to prepare for the foreign field. Of course, I want a college course and then perhaps some medical study, and certainly Bible study, at Moody Institute perhaps.[7]

The next stop was China. His love of yachting and boat life made him especially interested in Canton's river population. William was accustomed to narrow quarters on the Borden family boat, but never had he imagined that people could be born, married, rear their families, and marry off their children without ever having a home on shore! There were at that time 350,000 boat people in Canton. He reported:

A boat perhaps twenty feet long will hold a family of six or seven. I couldn't see where they stowed themselves away, but they do it somehow. A great many keep chickens as well, hung out over the stern in a basket which serves as a chicken-yard. Some of the kids and women have empty cans tied to their backs to act as life-preservers if they should fall overboard. For one Chinaman will seldom rescue another, because the rescuer has to keep the rescued for the rest of his life, if he happens to want to be kept. And sometimes they will bargain with a drowning man before pulling him out![8]

William recounted a conversation he had with a young Canton businessman who said he was a Christian. He made it a great point that he always went to church. However, it turned out that he did not believe in anything the Bible said. William reported, "I told him what I believed and he said I was young and didn't know better, that in a few years I would think differently. I managed to quote a few verses to which he could not say anything but I didn't put up a very good argument as I got rather fussed and excited. I wished at the time that I knew my Bible better."[9]

This statement shows that William recognized his need for a greater knowledge and understanding of the Bible.

I read *Borden of Yale '09* on a Sunday afternoon more than sixty years ago. I was home for the summer from Wheaton College, class of 1938. I had spent the summer working ten-hour shifts on a hay-bailing crew in the Willamette valley near Portland, Oregon. My job, along with a partner, was to pile hay onto a platform where another crew member swept it into a hole where it was crushed into a bale by a gasoline-powered chunker. Every thirty minutes was a "rest break," which meant carrying the bales away by hand and piling them up until the horse-drawn wagons were ready to take them to the barn for storage.

Sunday was a workday for our crew, but my father, a Presbyterian clergyman, had asked me not to work on Sundays. When I explained the situation to my boss, who was a member of my father's congregation, he excused me from the Sabbath labor, and that is how it happened that I was reading a book on Sunday afternoon instead of sweating in the hayfield.

After church and Sunday dinner, I picked out the book from our library shelves, being attracted by the title. Here was the story of a university student, and I, as a college student, was naturally interested in his experiences at Yale. As I read I became even more interested, for Bill Borden was on the wrestling team at his school, just as I was at mine. Bill was a Christian, and so was I. He was a class leader, and I, too, had been entrusted with leadership responsibilities by my fellow students.

There was, however, a big difference in that Bill was a millionaire! My hayfield wages were twenty-five cents an hour, and my father was far from being a millionaire.

I was fascinated to read about Bill's desire to become a missionary—something I had no desire to do. I was a lower-middle-class American, and I wanted to move up the economic ladder, not down. I was almost sorry to read of Bill's decision, for it was a rebuke to me. He had become a role model for me and I felt I was losing him.

Another conviction that dominated Bill's life was that the Bible from first to last is the inspired Word of God. His biographer quoted a letter from the Reverend James M'Cammon concerning this:

> To him it was the Book of books. He had not only an intel-
> lectual grasp of its teachings such as one may get in a theo-
> logical seminary, but he had the spiritual understanding of
> it which only comes through prayerful and devotional study
> in humble dependence on the Spirit of God.[10]

Bill Borden's father had left him a very large inheritance. But Bill didn't cling to his riches, because he felt that everything he had was a trust from God. He gave away many millions of dollars,[11] dividing the money among various Bible schools and other Christian enterprises, including the Yale Hope Mission, a rescue mission he helped begin while he was a college student. I was aghast. Since childhood I had thought being a millionaire was one of life's highest goals. But here was Bill Borden, a college senior, giving away great wealth.

He was a spiritual giant in other ways, too. He frequently talked with his classmates about God—that he had a plan for their lives, including the forgiveness of their sins through faith in Christ. The thought of talking with an unbeliever about Christ terrified me. Perhaps this was a reaction to my father's almost embarrassing readiness to tell others about the Savior. Yet here was my new hero, Bill Borden, preaching at a gospel mission to down-and-outers. He would go there on Saturday nights and put his arm around men who came forward, telling them about Christ's willingness to forgive and help them.

I also admired his experience on the Yale wrestling team; he knew some of the agonies I had experienced when pinned to the mat.

As I read more about this millionaire, athlete, and spiritual giant, I became uneasy. He was thinking of becoming a missionary, something I had decided I would never be—not because I had prayed to know God's will, but because I didn't want to go. I didn't want to give up the good things of life in America, and I didn't want Bill Borden to do it either!

Nevertheless, after graduating from Yale University, he attended Princeton Seminary and became greatly concerned about Muslims in China, for whom little was being done by mission societies. After being ordained in his home church, he was accepted by the China Inland Mission. He was assigned to a western province in China heavily populated by Muslims. In preparation for the assignment, he went to Egypt to study the Arabic language and Muslim literature. As I read this, I became increasingly uncomfortable. Suppose God were to call *me* to be a missionary. Would I go? I tried to put the question out of my mind.

Then I read that Bill became dangerously ill after only a few weeks in Egypt. I had heard of wonderful miracles of healing because people trusted in God, so I was entirely unprepared, as I turned the page, to find that Bill's fever grew higher and higher.

"Dear, God," I prayed in my intensity, as I continued reading, "*don't* let him die."

But God let William Borden die. I was overwhelmed with shock. Then a cold, hard resolution gripped me. "If that is the way God treats a man wholly devoted to him, then I want no more of such a God." It was a terrible moment as I deliberately turned my back on God. It was as if I were stepping off a cliff and plunging to the rocks below.

At that moment God showed his grace to me in a way almost beyond my ability to describe it. He reached out and grabbed me and pulled me back. I can't explain what happened, but suddenly I found myself on my knees beside the chair where I had been sitting. I was praying in deep contrition, "Lord, here is my life. Take it and use it in any way you want to."

I have never turned back from that decision—a decision that completely changed my life's direction. It was a decision that made it possible for God to lead me on a "guided tour" for the rest of my life.

What is it about *Borden of Yale '09* that proved life changing? Undoubtedly, God's Holy Spirit had prepared my life and heart, and reading the book was the next step in his spiritual process. Would anyone else be similarly affected? I do not know. God has many ways of attracting us into his lifelong blessings, and in my life the stories of people who followed God have been a major factor.

So it proved for me at the beginning of my adult life, at an age when I was choosing a life-determining direction. As I knelt at the chair where I had been reading *Borden of Yale '09,* I truly did turn my life over to God. I believe he has used me in ways he might not have done without the influence of this book and the decision it led me to make. Of course, I have refreshed that commitment many times and sometimes have strayed from my goal. But I am thankful that God led Mrs. Howard Taylor to write this biography. God continues to use the words that Mrs. Taylor wrote to change lives. He used those words to change mine.

Caterpillars, Butterflies, Books, and Community

Gary R. Collins

There's nothing at the top and it doesn't matter.
We can fly!
We can become butterflies!

—TRINA PAULUS, *Hope for the Flowers*

His name was Stripe.

On this world's stage he was not a big player. He was only a couple of inches long when he set out to explore his tiny neighborhood. And nobody knew his name.

After gingerly crawling down from the tree that had been his home, Stripe made his way through tall blades of grass, moving forward with no plan or direction except to explore. Little plants and dirt and holes and tiny bugs and other crawlers like himself all came into Stripe's expanding world, but he was looking for something bigger, something exciting, fulfilling, meaningful.

Invigorated by a sense of adventure, he kept going.

Stripe never imagined that someday people would learn about his adventures in a book that could be read in fifteen minutes and had more drawings than text. And had he been able to think about such things, Stripe never would have thought that someday a psychologist—me—would write about his story in a volume concerning significant books that have impacted people's lives.

I struggled about including Stripe's story as the core of this essay. I am writing for a book where my chapter might well be surrounded by scholarly discourses about deep theological tomes that have shaped the lives of evangelical leaders more spiritual and influential than I. How, I wonder, will these giants of the faith or the other readers of this book respond when my favorite volume has nothing to do with theology or psychology, but instead is a lighthearted tale about a lowly caterpillar that turned into a butterfly?

I looked over my bookshelves and was reminded of the better-known authors whose works have shaped my thinking. I discovered Swiss counselor Paul Tournier in the 1960s. He wrote about integrating Christianity and psychology before this was a popular topic. I read all of his books and spent seven months in Geneva getting to know him and writing a book about his life and work. He impacted me profoundly, but I was unable to identify just one of his books that has influenced my life significantly.

I looked at my Henri Nouwen collection. I first discovered *The Genesee Diary* about the time it was written, and I assigned it as required reading in many of the counseling classes I taught.[1] From the beginning I loved Nouwen's openness about his spiritual journey and his struggles. Once on a trip to South America, I was accompanied by *¡Gracias! A Latin American Journal,* but it is not one of the most significant books of my life. The same could be said about *Clowning in Rome: Reflections on Solitude, Celibacy, Prayer, and Contemplation.*[2] In preparing this essay, I was refreshed to reread a description of the priest-author's months in Rome. He wrote:

> I started to realize that in the great circus of Rome, full of
> lion-tamers and trapeze artists whose dazzling feats claim

our attention, the real and true story was told by the
clowns. Clowns are not in the center of the events. They...
don't have it together, they do not succeed in what they
try, they are awkward, out of balance, and left-handed,
but...they are on our side.... Of the virtuosi we say 'How
can they do it?' Of the clowns we say 'They are like us....'

The longer I was in Rome, the more I enjoyed the
clowns, those peripheral people who by their humble,
saintly lives evoke a smile and awaken hope.... I even came
to feel that behind the black, purple, and red in the Roman
churches and behind the suits and ties in the Roman offices
there is enough clownishness left not to give up hope.[3]

From Tournier and Nouwen I turned to my large collection of counseling and psychology books. Over the years they have been so helpful, so practical, often so insightful, but none is at the top of my list of most influential books. I reached the same conclusion as I looked over the books by theological and biblical giants such as Strong, Barclay, Trueblood, Lewis, Stott, Schaeffer, Willard, Packer, and a host of others. More recently I have been influenced by Rick Warren's *The Purpose-Driven Church,* Andy Stanley's *Visioneering,* and *Spiritual Leadership* by Henry and Richard Blackaby.[4] But none of these rises to the top of my "most influential" list.

Then I went to the books on leadership, business, globalism, and contemporary issues that have become the core of my reading in recent years. Perhaps like Paul in Acts 17, I have come to the conclusion that if we are to reach a contemporary world with the gospel, we need to be familiar with that world and engaged with its inhabitants. There are few who touch the pulse of our postmodern world with the insight and accuracy of those who write books on leadership and business trends. I fail to understand how counselors or church leaders can hope to impact others if they stay stuck in the past, consumed by dead theologies or irrelevant psychology, ignoring the emerging trends that are bringing radical changes into the world where God has placed us. Bennis, Drucker, De Pree, Coles, Blanchard, and several hundred others have shaped my thinking, but even here no single book rises to the top.

HOPE FOR THE FLOWERS

Through all of this exploring, I kept returning to the simple story of Stripe that has impacted me and several million others. First published in 1972, *Hope for the Flowers* by Trina Paulus still appeals to a large audience.[5] It describes how Stripe continued his journey until he spotted a group of caterpillars climbing on one another. He saw a pillar of caterpillars, a "caterpillar pillar," where hundreds, maybe thousands of crawling creatures were climbing on top of one another, each trying to reach the top of the ever-shifting column.

> "What's at the top?" Stripe asked some of his fellow climbers as he started his climb upwards.
> "No one knows," one of the caterpillars replied. "But it must be awfully good because everybody's rushing to get there. Goodbye; I've no more time." Then he plunged into the pile.[6]

And so did Stripe. The higher he climbed, the more aggressive he and the other caterpillars became, stepping on one another, never hesitating to knock others off the pile, driving to get higher. At one time, Stripe gave up, came back down the pile and rested on the grass. It was relaxing in the sunshine, but his curiosity would not let him rest. He needed to reach the top.

Eventually he did, only to make an amazing discovery. There was nothing there. Hanging desperately to his position, supported by a column of striving caterpillars each intent on knocking him off and taking his place,

Stripe saw mostly other pillars, each with individual caterpillars like him at the top, each hanging on for dear life.

But Stripe saw something else. It was a butterfly, a beautiful creature that was not caught in the climb, a creature that could fly. The creature believed that Stripe could fly too, but only if he would stop striving and become what he was meant to be.

A beautiful little caterpillar named Yellow turned into the butterfly and inspired Stripe to do the same. The second-to-last page of the book says "The End" and shows two butterflies soaring above the grass. And the last page has only three words: "or the beginning."[7]

Surely you have guessed by now that I identify with Stripe. His story is the story of too much of my life, driving to reach the top. I don't think I ever knowingly stepped on anybody. I never intentionally knocked others out of the climb. A lot of my life to this day has been to encourage other climbers, younger people from all over the world who have leadership, counseling, and ministry potential. These are people who thrive on encouragement. They are spurred on by the affirmation of those who have climbed higher but who are willing to cheer even when these younger colleagues climb to greater heights than their mentors. Looking back, however, I wonder if I have spent too much of my life climbing and encouraging others to do the same. Climbing won't accomplish our goal. To get to the top in this world, to have the greatest impact, we need to fly. And according to Stripe, "you must want to fly so much that you are willing to give up being a caterpillar."[8]

Careful readers of the Paulus book will note that her volume has a lot of New Age implications. It doesn't strive to reach the conclusion that I have imposed on it, but it has impacted me greatly nonetheless. When my grandson, Colin McAlister, was born, I presented him with a copy of this book the first time I held him. Inside I wrote an inscription even before he was twenty-four hours old. I urged him to refrain from the driving, competitive lifestyle that has tempted many people, including his grandfather.

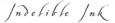

God protected me from falling, but the drive to reach the top has destroyed so many people. It has led thousands, maybe millions, to worldly and even ecclesiastical success but often exacts the terrible price of broken relationships, strained marriages, stress-filled lives, and ultimate emptiness. I urged my infant grandson to be like Stripe who ceased striving and who was able to soar because he allowed himself to be transformed into the creature God intended him to be.

THE HOLY AND THE DISCIPLINED

As he grows older, I hope my grandson will become familiar with some of the other books that have impacted me. As I looked over my bookshelves, two additional volumes stood out. Admittedly they are less enchanting than Stripe's story, and none contains captivating illustrations, but each of these authors captivated me with their words.

I don't know where I discovered A. W. Tozer's writings and first read *The Knowledge of the Holy.*[9] Perhaps it was when I was a graduate student at the University of Toronto and sometimes dropped into Avenue Road Church where Tozer served as pastor before I had ever heard of his name. First published in 1961, the book's message has proven to be prophetic. When we lose our sense of majesty, Tozer wrote, we lose our religious awe, our spirit of worship, and our "ability to withdraw inwardly to meet God in adoring silence.… It is impossible to keep our moral practices sound and our inward attitudes right while our idea of God is erroneous or inadequate.… A right conception of God is basic…to practical Christian living."[10] In twenty-three chapters, most no longer than three or four pages in length, Tozer described many of the attributes of God.

When I read Tozer's book, I was impacted profoundly. And the impact continues. I became a Christian as a child, but looking back I can see holes in my spiritual formation. I confess that I wasn't always listening to the sermons as I was growing up (too often I don't much listen now), but I never recall hearing about God's attributes. As a result, I was like the man that J. B. Phillips wrote about when he titled a book *Your God Is Too Small*.[11] Tozer gave me a bigger view of a bigger God, and my perception was changed permanently. I rarely read books more than once, but periodically I return to my well-marked copy of Tozer's book and ponder again the greatness of the God we serve.

Richard Foster did something similar when he introduced me to the spiritual disciplines in *Celebration of Discipline: The Path to Spiritual Growth*.[12] Early in my Christian walk I learned about prayer and Bible study, but I was well into my adult years before I began to see that solitude, submission, service, celebration, and other disciplines are crucial for spiritual growth. For years I attended weekly "worship" services where I never felt like I could worship. So much of the emphasis was on a person in the front of the room who waved his hands while we sang hymns with lyrics so familiar that we hardly ever thought about the words. Foster showed me that worship, private and corporate, is a key discipline for Christians, even though we may give glory to God in different ways and within different traditions. And Foster broadened my narrow view of the spiritual disciplines, giving me inspiration, direction, and the motivation to cultivate the other disciplines that deepen my Christian walk. As he writes: "Superficiality is the curse of our age.... The desperate need today is not for a greater number of intelligent people, or gifted people, but for deep people."[13]

The spiritual disciplines—taken together—are central to Christian spiritual growth and to anyone who wants to know God.

GROWING AND HEALING—IN COMMUNITY

In my early years as a psychologist, sandwiched between my discovery of Tozer and Foster, I came across the works of Elton Trueblood. I did not always agree with his theology, but in *The Company of the Committed* and *The Incendiary Fellowship*, Trueblood taught me about the importance of community.[14] Within the past few years, "community" has become such a familiar concept that it almost seems outdated, but forty years ago True-blood helped me see that Christians are meant for community. We grow in community. We grieve, care, learn, and thrive in community. We prepare in community to reach others who are outside the community of believers. And when there is pain, sometimes so severe that we need a Christian counselor, we still heal and mature best when we are in community.

Climbing on his pillar, Stripe learned about the stifling impact of self-centered striving. Of the authors who have impacted me, many have shown how we grow closer to God, impact our worlds, and fly like butter-flies when we cease individual striving and come together in community. It is then that we can be free to allow the Creator and Sustainer of the universe to transform us into the Christ-followers we are meant to be. It is then that we are able to soar—like butterflies.

FOURTEEN

Living with Longing
and Mystery

Luci N. Shaw

The experience is one of intense longing.... Though the sense of want is acute and even painful, yet the mere wanting is felt to be somehow a delight.... This hunger is better than any other fullness; this poverty better than all other wealth.

—C. S. Lewis, *The Pilgrim's Regress*

Last spring, reading the narrative of Acts chapter 9, I felt a sudden jolt of insight as I reread the account of Saul's riveting experience on the road to Damascus. I felt *I was* Saul. I could feel the immense clarity that engulfed him as "suddenly a light from heaven flashed around him,"[1] and gave him a crystalline sight of who he was from God's perspective, and the dramatic, life-changing reversal that was being asked of him. Entering that experience was like wine for me, or perfume, or the most warming sunshine. It was lucid, brilliant, vivid, unclouded. With Saul I had glimpsed God, and I understood with Saul that this energy from God was transformative. I could perfectly realize why he was never the same again.

The impression lasted in my imagination for about a day, as I revisited and reimagined it, with an intense longing to recapture it, to live it again—that reality, that sense of Presence. But, inevitably, its imprint faded, and all I had left was the memory of having felt for a moment something that had turned my world inside out. And now even the memory has paled. I remember having a memory, but that's all. It's like looking down a hall of mirrors to the small, blurred, primal image in the distance.

The electric pang of desire for God has always been a part of the awakening and reawakening of my own Christian imagination. There is both thrill and agony to it, a void created in me as by the powerful suction of a vacuum. Because, though intense, it is fleeting; it carries with it almost as much pain as pleasure. A longstanding and urgent desire in my Christian life has been of unquenched longing for the felt presence of God, and the sense of lack and loss when the longing goes unrequited. This may have something to do with my being a poet, with all the accompanying highs and lows.

Time and again, as I have voiced the struggle of my soul-loneliness for God to pastors and theologians, I have been assured that my doubts and questions, written or spoken, are my "gift to the church" or, alternatively, the thorn in the flesh that in my human-ness I must endure. Though this is reassuring—they seem to think I'm not, after all, a heretic—it's far from satisfying.

In some of his written works, C. S. Lewis described something similar. He labeled it *sehnsucht*, a poignant, holy, invisible beauty that is indescribable but for the conviction that when we finally find it, our joy will make sense of the heartache and despair of our present existence. In this idea I recognize the shape and substance of my own longing. This is perhaps most powerfully expressed in Lewis's preface to *The Pilgrim's Regress,* where he depicts the desire that shaped his own life. He wrote:

> When I wrote *The Pilgrim's Regress...*[w]hat I meant was a particular recurrent experience which dominated my child-

hood and adolescence and which I hastily called "Romantic" because inanimate nature and marvellous literature were
among the things that evoked it. I still believe that the experience is common, commonly misunderstood, and of
immense importance.... I will now try to describe it sufficiently to make the following pages [of *The Pilgrim's Regress*]
intelligible.

The experience is one of intense longing. It is distinguished from other longings by two things. In the first
place, though the sense of want is acute and even painful,
yet the mere wanting is felt to be somehow a delight.... This
desire, even when there is no hope of possible satisfaction,
continues to be prized...by those who have once felt it....
And thus it comes about, that if the desire is long absent, it
may itself be desired.... "Oh to feel as I did then!" we cry.[2]

Elsewhere Lewis admits,

There have been times when I think we do not desire
heaven; but more often I find myself wondering whether, in
our heart of hearts, we have ever desired anything else.... It
is the secret signature of each soul, the incommunicable and
unappeasable want, the thing we desired before we met our
wives or made our friends or chose our work, and which we
still desire on our deathbeds.[3]

In *The Pilgrim's Regress,* his first "Christian" book and admittedly one
that has proved "difficult" for many readers not acquainted with the mul-
titude of his literary or psychological allusions, Lewis presents a story, that
of a young seeker named John (Lewis himself, thinly veiled) whose youth-
ful experience with the church in Puritania, a region ruled by Stewards,

under the Landlord in the Eastern Mountains, seems so repressive and punitive that he longs to leave it. One day he catches a glimpse on the horizon of a remote western island, and in that glance he experiences the almost unendurably blissful vision described earlier. In his pilgrimage (Lewis clearly had Bunyan's Pilgrim in mind), John encounters individuals who represent a number of philosophical and theological stances, including Vertue, History, Wisdom, Reason, Mr. Broad, and Gus Halfways. He travels south, visits the town of Thrill, then journeys to the northern city of Eschropolis in a region called The Spirit of the Age. None of these satisfies him, or fulfills his longing; the early vision continues to draw him. He returns to the Main Road, and at the end of his journey, finally and reluctantly, he submits to the help of "Mother Kirk" (the Church) to cross The Grand Canyon. Once across he realizes at last that he has circumnavigated the globe and arrived back where he started, at the Mountain, now seen from the east and revealed by its contours to be the island of his longing. He gains a new and enlightened view of the Landlord who has thus drawn him back to himself.

> In one night the Landlord…had come back to the world,
> and filled the world, quite full without a cranny.… It grew
> upon [John] that the return of the Landlord had blotted
> out the Island: for if there still were such a place he was no
> longer free to spend his soul in seeking it, but must follow
> whatever…the Landlord had for him…more like a person
> than a place, so that the deepest thirst within him was not
> adapted to the deepest nature of the world.[4]

As a lifelong seeker and questioner, brought up in very conservative Christian circles, my own reading of this book has always had singular meaning for me. In many ways the legalistic Stewards, with their skewed interpretations of the Landlord's wishes, as presented to my impressionable young mind, brought me the same sense of fear and anxiety as it did to the preconversion Lewis. I became a Christian at the age of five, largely because of the fear of eternal punishment rather than because I was drawn by Jesus' love. Yet my deepest existential questions were neither answered (were there answers?) nor was their insistence quelled. In fact, the very asking of questions seemed to imply lack of faith and produced in me an ongoing sense of guilt and failure.

It was only in my late fifties that my journey led me into the Anglican Church, where mystery is sanctioned and celebrated, where the sacraments, and especially the Eucharist, that pointer to the unseen real, brought me into Christ's real presence, and where incarnational reality—the recognition of God's fingerprints in human lives and Scripture and the created universe—supplied me, not with watertight proofs, but with a willingness to wait and listen for God, and to leave ultimate answers to him in that realm of mystery.

In a letter to Dom Bede Griffiths, Lewis admits, "Our best havings are wantings."[5] I construe this to mean that our longings for supernatural reality and for God himself are what continue to *draw us toward him* and toward the eternal state where ultimate fulfillment dwells, and we will know as we are known.

An added note: Lewis's use of poetry in *The Pilgrim's Regress* has encouraged me in my own pursuit of the poetic muse. Lewis's poems, with their economy, music, rhythm, vivid metaphor, and precision, confirmed to me that poetry was a potent form for expressing ideas and communicating reality. At the beginning of *Regress* the poems appear infrequently, but as the narrative continues they become more numerous, appearing on nearly every page, as if Lewis couldn't say what he wanted to say even in story—he needed to employ the brilliance and power of poetic metaphor to illuminate his ideas.

Yet story seems to be an important aspect of God's communication to us. Jesus was called the Word, perhaps because God purposed in his Son's incarnation to reopen the huge communication gap between deity and humankind, his creatures with whom he had fellowshiped so openly in Eden. The Creator also provided us with the written Word, because we seem to need a black-and-white verbal record of his dealings with us to refer back to, to jog our faulty and selective memories. Each of us, if we are thinking seriously, is motivated to enter the narrative mode in order to make sense of the fragmentary and dis-orienting nature of human experience, the dis-junction brought about by the Fall, the break between natural and supernatural that compels us to ask Who? What? When? Why?

As to the question of Why? I return again and again to Annie Dillard's *Holy the Firm*, a book that never fails to set my imagination on fire.[6] Indeed, the theme of the book is fire and the pain it causes, or rather, the *why* of suffering, especially when the sufferer seems "innocent," undeserving of the degree of agony that, as the story unfolds, becomes an outrage to the writer and the reader both.

Summed up, Dillard's question is: Is God an arsonist, "a barn-burner... with a pittance of power in a match?"[7] And where is God in the world's pain? Is he cause or comfort? Or, in a strange, cross-deepened sense, is he both?

Behind that large, existential question of suffering an even larger question looms: Is the universe only an illusion? "How do we know...that the real is there?... [D]oes the skin of illusion ever split, and reveal to us the real, which seems to know us by name?"[8] And what is this *holy the firm* that, in Dillard's view, underlies everything that happens to us? Is it ultimately firm? And is it holy? And if the answer is affirmative, in what does its holiness consist?

Considering the magnitude of its themes, this is a surprisingly thin book. But it is thin only in size, not in substance. It is thick with meaning, and in it each word, like the words in a good poem, carries enormous weight. There are three sections, and the seventy-six pages encompass

"events" over a meager three-day period, but the import of the events staggers Dillard, staggers us, as we live through her eyes on the western shore
of Lummi Island in Puget Sound, where she wrote her questions.

Lummi Island, with its strange topography—humped and high on its
southern end, gently sloping and quilted with farmlands and island homes
at its northern tip—is one of my favorite places, and within reach. A
three-quarter-hour drive from my home in Bellingham, Washington,
through the Lummi Indian reservation to the ferry dock, and then a five-
minute ferry ride across Hale Passage to the leeward side of the island.
From there the road circles the northern tip and doubles back along the
windward beaches, sturdy with pebbles, and the fishing village from
which local fishermen endeavor to make a living from the dwindling
salmon population.

It's the beaches that fascinate me. Annie Dillard has said (in a brief
essay on "The Meaning of Life"): "We are here to abet Creation and to witness it, to notice each thing, so each thing gets noticed. Together we notice
not only each mountain shadow and each stone on the beach but we notice
each others' beautiful faces and complex natures so that Creation need not
play to an empty house."[9]

Creation seldom plays to an empty house in me. The created universe
is the truest, most potent, most vital of resources for my soul and spirit,
which has all my life long been seeking, in the concreteness of detail, ultimate meanings, even ultimate Truth. And of course, as Truth-seekers, what
we Christians are ultimately looking for is a Person.

At West Beach, Lummi Island

My boots crunch down the slope, clamber over
the bleached bones of trees. I conquer a tide of pebbles;
at wave edge I stoop and finger one, another,

fondling their flecks and facets, their skin soft as peaches.
Their colors burn my retina. Uninvited words leap into my throat.
I am astonished; from what pleat of brain tissue did they spring?

Schist, agate, gneiss, shale, scree, granite, quartz—they use
my lips to utter their abrasive syllables. God is in these
crystalline names, in the mineral click, the stony rattle

of gravel under the scrolling breakers. God speaks the language
of stones. I am a polished stone myself, and he is speaking
my name. With every ripple, every spit of rain that wets a pebble

into its real color, he tells me, I am washing you with salt,
I am grinding you smooth to my touch. With rain I caress
your oval shape, your apricot silk, and show you your true self.[10]

On that beach on an island, God speaks to me in syllables I cannot ignore. The ocean speaks his voice, with every sweep of waves and foam, and the clatter of stones as the waves pull back. Birds. And the silky wind. And the intricacies of bush and twig, the subtle grays of sycamores, the bronze of madronas. And I resonate with Dillard's telling of a different story, where she also seems to encounter the ineffable.

The informing image right at the beginning of Dillard's story is of a moth that flies into a candle flame, is burned to a crisp (the descriptive words themselves are onomatopoeic—*flamed, fried, crisped, crackled, spattered, kindled*), and whose charred body becomes, itself, a wick. The wax fills the hollow tube of the moth's abdomen and thorax and sends up a saffron flame, "like any immolating monk." Dillard, reading by this fragile light, tells how "[the moth] burned for two hours, until I blew her out."[11] Then the cat, Small, comes in, mouthing a dead wren. Death seems to be a prevalent reality here. And we sense there's more death to come.

The first section begins with these words: "Every day is a god…"[12] and closes with visions of each day as a god, with the writer's eye coloring in his lineaments and vestments in the tones of weather, and of fields and hills and ocean, and the shadows of grazing sheep, a pastoral landscape invested with a largeness of sky, and ocean, and eternity. Perhaps the presence of these "gods" is Dillard's way of suggesting the presence of power and reality beyond the capability of human observation or control. As in her novel, *The Living,* Annie Dillard feels this west coast of the North American continent to be the perilous edge of the real world, with its immense skies and scrolling seas.[13] And it is this view of immensity that catapults her into ideas about God and reality, which both seem, and are, unmanageable, and almost unimaginable.

Section Two begins, "Into this world falls a plane."[14] Like the randomness of the moth attracted to the flame, the randomness of the accident is horrifying; accidents, by very nature, are neither planned nor anticipated. "The plane's engine simply stilled after take-off…smashed in the thin woods…the fuel exploded; and Julie Norwich seven years old burnt off her face."[15] The irony is that the plane's pilot is Jesse, Julie's father (echoes of the Crucifixion, and the Father sacrificing the Son?). Once again, the people in the story seem too small to help, too close to tragedy to make sense of the god's "hugeness and idiocy" when seen from a human perspective.[16]

Only young Julie Norwich was damaged when the plane fell. "A gob of flung ignited vapor hit her face.…"[17] There she lay in St. Joe's, the hospital in town, "little Julie with her eyes naked and spherical, baffled. Can you scream without lips?"[18] To Dillard and the other human observers, there was no sense to be made of this; human reason shrank and withered in the blast of this absurdity. "You get caught holding one end of a love.…" Even love makes no sense when "the meanest of people show more mercy than hounding and terrorist gods."[19]

The exploding plane fuel, a sheet of flame, caught Julie in the face. Fire is always a devourer. In a passage about the orders of angels, Dillard zeros

in on seraphs who perpetually praise God, crying, " 'Holy, holy, holy'....
But, according to some rabbinic writings, they can sing only the first 'Holy'
before the intensity of their love ignites them again and dissolves them
again, perpetually, into flames."[20] Fire keeps taking over.

And the question of faith, what it consists of, how it is exercised, flies
into the author's mind, and ours, and becomes centrally significant. If God
is all good (a given in Dillard's mind and in orthodox Christian belief),
what is the meaning of all this pain? No answers are, or can be, supplied.
How can disaster happen so carelessly, as if God has turned his head or
blinked his eye, and, in that blink, calamity bared its teeth? Dillard, a God-
believer, a Truth-seeker, a world-disturber, makes no bones about her per-
plexity with Providence.

But the third section of the book is voiced in a tone of greater conviction if no less amazement. There is less questioning, more certainty, more
about God and his goodness. Faith seems to have reasserted itself. And
what is faith, if not belief that persists in the face of paradox and mystery?
A kind of coherence is achieved. Much of the fragmentation and shatter-
ing dis-jointedness of the earlier passages, which mirror the dis-junction
caused by catastrophe, drops away.

The language is no less luminous, but it feels more sure, of itself and of
the mysteries (which remain mysterious) and of the fierce firmness of holiness. "There is only this everything."[21] And the artist is the one who sees,
and sees this, with the all-encompassing eye of vision. Julie Norwich is, by
the pure coincidence of nomenclature, a figure of the Lady Julian of Norwich, the medieval nun and mystic. Julie, without a face, seems destined for
solitude and sacrifice. She will learn the Custody of the Eyes. "Held fast by
love in the world like the moth in wax, your life a wick, your head on fire
with prayer...you sleep alone, if you call that alone, you cry God."[22]

The idea of the substance posited by what Dillard labels Esoteric
Christianity and called Holy the Firm, which underlies us, "occurring...in
the waxy deepness of planets,"[23] hinges on our ideas about God's imma-

nence or transcendence. Does God intervene in our affairs? Is he so present (immanent) in material essence that that is all there is of him, or is he absolutely "other," apart, and uninvolved in his Creation? Neither, in Dillard's worlds. Christ is the link between immanence and transcendence. "Matter and spirit are of a piece but distinguishable; God has a stake guaranteed in all the world. And the universe is real and not a dream, not a manufacture of the senses; subject may know object, knowledge may proceed, and Holy the Firm is in short the philosopher's stone."[24]

Through the book are snatches of story that nail down all the questioning to a kind of particularity. One of these incidents revolves around the need for communion wine for the Congregational church that Annie Dillard attended while living and writing on Lummi Island. She volunteers to buy the wine for a Sunday Eucharist, then carries it to church in her backpack. "Here is a bottle of wine.... Christ with a cork.... Through all my clothing...and through the bottle's glass I feel the wine.... It sheds light in slats through my rib cage, and fills the buttressed vaults of my ribs with light pooled and buoyant."[25] It is fire again, but purgative and redemptive, healing rather than damaging. This lambent image calls us back to the incarnational reality of Christ, how he shines through our materiality, how his power is manifested in human activities and phenomena that seem mundane, even insignificant, but are shown to have large significance once we become aware of them and pay attention to the ways of God manifested in our living.

In my wanderings on the island I have often stood in silence in front of the small, wooden, white-painted church where Dillard worshiped and partook of the Eucharist during the seven years she lived on Lummi. I wrote about that, too, and about what the sacramental feast signifies to me:

Two Stanzas: The Eucharist

Annie Dillard speaks of Christ corked in a bottle: carrying the wine
to communion in a pack on her back

she feels him lambent, lighting
her hidden valleys through the spaces
between her ribs. Nor can we
contain him in a cup. He is always
poured out for our congregation.
And see how he spills, hot, light,
his oceans glowing like wine,
flooding all the fjords among
the bones of our continents.

Annie Dillard once asked: How
in the world can we *remember* God?
(Death forgets and we all die.)
But truly, reminders are God's
business. He will see to it,
flashing his hinder parts, now,
then, past our cut in the rock.
His metaphors are many, among them
the provided feast by which
our teeth and tongues and throats
hint to our hearts of God's body,
giving us the why of incarnation,
the how of remembrance.[26]

To try to summarize Dillard's ideas in plain words is to reduce them, to suck out their juice. Their very wildness and eccentricity is their genius. Throughout *Holy the Firm*, almost every word and phrase seems to fit into its lines like poetry. Indeed, many of the lines are poetry. But Dillard's style, as always, is idiosyncratic. Her grammar, syntax, word choice, and word order are often astonishing, unnerving. They seem on the edge of irrationality, designed to catch us, the readers, off guard, or throw us off balance so that, teetering on the edge of her meanings, we may fall and find the firmness of the firmament and God underneath it, bearing it up, to be our reality. In dealing with mystery, she never renders it less mysterious. But in one crucial moment in the book, she uses the simple words "I know"[27] to affirm her own sureness of Christ's centrality in the real. "Everything, everything, is whole, and a parcel of everything else."[28] Its co-inherence and coherence are in evidence, through the senses, through intuition, through an internal knowledge, which we can only identify as faith.

I have read this book again and again, in all its elegant oddity, often when my quotidian rhythms seem too ordinary and superficial to have lasting meaning for me or anyone else. *Holy the Firm* always beckons me back into the arena of the invisible real that haunts and draws us toward that which will ultimately satisfy our desire.

Guides for the Imaginative Life

Phillip E. Johnson

Few can foresee whither their road will lead them, till they
come to its end.

—LEGOLAS, from J. R. R. Tolkien's *The Lord of the Rings*

Most books are read for information or pleasure and are then returned to
the shelf and soon forgotten. A very small number live on in the reader's
imagination and become a part of the apparatus through which he or she
views the world. The Bible serves this role for many of us, so that we sort
our experiences by biblical models and express our thoughts or feelings
about them in biblical language.

When I was in the hospital last year following a stroke, I instinctively
expressed my despair and hope in the words of Psalm 23 that I had learned
as a child, for I seemed truly to be living in the valley of the shadow of
death. I evaluated the catastrophe against the model of Job. I could go on
to explain how I turned to biblical language during the months of strenu-
ous therapy that followed, to express my growing awareness that, for those
who place their confidence in what God has done and promised, even a
stroke has its positive side. My assignment in this essay, however, is to
describe some book other than the Bible that has played an important role

in my life. I have interpreted the terms of the assignment liberally, however, as you shall see.

The three books considered here—*The Lord of the Rings, That Hideous Strength,* and *Not of This World*—have become part of the furniture of my mind, to the extent that I rely on them daily to provide an imaginative background for interpreting my own experiences.

I will start with the book that is probably least familiar to readers of this essay—*Not of This World.*[1] This biography of the American Russian Orthodox scholar-monk Seraphim Rose was given to me by a young man who had become acquainted with the biographer, Seraphim's brother monk and protégé, Father Damascene.

Few people outside the Orthodox world are likely to have read this massive biography, but I was sufficiently fascinated by its subject that I read every page. Seraphim grew up in San Diego, attended public schools, and then began a lifelong pursuit of truth that took him through Eastern religion, past an intellectually and spiritually desolate academic world, and into a life of contemplation, prayer, and original scholarship that produced insights unlike any I have encountered elsewhere.

After his death in 1982, Seraphim became renowned and beloved throughout the Russian Orthodox world. His life and thinking became more and more present in my imagination as I also left academic respectability to pursue truth, until I found myself thinking of him as a sort of spiritual elder brother and wishing I could somehow meet him in person so we could have long conversations (perhaps in heaven). Seraphim's biographer and his monastery brothers may also have sensed this spiritual relationship, because they asked me to write an introduction to a collection of Seraphim's writings on Genesis and treated this unenlightened Protestant almost as an honorary member of their brotherhood. A new edition of Seraphim's biography, titled *Father Seraphim Rose: His Life and Works,* will incorporate several more years of research into his life and times. I recommend it, if you would like to become acquainted with an impressive individual who illuminates something about the rest of us just by being completely different. Perhaps not *completely* different, because Seraphim, like me, went to ordinary public schools, adopted fashionable agnostic philosophies for a time, had the gifts necessary for a successful academic career, but in the end turned away from any conventional measure of success to pursue the truth about God and Christ, a subject about which our intellectuals no longer seem to care.

Likewise, I carry around in my imagination images and ideas from a very different work of literature. I first remember reading *That Hideous Strength* in my late thirties as a new Christian and disillusioned academic careerist wishing for some noble adventure that would give purpose to my life.[2] It is by far my favorite of C. S. Lewis's space trilogy. It seems like an old friend because it is set in a university town. The premise involves a technological institute whose program eerily anticipates the utopian fantasies that contemporary science writers spin from the as-yet-unfulfilled promises of the Human Genome Project or from the dreams of Silicon Valley visionaries that one day it may be possible to download our memories into machines and thus transform humanity from its perishable body of flesh and blood to effectively immortal silicon.

In Lewis's novel, everything cozy and comfortable must be destroyed to make room for the soulless future envisaged by technology-obsessed utopians who are secretly in the service of evil spirits. The technocrats seduce the careerist academics, so the power of evil is resisted only by a ragtag assortment of ordinary people led by a man who was made lame by a wound from a previous adventure. The group is assisted by a talking bear and by Merlin, the legendary magician, revived after centuries of enchanted sleep. It is all fantastic, and yet most of the villainy could be taken from today's news reports.

As my own motley band of Intelligent Design theorists has gained in confidence and influence, I have reflected often on how our situation could be compared with that of the characters in Lewis's novel. The biblical model for the Lewis novel was the Tower of Babel story, and *Tower of Babel* is the title of a book from the Darwinist camp attacking Intelligent Design, written by an earnest but unpersuasive author who could not have realized how ironically appropriate a title he had chosen.[3] The parallel to Lewis's novel became still more compelling to me after I was wounded by a stroke just when the Intelligent Design struggle seemed at the verge of success. Perhaps that stroke was not the impediment to accomplishing my mission that it had seemed at first, but some experience I needed to have if I was to overcome the spiritual immaturity that limited my effectiveness as a follower of Christ and a leader of men.

Once again, life mirrors art. The ultimate story of a quest by humble people that succeeds in overcoming the power of evil is J. R. R. Tolkien's *The Lord of the Rings*.[4] This three-decker novel will always find a new generation of devoted readers who are undaunted by the sneers of haughty literary critics who don't realize that a great story is much more to be valued than a collection of sophisticated puzzles that provide suitable material for doctoral dissertations. I first read Tolkien at the age of nineteen when my sister, who worked for the author's American publisher, brought the three volumes home. I will never forget the combination of joyous anticipation and dread I felt as I turned the pages of the third volume—joy that I would soon experience the climax, and dread that I would soon have no more Tolkien to read for the first time. Such is the power that Tolkien exercises over one's imagination.

More than thirty years later, I encountered on the Internet a struggling young philosopher who was to become one of my favorite colleagues and my spiritual adopted son. I recognized a kindred soul when we shared our respective fantasy lives, and ever since, the two of us have shared our experiences by playing roles borrowed from Tolkien. Some years later, when my young friend had become a successful professor and revered director of his own college program, I was able to suggest that he and his students would love the novels of Anthony Trollope. Given what I knew about his imagination, it was a sure thing.

I recall that Benjamin Disraeli once said something along these lines: "The trouble with the utilitarians in philosophy is the same as that of the Unitarians in religion. Their system leaves out imagination, and yet imagination rules the world."[5] To recognize that imagination rules the world is not in any way to denigrate the value of the great critical tools of science and logic. Imagination can produce bad ideas as well as helpful ones, evil as well as good. In my legal career, and then in my second career as an author of books about evolution and creation, I have tried to cultivate the skills of critical reason. If we are truly reasonable, however, we know that critical reason only goes to work after imagination has provided the raw material. Imagination comes not only from the mind but also from the heroes and villains of the stories that supply its furniture.

Heroes come in diverse forms, and the three books I recommend here provide heroic models for, among others, a scholar, a faithful servant, and a wife. It is not vanity to imagine ourselves in some heroic or glorious role, if we also keep our feet planted firmly in reality. Somewhere within each humble or misguided person lies the capacity to find the true path and to accomplish feats of heroism. We may never find that buried capacity if we do not first savor it in our imagination.

Any Old Bush Will Do!

Luis Palau

> You are not called upon to commit yourself to a need, or to
> a task, or to a field; you are called upon to commit yourself
> to God!
>
> —MAJOR IAN THOMAS, *The Saving Life of Christ*

My first encounter with Major Ian Thomas was not through a book he had written, but through a sermon. It was a challenge to make out all the words through his thick British accent and staccato delivery, but God brought the clarity I needed to understand his life-changing message.

Ian Thomas came into my life at a time when I had wrestled every aspect of my faith into a frustrating question. I was searching, but nothing was getting through until I heard Thomas speak. He came to the graduate school where I was studying. He was on a promotional tour and spoke from his classic book *The Saving Life of Christ*.[1] It was a book I had not yet read but soon would not forget!

Let me provide some background from the years prior to this first encounter to help you understand why Thomas's message made such an impact. For a couple of years before I heard Thomas speak, I'd fought a losing battle for personal holiness. Whenever a great preacher came to our church in Argentina, some of my friends and I would try to schedule an interview with him. Our questions were always the same: "How can we get victory over temptation? How can we live holy lives?"

Usually the visiting preacher would ask, "Are you reading the Bible?"

"Yes, we get up at five o'clock every morning before going to school or work. We read several chapters every day."

"Great! But are you testifying for Jesus?"

"Yes. We hand out tracts, teach children's classes, and even hold street meetings."

"That's terrific! But are you praying?" the preacher would ask. So we'd tell him about our all-night prayer meetings.

We were urged by preacher after preacher to rededicate our lives to Jesus Christ. I did as they suggested, but still I struggled with many of the same feelings of frustration and inadequacy. *Maybe there's some area of my life I still haven't dedicated to the Lord,* I thought. So I went to the altar and re-rededicated my life. A year later I super re-rededicated my life! But something still wasn't working.

"What else do we need to do?" we'd ask the next visiting preacher.

"Well, pray some more, witness some more, read the Bible some more." So we did. We just about killed ourselves, we were so eager to be holy.

Later, during my first semester in seminary, I was on the verge of giving up. Not because I saw a lack in God, but because I was weary of fighting and struggling and seeking on my own to persevere through sheer dedication.

When am I ever going to catch on? I wondered. *Will I give up now, after all I've been through?* I wanted to please and love and serve God. I wanted people to be saved. I would sing, "Oh, Jesus, I have promised to serve Thee to the end," and I would think, *Even if it kills me.*

One day I was invited to view a brief film of Billy Graham speaking to Christian leaders in India. Although he was speaking in front of a crowd of tens of thousands, he seemed to be staring right into my eyes as he quoted

Ephesians 5:18: "Do not get drunk on wine, which leads to debauchery. Instead, be filled with the Spirit." It was as if he was shouting at me: "Are you filled with the Spirit?"

I knew that was my problem—I wasn't filled with the Holy Spirit. That was the reason for my up-and-down Christianity. That's why I had zeal and commitment but little fruit or victory. When would it end?

I found my answer in the United States after several frustrating months in seminary. I came to the States through the patient prodding of Ray Stedman, pastor of Peninsula Bible Church in Palo Alto, California. The first two months I lived in his home. I was argumentative and wanted to discuss theology and doctrine for hours. I had come to learn, but maybe I wasn't yet ready to admit that I didn't have all the answers.

After two months with the Stedmans, I went to what is now Multnomah Biblical Seminary in Portland, Oregon. Multnomah is a demanding graduate school, and I found the first semester particularly rough.

The professor of our spiritual life class, Dr. George Kehoe, only added to my frustration when he began every class period by quoting Galatians 2:20: "I have been crucified with Christ and I no longer live, but Christ lives in me. The life I live in the body, I live by faith in the Son of God, who loved me and gave himself for me."

I was still frustrated with not being able to live the lifestyle I saw in men like Ray Stedman and several others. Their lives exhibited a joy and freedom that I found attractive. But the more I sought it, the more it eluded me. I continued to grapple with the desire to be holy. I studied, I prayed, and I waited. I thought I was taking all the right steps, but I was still lacking. My faith was a quest for knowledge, but not a spiritual longing. When I lost my first excitement and love for Jesus Christ, it was as if someone pulled the plug and the lights went out. Perhaps I let a cynical attitude get in the way.

My spiritual journey seemed like a climb up a tall cliff. I clawed every inch of the way only to slip and slide back down. Although I had experienced times of blessing and victory, for the most part I felt the struggle was impossible. I *thought* I had dedicated my life to the Lord, but I had gone only three-quarters of the way up Calvary's hill, stopping short of the cross. I couldn't go on that way. It was my secret, private death, and I didn't realize that the death I needed was death to my pride, death to my selfish ambitions and dreams.

In those days I was envious, jealous, and self-centered. I was smug about other speakers, silently rating their illustrations or delivery against my own. That left me feeling mean and petty. No amount of wrestling with myself would rid me of those sins. And yet I tried. I felt despicable; I hated the idea that I was a hypocrite. I felt like Ian Thomas's description of Moses, "In his sensitivity to the presence of man, Moses became strangely insensitive to the presence of God."[2]

Maybe that's why I was getting annoyed by Dr. Kehoe's daily quoting of Galatians 2:20. *It can't be a Bible verse that gets you so upset,* I told myself. *It must be you.* Rather than let that verse penetrate my pride, however, I decided that the verse was self-contradictory, hard to understand, and confusing—especially in English.

I was weary of struggling and seeking to persevere through sheer dedication. I was exhausted, and exhaustion can breed cynicism. I knew that the other side of life is hopeless. But there is a monumental emptiness when you know you're looking in the right place and still not finding the answer.

Shortly before Christmas break, Ian Thomas, founder and director of Torchbearers, the group that runs Capernwray Bible School in England, spoke at our chapel service. I usually sat in the back and dared the speaker to make me pay attention. If he was good, I'd honor him by listening. Otherwise I would daydream or peek at my class notes.

But when Thomas spoke and pointed a finger that had been partially cut off, I was intrigued. *Now here's an interesting man,* I thought—probably because he wasn't afraid to use that finger for gesturing each time he made an important statement. But as soon as he had me hooked, his short message spoke to the core of my being.

Thomas talked about Moses and how it took this great man forty years in the wilderness to learn that he was nothing. Then one day Moses was confronted with a burning bush—likely a dry bunch of ugly little sticks that had hardly developed—yet Moses had to take off his shoes. Why? Because this was holy ground. Why was it holy ground? Because God was in the bush!

In essence, God was telling Moses: "I don't need a pretty bush or an educated bush or an eloquent bush. Any old bush will do as long as I am in the bush. If I am going to use you, I am going to use you. It will not be you doing something for me, but me doing something through you."

I realized immediately that I was that kind of bush: a worthless, useless bunch of dried-up sticks. I could do nothing for God. All my reading and studying, asking questions, and trying to model myself after others was worthless. My studies and questions were important steps in growing faith, but I was focusing too much on the knowledge I could gain and the person I felt that I should become. In the midst of my studies I forgot to let God mold me. Instead, I was trying to pave my own path.

After hearing Thomas speak, I read his book. It was profoundly significant to my spiritual life. God knew I needed to hear those words at that point in my life. It was as if Thomas were speaking directly to me when he wrote: "You have felt the surge of holy ambition. Your heart has burned within you. You have dreamed dreams and seen visions, but only to awaken again and again to a dull sense of futility, as one who beats the air or builds castles in the sky."[3]

Everything in my ministry was worthless, I realized, unless God was in the bush. Only he could make something happen.

Thomas told of many Christian workers who failed at first because they thought they had something to offer God. He himself had once imagined that because he was an aggressive, winsome, evangelistic sort, God would use him. But God didn't use him until he came to the end of himself. *That's exactly my situation,* I thought. *I am at the end of myself.*

Thomas closed his message by reading—you guessed it—Galatians 2:20. And then it all came together for me. "I have been crucified with Christ and I no longer live, but Christ lives in me." My biggest spiritual struggle was finally over! I would let God be God and let Luis Palau be dependent upon him.

I ran back to my room and in tears fell to my knees next to my bunk. "Lord, now I understand!" I prayed in my native Spanish. "The whole thing is 'not I, but Christ in me.' It's not what I'm going to do for you, but rather what you are going to do through me."

I stayed on my knees until lunchtime, an hour and a half later, skipping my next class to stay in communion with the Lord. I realized the reason I hated myself inside was because I wrongly loved myself outside. I asked God's forgiveness for my pride.

I had thought I was a step above my countrymen because I had been well educated and was fluent in English; I had worked in a bank and spoken on the radio, in a tent, and in churches. I got to come to the United States and mingle with pastors, seminary professors, and other Christian leaders.

I thought I was really something! But God was not active in the bush. I hadn't given him a chance. Up until that point I had failed to answer some important questions. "Will I truly dedicate my life to Jesus Christ? Will I make everything else secondary and live for him? Will I seek first the kingdom of God and his righteousness? Is it true for me that 'to live is Christ'?" These questions had been burning in me without answers for so long. Finally, I was ready to face the commitment, to give to the Lord in total sacrifice, maximum surrender, the end of "me," and let him burn in me.

God still had a lot of burning to do, but he was finally in control of this bush. Slowly I was seeing that, although I might fail God many times, he would never fail me. I was learning, step by step, what it meant to live a godly, joyful, fruitful life. He wanted me to be grateful for all the things he had put in my life, but he didn't want me to place my confidence in those opportunities to make me a better minister or preacher. He wanted me to depend not on my breaks, but on Christ alone—the resurrected, almighty, indwelling Lord Jesus Christ, my Savior!

That day marked the intellectual turning point in my spiritual life. The practical working out of that discovery would be lengthy and painful, but at last the realization had come. I finally realized that when Jesus calls us to consecrate our lives, he is asking for a loyalty and love next to which all other loyalties pale into insignificance and all other loves appear to be hatred. It was exciting beyond words. We have everything we need when we have Jesus Christ living in us. It's his power that controls our dispositions, enables us to serve, and corrects and directs us.[4]

Major Ian Thomas gave me, in his book, the greatest understanding I could gain about my duty as a Christian:

> You are not called upon to commit yourself to a need, or to
> a task, or to a field. You are called upon to commit yourself
> to God! It is He then who takes care of the consequences
> and commits you where *He* wants you.[5]

I could finally relax and rest in Jesus Christ. He was going to do the work through me. What peace there was in knowing I could quit struggling! By gladly choosing God's will, I was free to move ahead with renewed vigor. I understand now that this process involves continuous, ongoing obedience and submission to God. It means repeatedly surrendering my rights for the greater spiritual good. Every time my will crosses God's revealed will, I am forced to make a decision. If I choose his revealed will over my own, I am surrendering, allowing God to burn in this bush. And that, as Ian Thomas so forcefully points out, is what it takes to follow Christ.

Bishop J. C. Ryle
and the Quest for Holiness

John R. W. Stott

> Of all sights in the Church of Christ, I know none more
> painful to my own eyes than a Christian contented and satis-
> fied with a *little* grace, a *little* repentance, a *little* faith, a *little*
> knowledge, a *little* charity, and a *little* holiness. I do beseech
> and entreat every believing soul that reads this tract not to
> be that kind of man.... Let us *aim at eminent holiness.*
>
> —J. C. RYLE, *Holiness*

Thinking back on my Christian pilgrimage, several books come to my
mind as significant signposts in helping me find my way. One of the most
formative of these books was *Holiness* by J. C. Ryle, published at the end
of the nineteenth century.[1] I am almost sure that I first read *Holiness* when
I was an undergraduate at Cambridge University. I had become a Christian
about two years before going up to Cambridge, so I was in my early twen-
ties physically, but still a child spiritually.

After the first flush of enthusiasm following my conversion, I experienced not exactly an anticlimax, but at least some disappointment. Jesus

Christ had undoubtedly entered my life when I opened the door and invited him in. I was a changed person. I remember walking down the road at Rugby School one day and suddenly realizing that I was in love with the world. All the old boyish hostilities and rivalries had dropped away from me, and I had no enemies left. In spite of such authentic experiences, which were evidences of the new birth, I was still the same person with the same temperament and the same temptations, and the lordship of Jesus often seemed to be more fantasy than fact.

When I was in this vulnerable condition, I was introduced to a variety of holiness teachings that promised me an easy way to the victory I longed for. Romans 6 was interpreted to me as meaning that I could become "dead to sin" in the sense of becoming insensitive to it. But this wasn't true to my experience. More important, it wasn't true to Scripture. For the exhortations in Romans 6 that we not allow sin to reign in our bodies proved that it *could* reign there. Otherwise, why should Paul exhort us not to let it? So I was not "dead" to sin.

Then there was the emphasis among holiness teachers that often is summarized as "let go and let God." It was essentially an exhortation to adopt a passive stance, in which we were told to relax and trust and leave the fighting to Christ or the indwelling Spirit. Any activity on our part—fighting, striving, struggling, wrestling—was frowned upon as "legalism."

A third popular holiness doctrine is a "second blessing" teaching. It insists that conversion is not enough, but that a second stage is needed, variously identified as "full salvation," "perfect love," "the baptism of the Holy Spirit," and so forth.

So here were three holiness promises that were jostling with one another in my mind, a "death to sin," a "let go and let God," and a "second blessing." I do not doubt that fuller and richer blessings can be experienced in the Christian life. It is the stereotype of two stages of Christian initiation that I could not (and still cannot) accept.

It was only after having been introduced to these teachings that I came upon Bishop Ryle's *Holiness*. By careful exegesis, accompanied by clarity of expression and a vigorous style, he demonstrated conclusively that the New Testament depicts us as thoroughly active in fighting against sin, pursuing after righteousness, and laboring to be holy. Bishop Ryle clarified for me the differences between justification and sanctification. One of them is that, although we are justified by faith alone *without* works, we are sanctified by faith *and* works. And he showed that whereas justification is a crisis, sanctification is a process, in which there may be many deeper experiences. One of Ryle's catchwords or slogans is that there are "no gains without pains."

Knowing Bishop Ryle's role in the history of the Church of England increased my respect for his writing. I knew, for example, that he was Bishop of Liverpool from 1880 to 1900. Evangelical bishops in the Anglican Communion were so rare toward the end of the nineteenth century (things are different now) that I was intrigued to read and listen to him. I also knew that a number of his other books were sometimes to be found in second-hand shops, so I gradually collected them. I am thinking of books such as *Knots Untied*, subtitled *Being Plain Statements on Disputed Points in Religion from the Standpoint of an Evangelical Churchman*, and *Principles for Churchmen: A Manual of Positive Statements on Some Subjects of Controversy*.[2]

Ryle also wrote historical books; for example, *Light from Old Times*, being thumbnail sketches of sixteenth-century reformers and martyrs, and *The Christian Leaders of England in the 18th Century*, biographical pictures of Whitefield, Wesley, Grimshaw, Romaine, and others.[3] All this built up my confidence in him as a reliable guide and mentor.

Looking back on my life and ministry, I have sometimes wished that I could ask Bishop Ryle for his wisdom in relation to issues that have been particularly difficult. For instance, I would ask him for his assessment of the Christian church in the twenty-first century, and in particular, how he would evaluate the rise of the Pentecostal churches and the charismatic movement. What Bishop Ryle set himself against, that is, the search for Christian growth and fulfillment without acknowledging the cost of Christian discipleship, is still a major temptation today. Is this perhaps the Achilles heel of many charismatic movements, which are spreading so rapidly throughout the world? If so, how can we somehow ensure in the twenty-first century a biblical teaching that neither insists on a double initiation into Christ nor undervalues the place of effort in the process of sanctification? If I had the chance, I would ask Bishop Ryle which passages of Scripture he would recommend in order to secure such balance.

Holiness, though written more than one hundred years ago, is not an out-of-date read. Having been shaped by his writing myself, I would hope that other young Christians would read him. If one should pick up his book, watch for the theme "no gains without pains," which runs like a thread throughout *Holiness.* Another similar theme is the Puritan emphasis on "the means of grace." These are such practices as prayer, Bible reading, public worship, Sunday observance, fellowship, and the Lord's Supper. God has given us these privileged activities as means by which his grace comes to us and sanctifies us. But they do not operate mechanically. In each we have our part to play. So the Puritans stressed the need for "a disciplined use of the means of grace." It is still grace—there is no holiness without the grace of God. But we must be disciplined in making full use of its means. I hope that a reading of Bishop Ryle would challenge readers, as it has challenged me and continues to challenge me, to maintain a biblical balance in the process of sanctification between God's work and ours, and not to separate what God has united.

In closing, I share some excerpts from *Holiness* that have been especially significant in shaping my understanding of the holy life. May God grant us the grace and strength to heed these important words.

On a diligent use of the means of grace:

> I lay it down as a simple matter of fact that no one who is
> careless about such things must ever expect to make much
> progress in sanctification. I can find no record of any emi-

nent saint who ever neglected them. They are appointed
channels through which the Holy Spirit conveys fresh supplies of grace to the soul, and strengthens the work which
He has begun in the inward man. Let men call this legal
doctrine if they please, but I will never shrink from declaring my belief that there are no "spiritual gains without
pains." I should as soon expect a farmer to prosper in business who contented himself with sowing his fields and
never looking at them till harvest, as expect a believer to
attain much holiness who was not diligent about his Bible-
reading, his prayers, and the use of his Sundays. Our God is
a God who works by means, and He will never bless the
soul of that man who pretends to be so high and spiritual
that he can get on without them.[4]

On humility as the goal which a holy person follows after:

He will understand something of Abraham's feeling, when
he says, "I am dust and ashes"; and Jacob's, when he says,
"I am less than the least of all Thy mercies"; and Job's, when
he says, "I am vile"; and Paul's, when he says, "I am chief of
sinners." Holy Bradford, that faithful martyr of Christ,
would sometimes finish his letters with these words, "A
most miserable sinner, John Bradford." Good old Mr.
Grimshaw's last words, when he lay on his deathbed, were
these, "Here goes an unprofitable servant."[5]

On justification and sanctification:

I fear it is sometimes forgotten that God has married
together justification and sanctification. They are distinct

and different things, beyond question, but one is never found without the other. All justified people are sanctified, and all sanctified are justified. What God has joined together let no man dare to put asunder. Tell me not of your justification, unless you have also some marks of sanctification. Boast not of Christ's work *for* you, unless you can show us the Spirit's work *in you.* Think not that Christ and the Spirit can ever be divided.[6]

On the cost of discipleship:

But it does cost something to be a real Christian, according to the standard of the Bible. There are enemies to be overcome, battles to be fought, sacrifices to be made, an Egypt to be forsaken, a wilderness to be passed through, a cross to be carried, a race to be run. Conversion is not putting a man in an armchair and taking him easily to heaven. It is the beginning of a mighty conflict, in which it costs much to win the victory. Hence arises the unspeakable importance of "counting the cost."[7]

On the importance of having strong convictions:

For your own soul's sake dare to make up your mind what you believe, and dare to have positive distinct views of truth and error. Never, never be afraid to hold decided doctrinal opinions; and let no fear of man, and no morbid dread of being thought party-spirited, narrow, or controversial, make you rest contented with a bloodless, boneless, tasteless, colourless, lukewarm, undogmatic Christianity.[8]

﹙☙﹚

God's Work Done in God's Way

Edith Schaeffer

[Hudson Taylor] saw that the faith-principles of the Mission
must be carried to the point of making no appeals for money
nor even taking a collection. If the Mission could be sustained
by the faithful care of God in answer to prayer and prayer
alone, without subscription lists or solicitation of any kind for
funds, then it might grow up among the older societies without the danger of diverting gifts from their accustomed channels. It might even be helpful to other agencies by directing
attention to the Great Worker, affording a practical illustration
of its underlying principle that "God Himself, God alone, is
sufficient for God's own work."

—DR. AND MRS. HOWARD TAYLOR,

Hudson Taylor and the China Inland Mission

I was born in Wenshow, China, to missionary parents (one from New
York, the other from Pennsylvania). My parents met in China and married
in Shanghai in 1906. Given their heart for Christian ministry in China, the
story of Hudson Taylor made a grand impact on them. Of particular interest was the effect his speaking had on seven Cambridge students who gave

their lives to spread the gospel in inland China. Prior to the decision made by those young men, the church missionary society only preached in China's coastal towns. This new mission became known as the China Inland Mission, and it focused on a previously unreached portion of the country.

A book about this ministry, *Hudson Taylor and the China Inland Mission,*[1] written by Dr. and Mrs. Howard Taylor (Hudson Taylor's son and daughter-in-law), has remained a source of inspiration for me throughout my life. I began to devour this book when I was twelve years old. It especially intrigued me because I was born in the first compound of the China Inland Mission.

The book gives a vivid account of the ups and downs of the beginning of that work. It also gives example after example of how God works in answer to prayer. Prayer opens the eyes of understanding as well as providing for the material needs of everyday life for both individuals and Christian organizations.

The story of Hudson Taylor and the mission played a significant role in my life when Francis, my husband, and I left our home in Pennsylvania and ventured overseas to Switzerland. It was during these years that I most often found myself going back to that story, both in its pages and in my mind. Our story was, in part, shaped and encouraged by Hudson's. Francis had a chance to meet him in college, and I still have the old maps of China that he gave Francis. Written in the margin in Taylor's handwriting is the exhortation, *Serve the Lord with gladness.* His encouragement meant so much to both of us, and it is a theme that Francis and I always tried to carry out in our ministry.

Dr. and Mrs. Taylor's book put me on my knees concerning our own work in the three pastorates we had in the United States. When Fran was asked by his denomination's missionary board to survey thirteen European countries in 1947 and report on how the war had affected theology in the various denominations, we took our first trip to Europe. When asked by his mission board a few months later to work in Europe, he chose Switzerland as his headquarters. Fran and I traveled to a number of countries with the purpose of helping churches start children's work. After a year in the city of Lausanne, we moved to the mountain village of Champéry, where we had services for young people who came there to ski and to whom we opened our home for further discussion. This new work also had its roots in Hudson Taylor's life, in that both he and we had no idea what was to come as a result of trusting God alone. In our case, God opened the way for us to begin the work of L'Abri.

When we were going through dramatic times in Champéry, I reread *Hudson Taylor and the China Inland Mission* often. Champéry was a Roman Catholic village without any Protestant church services except for those of visiting English schools that came en masse for skiing. A church had been built there by an Anglican mission society for visiting skiers. Francis made a habit of speaking with villagers about who Jesus is and what the Bible says. After some time one leading man from the village became a Christian. He bought a Bible and was reading it so much that his family became alarmed and stirred up trouble. The village priest worked behind the scenes to get us evicted, and we soon received an official notice stating that we had thirty days to leave.

At that time there had been tremendous snowstorms, which caused snow to pile up on the mountainsides above Champéry. Without warning the weather changed, bringing a thaw and driving rain. The snow melted and the mountainside turned into unstable mud, which slid against the village, including our chalet. Fran helped the men of the village as they tried to divert the swell away from the houses. To make matters worse, our two-year-old son had just come down with polio. I felt like Job as the calamities multiplied.

As American citizens, we had to report the eviction order to the American embassy. After a three-hour train trip on a cold, rainy morning, I arrived in Bern and made my way to the embassy. The door had not yet opened to the public, and a young man who was standing there snarled, "What do you want?" I replied, "I have to see the consul." With complete apathy he snorted back, "He's far too busy to see you. There is trouble at the Belgian Consulate, and he has to be on his way in a few minutes." However, the young man led me upstairs to the consul's door. As I knocked, the consul himself opened the door, and I handed him the eviction papers. He read my husband's name: *Francis August Schaeffer*.

"Where did he live?" he queried.

"In Germantown, Philadelphia," I answered. I hardly expected his response.

"Oh, that's where I lived! Where did he go to school?"

I informed him that Francis had attended Germantown High School, and it became clear that the two men had not only attended the same school but also had graduated in the same class.

Then the consul exclaimed, "Francis Schaeffer was president of our class, and I was secretary. How amazing. Do come in." He offered me a comfortable chair and then telephoned his wife. "Dear, I'm bringing someone home for lunch. It's the wife of my old high-school friend." Then he turned to me and said, "What is the problem? Tell me from the beginning."

I could not help thinking of Hudson Taylor's impossible situation when he had been told that an English missionary would never be allowed into inland China, and of how he took passage on the Yangtze River from Shanghai to Wenchow. Everyone said the odds were so completely against him that nothing would ever take place in that southern town. The same God who led Hudson was leading us at that point, and it was a comfort to know that odds, no matter how great, were nothing that God paid too much attention to.

I read aloud these parts of Hudson Taylor's story to my husband as we approached the date of our being taken by jeep out of Champéry and the canton of Valais. The eviction order stood, and we were to be out by midnight of March 31. The reason given was: "You have had a religious influence in Champéry." As I quoted from Hudson Taylor to Fran, we spoke about the impossible situation this young English missionary found himself in standing at a bank in Cambridge. Starting a bank account with all the money he had, which amounted to ten pounds, he considered the teller's question: "In what name shall I start this account?" Hudson Taylor, who had never realized that the account needed a name, took a deep breath and stammered, "The China Inland Mission." His faith, which essentially launched a mission on next to nothing, only grew—and so did God's provision. When he would speak about China's needs in meetings all over England, he refused to take a collection, stating, "God's work done in God's way will receive God's supply." How Fran and I prayed that we would have this same faith.

Prior to our departure from Champéry, Fran instructed me, "Go look for another place to stay outside the canton of Valais, and I'll start packing." George Exhenry, the local man whose conversion prompted our eviction, had a good friend who was president of a local department, which was Protestant, and was located on the other side of the Rhone River. George called his friend and arranged a time for me to meet with him.

A little red train took me through beautiful woods and farmlands, arriving at the village of Gryon, where the Swiss writer Juste Olivier had lived. His former house was for sale, but it was not big enough for our large family, and there was no school in the area for students who might have been interested in coming to us for Bible study. The two sisters of Juste Olivier advised me to go on to Villars. As I inquired at various places, I found myself pushed out rather than welcomed. At four o'clock in the afternoon I had no place to go. I went up the steps to a hotel, and a woman came to the door. I asked how much it would cost to stay the night and told her my story. She burst out, "I have just been saved in a Billy Graham meeting. I went up front and am now being 'followed up.' You can stay in 'the prophet's chamber,' and it won't cost you anything." Not only was there a sparkling clean bed with a big Swiss feather puff, but a little table with a white cloth had been set. On it was a pot of tea, a pitcher of hot milk, and a plate of bread and cheese. That day I prayed, *Thank you, God, for setting a table for me in the wilderness.* There was no answer yet as to where we could live, but I went to bed encouraged.

In the morning, after being generously provided with a Swiss breakfast of bread and coffee, I set forth on my way to find a house. I had not walked far before I met Monsieur Gabus, the real estate dealer who had told me the day before that he had nothing in the price range I had mentioned. Seeing me, he called out, "Would you mind living in Huémoz?" I had never heard of that village but answered that it would likely be fine. I got in his car and we drove to a dismal-looking chalet. He led me up a set of dirt steps and unlocked the door of a ground-floor apartment. "This chalet has three apartments," he said, "rented to skiers in the winter and to hikers in the summer. It has not been well kept because it hasn't been a home." I had prayed that if the Lord wanted Fran and me in Switzerland, he would take me to a chalet that would be within our means. When we had finished looking around, Monsieur Gabus jumped into his car and shouted out the window, "A bus stops here and connects in Ollon with a train going to Champéry. Goodbye, and bring your husband to look at it tomorrow morning at ten." I shouted back, "Oh, Monsieur Gabus, how much is the rent?" He answered, "It's not for rent; it is for sale." And with that he was gone.

As I boarded the bus, I almost collapsed into a seat from exhaustion and discouragement. But again the example of Hudson Taylor came to mind. Was I any worse off than he when he banked his ten-pound note and began looking for seven Cambridge graduates who would accompany him to China? Our God is able to do all things. Trust is a word that cannot be used when we can see exactly what is about to take place. We trust as we walk along a dark road, holding the arm of someone who knows the way. To trust the person leading us means that we are not able to go it alone.

Arriving back in Champéry, I walked through the village and turned left down the road that ended at our chalet, all the while thinking of

Hudson Taylor and his various experiences. Thankfully, the lives of others who have traveled down the road of life are written down for us to be encouraged and spurred on by.

The children jumped up and down as the door opened. "Mommy, Mommy, did you find anything?" I replied, "Yes, but Daddy will have to come and see it. We need to take the early six o'clock train." It snowed heavily through the night, and the postman was making an early start on his rounds the next morning. He handed us three letters on our way out. I had not yet told Fran that the chalet was for sale and not for rent. As the train started chugging down the cog rail, I opened the three letters. Two were from people saying they were praying for us. The third one, from a couple in Ohio, contained a check. The letter told the story of how the woman's husband had received a bonus from his company—he had never received such a thing before—and how they had prayed that the Lord would show them what to do with the money. When they finished praying, they spoke spontaneously to each other: "Let's send this to the Schaeffers toward the buying of a chalet." I nearly burst into tears as I told Fran that the chalet was not for rent, but was for sale. Then I unfolded the check and saw it was for one thousand dollars. As Mr. Gabus showed us through the house, we realized there was plenty of room for our family and for students, who we prayed would come to ask questions about the existence of God and the purpose of life.

March 31 found us in a jeep with boxes and trunks precariously tied on. We asked the driver to stop after we crossed the bridge over the Rhone River, which separated the Roman Catholic canton of Valais from the Protestant canton of Vaud, so that we could give thanks to God for providing us with a destination.

Within a few days of our arrival, our daughter Priscilla started her courses at the University of Lausanne. The first week she met an American student who was studying Buddhism and oriental religions, searching for meaning. Priscilla telephoned home and said, "I want to bring a girl home for the weekend. She has questions and wants to ask Daddy. She's very sad, even though she comes from a wealthy family." I thought, *Oh no! We're in the middle of unpacked boxes and trunks, and I have three little kitchens, each one on separate floors, and only a strange assortment of dishes and cooking pans. We're not ready for visitors.* But I told Priscilla it would be all right if she and her friend came.

On Friday Priscilla arrived with her friend Grace. At the dinner table Grace's questions poured out. Although we didn't know it just then, L'Abri had begun. Upon returning to the university, Grace told her friends, "You can't imagine where I've been this weekend. I've had so many questions answered—hard questions about the meaning and purpose of life—at this little chalet in the mountains." John Sandri (Priscilla's future husband) was one of those Grace spoke to.

Several weeks later Priscilla met me at the door and said, "Guess what, Mom, two singers have just arrived from Milan. They're not gospel singers, but opera singers." Jane Stuart Smith had arrived in town, and her first words to us were, "I heard you have a place where people can come and ask questions about life, purpose, and truth. I have so many questions, so I've come." Others came, including American soldiers serving in Germany. One gentleman, Bill McColley, stayed for a weekend. Some of his army friends had told him that only dumb people believe that Christianity is true. When he went back to Germany, he shared with others that he was now intellectually proud of being a Christian.

As Hudson Taylor's story had filled me with courage, I began to see the pieces falling together in the beginning of L'Abri's history, just as it had with the history of the China Inland Mission. Hudson Taylor had also stood alone, facing impossible difficulties, far from the coastal areas where many Anglican missionaries lived and worked. He strongly believed that he was not alone, but that God, who can penetrate all walls, was there beside him. Francis and I had our own walls that needed to be penetrated. Would we have food to feed those who were coming? Would the garden grow?

Would the rest of the money come to buy the chalet? Would we get a permit to live in the village? I found myself returning to Hudson Taylor's life story to remind myself of how God had worked in his life, praying that He would work as mightily in ours.

As the days passed and more and more university students were coming, we also received more donations. Priscilla drew a thermometer on white poster cardboard, and we posted it on the kitchen wall. As the money came in, she drew a line and colored the thermometer red up to that line. She also indicated the amount of each gift. The postlady became interested in the thermometer and came to realize that the mail she was delivering was contributing to this image on the wall. One day she handed me a little blue envelope, which looked like an invitation. Inside was a check for five hundred dollars! I called everybody together in the dining room. As we sat in a circle, I put the check on the floor and said, "We should give thanks to the Lord for answering our prayer." After several of us had prayed, Franky, age two, said, "I think we should clap," which we all did, clapping our thanksgiving.

The final payment was due in two months' time. We felt strongly that we should make no appeals for money. Instead, we called for a day of prayer and fasting. Through the years we have continued to set aside days to devote to time with God, putting aside our daily activities (cooking, washing dishes, cleaning, even table conversations). These days give everyone the opportunity to go out with their Bibles and a prayer list and pray all day. We close these days in the late afternoon with joint prayer.

Over the weeks money came in, and we had received nearly enough to make the payment at the notary public in Aigle. We lacked only three hundred Swiss francs. Alice, the postlady, arrived as we were rushing down the steps to catch the bus. She waved a letter to us and said, "Hurry, open it up. Perhaps this is it." The letter was from Monsieur Exhenry in Champéry. He wrote, "You were put out of your home and your village because of my salvation. Now I want to buy a door that will always be open for people like me who need to find the truth." The amount was exactly three hundred Swiss francs! We arrived in Aigle with much thanksgiving and placed the money into the notary's hands. We felt as though one of the walls at Jericho had come tumbling down.

Still, there was no possibility of continuing to live in the chalet and receive students unless we could obtain a Swiss *permis de séjour*—permission to live in that village and canton. This was the next wall that had to fall. We tried many contacts with little results. Then I was invited to have tea with the Mesdemoiselles Chaudet who lived next door to our new home. They gave the appearance of being humble ladies who ran a little boarding house. As we drank tea, they asked pointed questions as to why we had moved to Huémoz and what we were going to do there. Our story of the past few months gradually unfolded. I let them know that what we now needed was a permit to live in this village so that students could come and raise their questions. The ladies looked at each other and said, "We'll ask our brother." I thought, *What can their brother do about it?* When Alice arrived with our mail the next day, I asked her who the brother of the demoiselles Chaudet was. Somewhat taken aback, Alice answered, "He's one of the seven men of the Federal Council." Each year in turn, one of the seven becomes President of the Confederation, and Monsieur Chaudet happened to be president that year. The ladies next door were going to tell our story to the president of Switzerland! Indeed, he could do something, and he did. He arranged for us to have a permit and it became official.

L'Abri continues to work on the basis of prayer. Month by month we see students coming, gifts arriving, and workers being provided for in the seven L'Abri centers (two in the United States and the others in Switzerland, England, Sweden, Holland, and South Korea) and also in the work of the Francis Schaeffer Foundation in Gryon, Switzerland. Little did I know when we were going through those difficult times that there would be an amazing harvest around the world over a forty-six-year period (so far).

What do I feel *Hudson Taylor and the China Inland Mission* teaches us?[2]

Our eyes should be fixed upon our heavenly Father, and we should be filled with wonder as centuries go by. We who are His children by faith in Christ can call upon Him in prayer for guidance and understanding and for the means to do what He has asked us to do. My husband often said in the early days of our work, "I am so glad we have no endowment because I can trust God's leading through the money coming in or not coming in."

At L'Abri we continue to look for the place God would have us to be. God communicates His will for our lives step by step, giving direction just as we need it to follow His lead.

Hope Grows Best
in the Garden of Despair

An Interview with Walter Wangerin, Jr.

Until I am a nothing in a nowhere...

—ANONYMOUS, *The Cloud of Unknowing*

Scott Larsen: Before we discuss the books that have influenced you the most, do you have any general thoughts to share about the ways books shape us?

Walter Wangerin: When books work well, it isn't just that we memorize them and then, by our will and our personal wisdom, shape our lives to follow them. Rather, when books work for us, we begin to walk beside the mind that created the book. That mind may be so much wiser than ours, but we walk beside it until soon we are walking like that one.

That sounds like a dynamic relationship, where the reader is being continuously shaped to be more like the mind of the one who wrote the book. It makes us seriously consider the stuff we choose to read!

The question becomes, Who is going to teach you both how to interpret

the world around you, to see it in small, and to come to a true understanding of it, organizing the context in which you live?

A child enters the world and really doesn't make sense of it but lives in
sort of a senselessness of existence. The kid first begins to know her little
house and her parents, and they become the whole world to that child.
You pull a child apart from that house and that well-ordered, nicely con-
structed, beloved family, and the kid is lost—literally lost. As the kid gets
older, it becomes the kid's business to read the events and the details of the
universe in such a way that she puts them together so that they make sense.

The universe is infinitely various and infinitely filled with stimuli, details,
shapes, and motion—both spiritual and material. So you see how various
and how cluttered the universe is, and what a mess it is unless you know how
to put it into some kind of order and interpret it. When we see, we either discover order or we impose an order upon the mess of this universe.

Let me pause here and highlight some early meanings of the word *poet*.
It comes from *poētēs*, a Greek word that generally means "the one who creates, who makes things, who makes." But I like the older Sanskrit meaning of this word, which means "a heaper into heaps and a piler into piles."
The poet comes upon human mess, human beings who are despairing,
feeling lost, anxious, and believing that the world around them is destroyed. They don't know what they control and what controls them. The
poet then begins to sing a song that gathers the details of the mess and
names the name of him who died. But the poet names that name in such
a way that the one who died begins to take up a place in the old stories, the
old songs. As the people close their eyes and listen to the song, they find
that the pieces of the story are literally the pieces of their lives, but the song
in the story put the pieces together into a sensible order. The people
become less confused and more put to peace. They feel that they are no
longer aliens in the universe, but citizens of a universe they can somewhat
understand.

Think about another word for poet, the Old English word *scop* (pronounced "shop"). It is related to our word *shape*. The Old English understanding of scop was this: The singer of songs, the artist, the writer of books is the one who will take your mess of a day when you're lost and incapable, and this poet will sing shape to it—and sing you into that shape.

So the question becomes, Who are you going to allow to become your "heaper into heaps" and your "piler into piles"? Who will shape the world that you enter into and dwell in? Are you going to allow football to do that, so all the world is seen in a contest? Are you going to allow simpleminded understandings—like the cartoons, newspapers, or the government—do that for you? Or are you going to enter into the sweet complexity of minds, this living treasure of singers and writers who embrace more details with greater richness of beauty, deeper understanding of what is truly evil, what is good, and what is the procession of human experience? You want the minds of those who have created whole cultures of insight. The more complexly we see the world, the more capable we are of admitting many people into that world—people who are not like us. Books open our eyes to the complex truths that simple, mindless stories simply have no names for. So why not pick the best?

I don't mind the people who read romances, but that's formula fiction. It repeats the same world over and over again, and it's a profoundly limited world. And every one of the people who loves romantic fiction has a mind better than the world that it shapes. We call that escapism. Gerard Manley Hopkins offers his poetry as *inscapism*—to escape into things, truly, not escape from them.

That's the influence of great books; they teach us how to see the world that is.

Moving on to specific books, which ones have played the role in your life that you just described?
Depending upon where I am and what I'm feeling, there are a number of very important books in my past. However, I think I would almost always

choose two writings of Fyodor Dostoyevsky—*Crime and Punishment* and *The Brothers Karamazov.*[1]

I read *Crime and Punishment* while I was in high school. It wasn't assigned; my brother had it at home, and so I read it.

My father was a pastor, and so religion was a great deal of everything we did. I wouldn't say that I didn't have faith throughout that experience, but I dealt an awful lot with questioning, sort of a joyful questioning early on. I was wrestling with questions of law. That's why *Crime and Punishment* was so important. It is a dazzling book that gave me scope and gave me privilege for questioning exactly as I was. This book, along with *The Brothers Karamazov,* confronts issues dead-on and fearlessly.

When I read *Crime and Punishment,* it was the first time I had seen a knockdown author—a *powerful* author—deal with the themes of sin and whether a person can get freed of sin at all. The greatest part of that book is when Raskolnikov gives the most profound argument for freedom from the law. He is a young man with the intensities of young students in Russia, and he believes that an individual of perfectly good intent—and also with the freedom to act untrammeled—can break a law in order to do good by the whole of society. This is the argument of the *Ubermensch,* the "over-men" or "over-people," whose concept was originated by Nietzsche, the philosopher who said there is no God.

Dostoyevsky was fighting with Nietzsche, who had again raised the issue that there could be certain human beings who could be above the law and benefit all of society by acting above any law. Dostoyevsky took him on by positing an individual, Raskolnikov, who believed he could act above the law. He, in fact, is a good man, and his act of murder is genuinely to get rid of an evil in the world—a terrible old woman in whom there is not a redemptive bone. She is literally ugly. Raskolnikov kills her. Dostoyevsky describes this scene so powerfully that even as a sophomore in high school I became hooked.

Thereafter, a police detective focuses on Raskolnikov as a potential murderer, and they have long discussions in which they put to one another hypothetical questions with regard to freedom and the law. Raskolnikov answers with Nietzsche's attitude that there are some people free like that, but he never quite gives himself away. It is a dazzling dance of minds. Raskolnikov argues overtly that he didn't commit the murder, but covertly that he had the right to do it. The detective, of course, just quietly plods with the law.

As the book continues, what happens to Raskolnikov is what Dostoyevsky actually felt would happen to people who have sinned grave sins—even if their sin was committed to save other people. Raskolnikov begins to feel more and more isolated, afraid, filled with anxiety and, as Dostoyevsky would have it, more and more guilty. You can't escape guilt. The crushing weight of his own guilt is infinitely more powerful than the accusation and the punishment of the law.

Sonia, who loves Raskolnikov, persuades him to declare unto the people his sin. She says something like the following: "Get down in the center of the street at the crossroads and say unto everyone who passes by, 'I'm sorry. I am sorry. I confess my sins.'" He does this, and in doing so discovers how freeing it is to make confession. He then begins to believe in the potential of forgiveness. Ultimately, he is sent to Siberia but is sent with the freedom of spirit, because the greatest punishment is past.

What impact did *The Brothers Karamazov* have on you?
The high school I went to was a prep school for Lutheran ministry. It was all male, and there was a general sense of the law all around us. So when I read Dostoyevsky, I didn't feel like the issues he dealt with were far away from me. But *The Brothers Karamazov* took all this much farther. It really peered at the issue of goodness on earth and what it looks like, what Christian goodness looks like.

Fyodor Karamazov is an older man with enormous appetites—sexual, physical, mental. He also owns enough money to be independently wealthy, though not necessarily enough to make all of his sons wealthy. He is, as the book goes on, a bad man. He's not a terrible man, but a burping, sodden, drunken, rich, bad man.

Karamazov has produced three legitimate sons and most likely one illegitimate son. The oldest is Dmitri, who is a passionate individual and is closest to his father with regard to appetite. His emotions and his energy for life are consuming. He loves people. He is not bad; he does not live the way his father does, though the potential is there.

Although he doesn't sin terribly, I have never read a scene that more truly describes how true repentance and confession feel than the scene in which the police have Dmitri strip bare naked in front of everyone. The police kept questioning him. He thought they were asking about some money that he had kept in a pouch over his chest. But they were actually questioning him about a much larger thing, and that was the stealing of a great deal of money and the murder of his father. So he makes a confession to a little thing, which is very devastating to him. But he is only guilty of a little thing. What most shames him, as he is standing naked, is one of his toenails, which he says is rugged, tough as a slug. It embarrasses him deeply that it should be seen amongst individuals who are all dressed. That's the first I remember being blown away by thinking that this is exactly what confession is. It is a complete stripping down, even to the things that most embarrass us, and it's done in public.

Immediately following this scene, Dmitri falls asleep. When he wakes up the next morning, he finds that somebody had placed a pillow under his head, and he almost weeps. "Who," he said, "did this? Who did such a kindness to me as to put a pillow under my head?[2] Even as young as I was, I was moved by seeing what follows true confession. When you come to a point of saying, "I am worthless. I am nothing," then any kindness done unto you has the full weight of miracle because you don't expect it. A pillow, in fact, is like the presence of an angel.

Ivan, the second brother, lives in the coolness of the mind and, in fact, explains all things of the world from what he perceives to be rationality, believing nothing that cannot be weighed, measured, proved, or reasoned. He argues for a rational God, not the God of the Bible and not the God of Christ.

Then you have the other extreme in the youngest brother, Alyosha, who is the spirit. Dostoyevsky's characterization of the three sons is not unlike Plato's distinction of the three parts of a human being—the reason, the body, and the spirit. Alyosha is the sweet-spirited one. He is the one who draws his strength and understanding from the Bible and from the church.

Alyosha is pure goodness. When some boys start throwing stones at him and he doesn't throw any back, they get angrier and angrier until finally one boy throws a stone so hard at him that this good man falls to the ground. The boy, when he sees what he has done, breaks into tears and runs away weeping. When goodness confronts evil and does not pay evil back with evil, suddenly evil is made so apparent that even the evil one must recognize it. In my book *Paul,* I wrote a scene in which Paul presents himself to the knife of a bad man and says, "I love you," and keeps saying this to the bad man who wants to kill him until it breaks the bad man down. It is a total conundrum that when evil faces goodness, goodness doesn't fight it back but declares love for it. I learned this first from Alyosha and Dostoyevsky.

In *The Brothers Karamazov,* there is a man who lives in the house with the brothers who has epilepsy, and his name is Smerdyakov. He's sort of smiling, snide, wears his hair greasy with spit curls, pomades himself, and makes himself humble. But all along he's seething with anger because it is presumed that he is the illegitimate son of Fyodor Karamazov who's going to get no money—nothing—when the father passes, which the father does. That's the structure of the book itself, and the profound question becomes, Who murdered Fyodor, the father?

You mentioned a time of questioning earlier in your life. Were there any books that were particularly important in your experience of finding answers?

At a critical point when I was returning to the faith, a book that opened up the potential of contradiction and paradox in faith (as opposed to clean and pure rationality)—which was absolutely crucial for me to accept the faith—was Søren Kierkegaard's *Fear and Trembling*.[3]

When I went to graduate school, I, in effect, realized that I was not a man of faith. For several years I had lived a very clear presumption with regard to God, myself, humankind, and so forth, but it was not Christian. When I returned to the faith, the books that I tended to read were ones that allowed for contradiction and paradox.

At that time I read *The Dark Night of the Soul*, by St. John of the Cross, which is a work about mysticism.[4] Both this book and Kierkegaard's *Fear and Trembling* deeply shaped my faith and allowed for me this profound sense of mystery and paradox. The two books need to be put together to explain their collective influence.

John of the Cross was a mystic who understood that in order to go toward God, sometimes you go through a wasteland. Not only sometimes, but almost always. You go toward the darkness to find the light. A genuine approach to God seems paradoxical.

Actually, John began writing *The Dark Night of the Soul* in order to interpret a hymn. By the time he got to the third line of the hymn, he was up to forty pages, and soon he abandoned the hymn and just went furiously forward with the idea of the *asceses,* the ascetic way of life. In this way of life, one begins denying the flesh comforts but does so in order that all one's attention may be placed upon God. God is ultimately the *mysterium tremendum,* the Immense Mystery—beyond our knowing. That God is beyond our rational knowing is part of the issue that John of the Cross understood. We are creatures and God is the Creator.

While certainly God is beyond our complete comprehension, would you agree that we can know rationally that which God has chosen to reveal to us?

Well, that's the paradox. There are things that we know rationally. This is a very Thomistic understanding of God and theology—that reason is the highest thing we have with which to work.[5] It's the highest thing that God put into Creation. Not only are we the highest thing created, but our reason is one of the sweetest, most precise tools we have to work with. And so, when we teach, when we develop doctrine, when we talk about the Trinity, when we talk about the person of Christ being both human and divine, we are using our rational mind—and we need this so that people don't go off half-cocked, just wild-eyed any way they want and think they're near God. But those who depend upon that, and that alone, will end up in a legalistic system. They'll end up with the law and not grace because grace is the least rational thing there is.

To get back to the work of St. John of the Cross, then, you are saying that we can't truly approach God apart from contradiction and paradox—both of which defy human reason.

My image for this is that for us to know the Creator directly and head-on would be the same as one of my fictional characters rising up out of my novel and greeting me. My novel and I are on such different planes—even the characters that I make up out of whole cloth. I may know them completely—I may know them extraordinarily well—yet I don't altogether control them. When I write a novel, sometimes I follow the characters rather than drive them. We are the book that God writes, and God may release us in freedom, but what we cannot do is rise up out of this context in which we live and peer at the Creator. It is as impossible as it is for Chanticleer to rise up out of *The Book of the Dun Cow* and peer at me.[6] It couldn't happen. Now, Christians say that God breaches this wall of impossibility by sending his Son into the world. This is like saying that I could dive into my own novel, which I can't do. Only God can do that sort of thing.

On the other hand, the mystics, including John of the Cross, say we shall meet God face to face, or that we shall come as close to God as possible. They remember God's admonition to Moses—you can't look directly at God; you can only see God walking away.[7] (They take that seriously. You only see God glancingly, and only walking away, which is almost as terrible as Orpheus must have felt as he was climbing up out of the pit in my book *The Orphean Passages*.[8]

In the case of my book, the mystery is that Orpheus will have Euridyce. Euridyce will come up to live with Orpheus after she has died, so long as he doesn't look back to see whether she's following. He is climbing up through darkness without the least hint, sound, or stone rattle that she's behind him. If he should stop and listen, he hears absolutely nothing. He can't detect any breathing. And the farther he climbs (it's very clear to his senses), the farther he goes from his beloved Euridyce. When he gets to the top, he decides he can't stand it anymore because he thinks he's lost her. He turns around and looks, but as soon as he looks at her he loses her. She had been there all along. Orpheus's experience is very much our experience of faith, this mystery experience that I got from Kierkegaard and John of the Cross.

But aren't things somewhat different from this analogy when we are approaching God?

Sure. On the one hand, there really is a sense that we lost God by looking around. It means that we're looking for some kind of a tangible proof of the existence of Jesus. We're looking for something that we can weigh in our hand, touch, and measure. We really hunger for this, and so we look to other people of strong faith, and we want them to be the proofs to us that God exists. This is why people so desperately hunger for miracles, like the healing of someone who should have died. They grasp that and hold on to it, but the more they hold on to those things (if they're being honest with themselves), the less those things can support the whole issue of salvation and the presence of God.

Turning around and looking is not the end of the process; that's about the middle way through the process. Because when God seems then to recede from you, you go into a real sense of despair. To be without hope is what that word means. So, that's the difference between my analogy and approaching God. When you approach God, of course, God does not recede, but you don't know that. And that's where faith becomes such a profound paradox in the end.

We will seem, as we approach God, to move more and more into the silences. The still small voice of Elijah's experience at the mount in Hebrew is translated "a silence in the center of silences," the most silent place.[9] If we use our natural body's senses to prove to ourselves that God is near, we will fail at it. Either we stick with all the signs, senses, and rationality—the signs of the Catholics, and the rationality of the Protestants—and we allow those things to comfort us that God is near, or we realize that God is greater than all those things. He's on a completely different level, and as we approach God, each one of those things that used to comfort us carries less and less comfort. It becomes a profoundly lonely thing. But in that seemingly farthest of moments from God, God is immediately present, and our hearts are filled with the quality of love, which is the sign of the presence of God.

Where does Kierkegaard's *Fear and Trembling* fit into all this, or does it? Where Kierkegaard deals with this paradox of seeming to go *from* God in order to go *to* God, he talks about the knight of faith, who is the most common individual on Earth. The knight of faith is always living in the light of the love of God and is absolutely convinced that God is there. He has the capacity to understand, or behold, or embrace the hugeness of the glory of God—that very thing that distinguishes God from all the rest of creation—and at precisely the same time to walk as if he were a normal butcher, and, in fact, genuinely be a normal butcher.

Kierkegaard represents the knight of faith as Abraham. Abraham has been commanded to take his son up to the mountain and slaughter him in the name of God. As he goes up the mountain, he knows he must keep this terrible commandment, and he is prepared to kill his son. At precisely the same moment, he also knows that God is a God of mercy and he will not require him to kill his son. Western minds, reasonable minds, will diminish one or the other of those two propositions. They'll say, "Yeah, but because Abraham knew he didn't have to kill his son, then he wasn't really thinking he would go through with it." But that's not what Kierkegaard says, and this is what drew me back to the faith. There may be these ideas that are completely contradictory, and both of them are right.

The knight of faith lives with the greatest adroitness in these two oppositions of the demands of the divine: (1) that you shall give your life up completely, and (2) that you shall (Kierkegaard does not touch this, but it comes in Luke), if you follow Jesus, hate your mother and your father, your wife, your brothers, your sisters, your children, even your own life. You will hate these things to follow Jesus, which sounds horrible to Christians, especially when we uphold family life. But the knight of faith hears that, believes it, makes an absolute, complete commitment unto God, and turns away from all of his family. And when his family returns, he smiles sweetly at the grace that they are there at all. But both are absolutely true.

I had not had that sense of paradox in faith before because I had been taught either/or-type laws. Either you're saved or you're damned. Either Jesus is this or he's that. Either it happens this way or that way. That, of course, is highly dogmatic, legalistic, and reasonable.

These books helped me enormously when I couldn't return to faith simply by orthodox doctrine only, nor by all the moves I had made at home and in school in preparation for Lutheran ministry.

What was the process you experienced as these books helped you return to the faith?

I found out that I had no faith because my belief had always been sup-ported by the strong structures around me. It was as if they held me and made me walk when I wasn't capable of walking at all. And when the struc-tures went away, then all gestures of faith left as well. I could not return at the level where I left, and this is the case for many people, I suspect. But many people in the church don't realize that. They think they just have to argue the person back to the same place where he was when he was such a faithful follower. That's not it. You have to enter at a different level. Because leaving the church is as much a part of the sequence of faith as staying with the church. The church often thinks that this person has now fallen and is out of the process altogether. What I declare is wherever that person ends up, these are stages of faith *too*. So my declaring that I was separate from God didn't mean that I had fallen. I don't take, in this particular instance, the word of Wesley, "backslid." That's not backsliding; that's dramatic for-ward moving. It's coming to the truth that you hadn't recognized before.

When I returned to the church, then, it did not work for me to come in at that simplistic level where all things are explained, and the things that are difficult are simply ignored. These two books helped me because they allowed precisely for paradox—that I could say two things, both of which seem profoundly true to me, and accept them both, despite the fact that they seemed completely opposed.

For example, when I was young the death and resurrection of Jesus all sounded very simple. Jesus rose from the dead, ascended into heaven, and took his place at the right hand of God. Now our Lord is King of all, back into the glory that we said he had at the beginning when Creation was made through him. At one point I thought that was really nice. I loved little baby Jesus. It was the beginning of this grand King, and, oh, he had stopped off on the way to save our sins by dying. In those days I believed in the death of Jesus the same way as I got through a visit to the dentist. I had horrible experiences with the dentist, but when I sat in the dentist's chair, I would fix my mind on *The Lone Ranger*, which was going to be on television that night. I would go through all this pain in my mouth, but I could survive it because I was going to see *The Lone Ranger*. And that's how I used to think of Jesus' death. Yeah, he died, but he knew he was going to rise again, you see, and he could always hold on to that. Or he knew he was doing good for the whole world, so at least he could have a good feeling about this terrible thing he was going through. He could hold on to that.

Well, the paradox, when you return again to faith, is that Jesus is not at the right hand of God helping all the good people and hurting only the bad people. It's much more confused than that! And in some respects Jesus still seems to be among the dead—literally. God is where people are hurting; Jesus remains the humiliated Son of God that Paul talks about in Philippians 2:6-8. There's something about that death that pervades us still.

I could not have returned to the church without coming to understand the absolute totality of the dying of Jesus and how he must have loathed what he had become bearing the sins of the world. He did not love himself at that point because he was the very thing he hated—he was sin. And this is a far different understanding from the "dentist's chair" approach to belief during my childhood.

But if I do return and recognize that there is both glory and the horrible dirt and dust of dying, and that God is fully as much among the dead, grieving them, helpless, weeping, as God is the King of the universe—Ah, I can return to that. That's how these great minds helped me come back to the faith.

One recurring theme is the need for the recognition of paradox in the Christian faith. Have you experienced any times in your life where paradox took on visible form?

I like the profound contradictions of things in the kingdom of God and the kingdom of the world. My whole parish ministry except for the very beginning was in the inner city at a black congregation. I'm white and my family at that point was all white. It was God who wanted me at this poor inner-city church. The people weren't necessarily poor, but the church was down to thirty-five members, and they were questioning whether they should shut their doors. My ministry at first was in an upper-middle-class white congregation in the same city, but not downtown. This little downtown church called Grace had come to the church I was with and had for two years been asking for help in deciding whether to continue. My first assignment at the big church was to work with the little church.

At that point in my ministry God forced my hand. He shut the door at the big white church and opened the door at that little black church. They gave me a call at the same time that the other church was about to dismiss me. It was as if I had no choice. Sometimes you don't question, you don't argue, you just go.

I was terrified of the inner city. When I took the position my salary dropped, we moved onto food stamps, and we moved into the inner city. From the outside it looked like I was a true knight of the church. On the inside it just scared the devil out of me. But I did it, and I did it in the sense of paradox.

First off, I decided that I could not drive to appointments in the inner city. If I was going to serve that place, then the wise thing to do was to go face toward it—almost Dostoyevskian. I made a pact with myself that I would walk everywhere in this almost ghettolike area. I would learn the names of people sitting on their porches and I would speak to them. I would learn where the poor were. In fact, when we at the big church were testing whether the little church should have a pastor, I sat down with a woman from Grace Church named Norma Malone. I told her, as I had said to other members, that it didn't matter whether their pastor was black or white. We were sitting in her living room and it was very dark. She only had one very low lamp in there, so I saw, as a crescent moon, that lamp strike light off her brown cheek, and I could scarcely see her face.

"It doesn't matter whether he's black or white," she said, "so long as he stands by us." And then she nodded and said, "Stands by us in the hospital.

Stands by us in the courtroom. Stands by us in the prisons. Stands by us in the streets. Stands by us before the city. Stands by us in the schools."

I had a feeling of anointing at that point. She was describing what I had to do. Knowing all this, I did the thing I feared the most to do—I walked from place to place. I never learned to love the prisons, but I went. Much of this comes out of this paradox of what I had been reading. I never put on my wall a little paradigm of these people and said, "Hmm, okay, I'll do it like that." These things don't come because you plan. They come because that's the way your heart has become—you don't even think about it. The paradox, then, is that I went toward my fear, not away from it.

Fear and Trembling and *The Dark Night of the Soul* permitted my heart to live in paradox. They talk about the fruitfulness of paradox, which is to say it looks like going into a wilderness. It looks like there shall be no fruit there. What you don't do is say, "Well, I'll hang here until I find fruit." What you do say is, "I'll work here in spite of the fruitlessness." The surprise is that if you do it right—if you do it in faith, not looking for success, not looking for some kickback or some sudden proof halfway through (such as God saying, "I am with you")—then, unexpectedly, the wilderness bears fruit. That's the paradox.

In the inner city, did you enter a wilderness and then find it later to bear fruit?

If you willingly go into the wilderness and happily work expecting nothing, then the pillow that someone places under your head is the fruit. It's the grace that comes unbidden. But you would not have seen that if you (1) had not gone to the wilderness, and (2) had not admitted that it was a wilderness, and that you'd work there without any gift or return or reward at all. It's only then that you begin to see how present is holy God in all those things. That's the fruit.

Too often, as preachers and writers, we continue to tell people of the world, "Oh, come to Jesus who will slake your thirst, who will bear your burdens, who will pat you on the back, who will keep you protected, who will watch over you... Come to Jesus!" And that's true, all that stuff. But if that's *all* we say, then this other entire element of the life of Christ in the world, which was a most fruitless life—a most failing venture, a most lonely thing—is lost. And we become profoundly comfortable Christians because we came to Jesus for comfort. We came for fruit.

People who are comfortable in the church are people who, when given a blessing by God, do not give thanks in a prayer that lasts their whole life. It's a quick, "Well, thank you. Another one for God!" Whereas when the one who is in the wilderness, and expects for the sake of God to be in the wilderness only doing work, is given a cup of water, that person thanks God for the rest of his or her life.

Do you have any closing thoughts concerning the value and power of books?
Reading short stories, novels, poetry, and so forth is like walking into a city. If I, as a writer, have done my city well, you'll find paths and directions through that city that I myself may not even have thought about. I will allow my book to be larger than I am. I tell my writing students over and over again, "Your books should be smarter than you. You should keep surprising yourself upon follow-up readings." For that very reason, the only thing I would ask when you enter any of the books that I have spoken of is, please, don't come with predispositions. Don't come thinking you know. Anybody who comes thinking that they know is going to close the book when they hit things of which they are ignorant, and that won't work. Too many of us read books to try to find something to back up what we already believe. We're unwilling to do the serious job of making our own paths, wrestling with, living with, walking with the author. If you come into an experience thinking you know, you will never know. You have to come with the risk of ignorance.

TWENTY

Reading: The Fingerprints on Your Soul

Ravi Zacharias

Lost somewhere in the enormous plains of time, there wanders a dwarf who is the image of God, who has produced on a yet more dwarfish scale an image of creation. The pigmy picture of God we call man; the pigmy picture of creation we call Art.

—G. K. CHESTERTON, "Lunacy and Letters"
in Robert Knille's *As I Was Saying: A Chesterton Reader*

I believe we greatly underestimate the weight of the influences in our lives, those realities that shape the development of how we think and how we live more purposefully than we ever realize. These influences come from two areas: from our reading and from our professors.

If I had even the faintest clue when I was younger as to how profound an impact books and professors would have upon my life, I would have kept a better record of my thoughts and emotions. Why? Because some books and teachers leave their indelible fingerprints on our souls. And when those fingerprints are left, it's as if our DNA has been changed. Our physical body takes on characteristics because of our chemical DNA.

Likewise, those whom we've read and those at whose feet we have studied will transform our passions, power, and purpose. So when I consider the books that have changed me, I am speaking not only of the fingerprints of particular words, but of the very lives of these authors as well.

WORDS THAT SHAPE ONE'S CALL

A book by Leonard Ravenhill is the first that shaped me beyond any dispute (outside of the Scriptures) and probably more dramatically than any other book I have read. An English revivalist born in 1907, Ravenhill wrote several books on the theme of prayer and revival, and *Why Revival Tarries* is the volume that impacted me.[1] First published in 1959, the book is a series of addresses that Ravenhill gave on the prayer life of the minister. Oh, the power of that book! I still remember reading it in the library at Tyndale College in Toronto, where I received my undergraduate degree in theology. I was twenty-two years old and felt the call of God upon my life. I had left the hotel industry, in which I was preparing for management, and went into theological training.

The shift in my life's trajectory did not occur quickly, however. There was a clear struggle in my heart. I came to know the Lord when I was seventeen, on a bed of suicide in New Delhi. In 1966, when I was twenty, my father sent my older brother and me to Canada to see if there was a future for us in the West. Jobs were difficult to find in India and the atmosphere was very competitive.

When I arrived in Canada, I had already completed two years of training in business management in the hospitality and catering industry. I find the food industry fascinating. It's a place where one can see and really meet the world philosophically without the rigors of academics. People's worldviews show very quickly in hotel rooms and in transient settings. They reveal their lives to you. Yet as I was working in banquet management, I felt the hunger to speak for the Lord. I was a new Christian, and wherever I spoke, things would happen. People would ask if I had ever considered that God had gifted me in the role of evangelism. It was natural to me, whether I was behind the pulpit or speaking with someone one-on-one. So I started taking part-time courses at a theological seminary in Toronto.

The more time I spent studying, the more I became restless in the hotel industry. This was especially true because liquor plays such an important role in the catering life. I had never even held a glass of it. Even before I was a believer, I had some disciplines that I kept, and for me personally, avoiding alcohol was certainly one of them. And when I saw the effect drinking had on some people, I thought, *Is this what my life is going to be reduced to—dealing with something that I don't even want to be responsible for on the other side of the counter?* As I wrestled with that reality, the burden to preach grew greater and greater.

Indeed, as God would have it, preaching opportunities came from hither and yon. So with this struggle in my heart, I informed my parents that I was going to give up my career in business. It would have been a very good career, for I was working for a major worldwide hotel chain. But I felt God's increasing call on my life—the pressure in the soul, as it were—to proclaim and to preach the gospel, although I didn't know what shape this call would take.

Looking back, it is interesting that at age nineteen, before I left India, I was asked to fill in for a young preacher representing Delhi at the Asian Youth Conference in Hyderabad. When the representative for Delhi didn't show up, I was conscripted at 1:30 in the afternoon to speak at 4 P.M. That was the first time I had ever spoken publicly, and I was given my subject only thirty minutes before. In the audience were Jay Kesler and Sam Wolgemuth, leaders of Youth for Christ in the United States and internationally. God used that message in my own life, and through that particular address—and to my utter shock—I was awarded the Asian Youth Preacher Award. Time and again when I was studying the Scriptures in

Canada, God brought that experience to my memory and said: *I have used you before without any of your training. This is where I want you.*

So in 1968 I left my business career and went to Tyndale College, where I graduated in 1972. When I was still a student, the Christian and Missionary Alliance invited me to speak in Vietnam. To see what God did during those meetings—where literally thousands came to Christ—was amazing. Several years later when revival historians recorded what happened in Vietnam, they traced the seeds of a great revival back to a twenty-five-year-old evangelist and his seventeen-year-old interpreter. I happened to be reading one of these accounts and was so stunned when I stumbled upon this description that I had to reread it! It was clearly the grace of God at work, and He confirmed to me that He was shaping my life.

God uses various means to guide us, including, as I said, teachers and books. I'll never forget laying my hands on the book *Why Revival Tarries.* From page after page, I made notes and wrote down what Leonard Raven-hill was saying. I got his tapes on prayer and revival and would listen to them at home. I still remember my mother asking, "Aren't you tired of that man's voice? Night after night you're hearing his voice. It's echoing through these walls." That was the effect that the book was having on me; I couldn't get enough.

Among the thoughts that shaped me most was the story Ravenhill told of the notorious British criminal Charlie Peace, who was going to his death on a capital offense. As the minister was reading from the Bible and another book, Charlie Peace asked him, "Do you really believe in such a place called hell?" The minister replied, "Yes." Charlie responded—and this is the thought that impacted me—"Sir, if I believed what you and the church of God *say* that you believe, even if England were covered with broken glass from coast to coast, I would walk over it, if need be, on hands and knees, and think it worth while living, just to save one soul from an eternal hell like that!"[2] That struck me. If what we lay claim to on these matters is true, then the dramatic influence in our lives is going to be inestimable.

"Even if England were covered with broken glass from coast to coast, I would walk over it." That is the kind of reality, and these are the words that shape one's call. This was the truth I was going to proclaim.

Ravenhill was a fire-and-brimstone preacher, no doubt about it. When I read him today, I wonder, *Will today's audience really listen to this kind of teaching?* But there was a time for him; there was an anointing upon him and a mission for him. And for me, *Why Revival Tarries* sealed my call to preach and proclaim, and it convinced me that this was a real message. I was not going to shirk from whatever sacrifice was required to take this message to the world. Little did I know that God was going to enable me to do just that.

PARADOX THAT PROPELS WONDER

Upon graduation from Tyndale College in 1972, I continued speaking as an evangelist. And in that year I sensed the need for higher training, because I wanted to address the skeptic. So in 1973 I went to Trinity Evangelical Divinity School and did my Master of Divinity. There, on my own initiative, I picked up the writings of G. K. Chesterton, C. S. Lewis, and Malcolm Muggeridge. It was Chesterton's *Orthodoxy* that most shaped my life and my apologetic.[3] It is one of the greatest books ever written. I disagree with Chesterton theologically on many points, but I agree with his existentially compelling arguments for the hunger deep within the human heart for that sense of wonder and awe.

As such, we missed a glorious opportunity in the 1960s when the existentialist thinkers, namely Jean-Paul Sartre and Albert Camus, were penning pointed phrases and screaming at the top of their lungs about the anguish of life. Wrote Camus: "There is but one truly serious philosophical problem, and that is suicide. Judging whether life is or is not worth living amounts to answering the fundamental question of philosophy. All the rest...comes afterward."[4] We read Camus's novel *The Stranger* and read

Sartre's two classic works, *Nausea* and *No Exit*.[5] These existentialists attempted to honestly consider life's paradoxes.

Likewise, and well before the 1960s, Chesterton dealt with the paradoxes of Christianity in *Orthodoxy* and, in fact, devotes an entire chapter to this theme. Now, I believe in the Law of Noncontradiction when I'm using the laws of logic, but I also know the paradoxes with which the human heart lives. Further, contradiction and paradox are not one and the same. The Law of Noncontradiction affirms that the same question cannot elicit two absolute answers that are opposite to each other. One of the two answers, if opposite to the other, would have to be qualified. A statement that makes claims to two things that are mutually exclusive is a contradictory statement. If the Law of Noncontradiction did not apply to reality, our law courts would be buried. When attempting to separate truth from falsehood, we seek to identify anything that is contradictory.

But a paradox is not a contradiction. Paradox involves two counterpoints on the same issue, both of which are not claiming an absolute nature. Consider, for example, the roles of emotion and will in marriage. Which element assures the success and longevity of a marriage, emotion or will? To be sure, without the will the marriage cannot survive. At the same time, without strong emotion a marriage would become drudgery. God brings the paradoxical roles of will and commitment and emotion and feeling to bear upon marriage. When you hold these in tandem, you will find that there is a beautiful blend of two seemingly different strands of your personality.

The classic illustration of this in theology is the paradox between the responsibility of man and the sovereignty of God. How can God give us the freedom to exercise our own will and still be sovereign over the universe? Western theologians tend to confuse the question by asking which one of the two is binding. The answer is "both are binding." This is a marvelous paradox that God brings to focus in the crucifixion of the God-man, Jesus Christ. Peter says in Acts, "This man was handed over to you by

God's set purpose and foreknowledge; and you, with the help of wicked men, put him to death by nailing him to the cross" (2:23). In the Crucifixion, God Himself was subject to evil men. Peter doesn't tell us where God's sovereignty ended and the responsibility of man began; he simply tells us that they are both real.

Another example is the paradox of Jesus weeping at the tomb of Lazarus, yet knowing that he would raise him in a moment. The fact that there is both pain and joy at the same time is a paradox and not a contradiction, for the emotions are not mutually exclusive.[6] What about the paradox of faith and reason? Are they mutually exclusive? Absolutely not. God has put enough into this world to make faith in Him a most reasonable stance, but He has left enough out to make it impossible to live by reason alone. Such is the paradoxical nature of Christianity, and Chesterton deals with it *in extenso* in his masterwork, *Orthodoxy*.

Although the human mind is engaged by mystery, we do not in turn know how to *engage it.* In other words, the paradox we encounter in matters of faith is not comfortable because we do not know how to hold the two parts of it in balance. Our compartmentalizing minds want to put everything into a box, and yet the claims of Christian belief are not mutually exclusive. God, in His divine sovereignty, has given to us liberties and freedoms. Since our sovereign God chose to grant us this privilege, it cannot be something that in any way diminishes His sovereignty. He circumscribes the limits of that freedom such that we cannot violate His sovereign plan and His will, but that does not negate the freedom that we enjoy. Paradox sits uncomfortably on our rational mind, but then so should the Incarnation, since it is the advent of a Person who is proclaimed to be very God of very God while also being very man of very man. How can God be entirely man while still being entirely God? It's a paradox of the highest order.

G. K. Chesterton has influenced my apologetic in learning to balance reason with emotion. I deal with the rigors of philosophical arguments in their classical tradition, yet I am much more of a cultural and existential apologist because I think most people live on the sharp edge of their feelings. Chesterton has shaped my apologetic by giving me the needed sense of direction. That is, in articulating the gospel I harness logic and emotion; I offer reasonable arguments while acknowledging our undeniable existential struggles.

I believe that sometimes the romantic side of Chesterton's nature overtook the theological side and provided a risky imbalance. But he nevertheless shaped my own way of argument, so that today I am not a classical apologist by any stretch of the imagination, but I'm very happy to be at the cutting edge of argument and persuasion in Christian apologetics.

One particular chapter in *Orthodoxy*, "The Ethics of Elfland," is one of the greatest chapters ever penned in the English language. Chesterton asserts that what he learned in the nursery stood him in greater stead in life than anything he ever learned by dabbling in philosophy. (Keep in mind, however, that the only reason he could state these points so cogently is because he understood philosophy so very well.) He straddled the line between the simplicity of a child and the sophistication of a thinker. If you can blend those two in apologetics you connect the heart and mind, because the human heart yearns for things simple and wonderful, while at the same time we struggle with the philosophical side of things. Chesterton marvelously blended the two.

In "The Ethics of Elfland," he writes:

> [T]he fairy tale founded in me...that this world is a wild
> and startling place, which might have been quite different,
> but which is delightful....
>
> This was my first conviction; made by the shock of my
> childish emotions meeting the modern creed in mid-career.
> I had always vaguely felt facts to be miracles in the sense
> that they are wonderful: now I began to think miracles in

the stricter sense that they were *wilful.* I mean that they
were, or might be, repeated exercises of some will. In short,
I had always believed that the world involved magic; now I
thought it involved a magician.... I had always felt life first
a story: and if there is a story there is a story-teller.[7]

Chesterton also gave me a bridge to literature and to the beauty and
romance of language, which is where Malcolm Muggeridge carried me
even further. I don't know if there has been a better exponent of the English language than Muggeridge. I must now discuss these men in tandem
because it would be unfair to acknowledge only one of them. Muggeridge
was the kind of person whose own life was a roller coaster between sensu-
ality and God. He was a modern-day Oscar Wilde—not in his life, but in
his thinking regarding pleasure and beauty on the one hand, and sobriety
and the Christian faith on the other.

These authors' use of language has reaffirmed for me how important is
the verse "In the beginning was the Word" (John 1:1). You see, God has
placed a huge value on language, and that is why He has given us His
Word, which abides forever. Yet the value of words has been lost in preaching, and we have witnessed as Jacques Ellul called it, "the humiliation of
the Word."[8] Modern-day evangelicalism particularly has sacrificed language at the altar of ecstasy, as it were. We want to generate the feeling but
do it mechanically rather than doing it thoughtfully. When feeling follows
on the heels of good thinking, it is wonderful. But when feeling is con-
trived and engineered without thought, once the emotion is gone, it leaves
you emptier than before.

Chesterton and Muggeridge taught me the significant roles of imagination, wonder, art, and language. These are important arenas in which
God has done His work and His revealing. And Chesterton shaped my
apologetic in the romantic side of life, the side that stirs one's imagination
and wonder.

BEAUTY THAT WHISPERS TO ONE'S SOUL

Of the books that have played the greatest role in molding me, the latest-comers to my arsenal of study are the volumes by the English writer F. W. Boreham. He authored more than fifty books of essays, studied at Spurgeon College, and was the last student approved by Spurgeon before the renowned preacher died. Boreham himself pastored in New Zealand, Tasmania, and Australia. He was not the classical preacher—not even a profound, deep preacher—but he was marvelous at seeing beauty in the simple things of life.

The book of his that has shaped my thinking most deeply is *A Bunch of Everlastings,* the first of five volumes in the Great Text Series.[9] In this series Boreham examines great men and women of the faith whose lives were shaped by a particular verse of Scripture. So we read of Martin Luther and the life-transforming influence of Habakkuk's announcement: "The just shall live by his faith,"[10] and of Thomas Chalmers and the prophet Jeremiah. Boreham considers the texts of John Newton, John Wesley, John Bunyan, David Livingstone, and Charles Spurgeon, among many others.

Of these writings, the greatest impact came through reading "William Carey's Text" in Boreham's book *A Bunch of Everlastings.* Missionary William Carey sailed for India in 1793. The verse that dug into Carey's soul was Isaiah 54:2, "Enlarge the place of your tent, stretch your tent curtains wide, do not hold back." And then Isaiah's marvelous conclusion: "Lengthen your cords, strengthen your stakes."

Boreham tells a wonderful story from William Carey's youth about his persistent curiosity. He climbed a large chestnut tree to look for a bird's nest, but he slipped and fell. He climbed it again and fell, and upon his third attempt he fell and broke his leg. Yet a few weeks later—with his leg still bandaged—young William climbed the tree and brought down the nest. Boreham imagines this exchange:

"You don't mean to tell me you've climbed that tree again!" (exclaimed his mother).

"I couldn't help it, mother; I couldn't, really! If I begin a thing I must go through with it!"[11]

Boreham relates this simple childhood incident to reveal to us the great man William Carey, who persisted and eventually succeeded in India despite repeated failure, for nothing would hold him back.

Anyone that I have introduced to the work of Boreham has never stopped thanking me for his brilliant nuggets of truth. He has an essay called "Please Shut This Gate" in his book *The Silver Shadow*. Boreham describes his wanderings through the villages of New Zealand and through meadows where one encounters signs stating "Please shut this gate." Landowners posted the signs to keep cattle or flocks from roaming into undesirable places. Boreham discloses how important that little lesson is in life—to shut the gate to certain things. He concludes,

> [T]he best possible illustration of my theme is to be found in the Old Testament.... [W]hen Israel escaped from Babylon, and dreaded a similar attack from behind, the voice divine again reassured them. "I, the Lord thy God, will be *thy rearguard*." There are thousands of things behind me of which I have good reason to be afraid; but it is the glory of the Christian evangel that all the gates may be closed. It is grand to be able to walk in green pastures and beside still waters unafraid of anything that I have left in the perilous fields behind me.[12]

Boreham takes a simple experience and anchors it in a marvelous truth from the Scriptures. He recognizes enchantment in common things and reminds us that beauty has the capacity to whisper to one's soul. I try to read an essay by Boreham every day to keep myself in tune with life's simple beauties, and to not get lost in the complexities of so many other things that my mind is prone to engage.

BOOKS THAT DELIVER FREEDOM

Do not underestimate the shaping power of the printed page and the voice under which you study. Recognize this truth and take seriously the process of remembering—and especially *recording*—what is going on in your life as these influences are molding you. As such, learning how to articulate and analyze what you read is one of the most vital things you can do. The concern of reading great writers only is that you might conclude that they alone know how to say it well. Don't fall into the trap of parroting someone else's thoughts. The great writers should serve as igniters and inspirers that enable us to express the way God has gifted us, and not make us feel inadequate.

Finally, though the writings of Ravenhill, Chesterton, and Boreham have had a great influence on me, I always encourage Christians to read extensively from many authors. When you read a diversity of authors, you complement your propensity with someone else's strength and are exposed to ideas you may not have otherwise considered. As the apostle Paul wrote to Timothy from his prison chamber, "Bring me the books."[13] For he knew that a book—and especially the Good Book—could break the mind out beyond the walls and deliver true freedom.

Learning to Love with Limits

Josh McDowell

> The Fall took who we really were and who we really were
> created to be and separated that person from God and others.
> That real person today longs for relationship and healing, but is
> unable to come into either one unless grace and truth are expe-
> rienced together. If relationship is real and honest, and God's
> truth is present and responded to, there is limitless healing.
>
> —HENRY CLOUD, *Changes That Heal*

There are so many books that have made a difference in my life, but aside from the Bible, one phenomenal book has affected my life more than any other. The book is *Changes That Heal,* previously titled *When Your World Makes No Sense,* by Dr. Henry Cloud.[1]

I first read Cloud's book several years ago when I needed help with a problem. There is still the thinking among many that Christians aren't sup-posed to have problems. Too often we project a sense that as long as a per-son knows the Lord, is filled with the Holy Spirit, and is sharing the faith with others, everything else should be fine. In reality we know that we are fallen people living in a fallen world. Problems are part of our human con-dition, and we need to go to the Lord for healing and restoration.

At any rate, I was dealing with a problem. I had a wonderful wife who loved me and whom I loved deeply. I had four incredible children. My ministry was thriving. But still, I needed help. Those who have heard my testimony know that my father was an alcoholic who abused my mother. When I was a kid, I would sometimes find my mother out in the barn, lying in cow manure where my dad had beaten her with a hose until she couldn't get up. I hated him and vowed that whenever I was strong enough, I was going to kill him.

One evening when I was a teenager, I came home from a date and found my mother lying in her bed weeping. "Josh," she said, "your father has broken my heart. I just want to live to see you graduate from high school and then I want to die." Two months later I graduated, and the following Friday she died. I blamed my father for what had happened…and I hated him for it.

Two years later, as a sophomore in college, I met the Lord. He changed my heart in so many ways, the most drastic of which was that He took the hatred I had for my father and turned it into love. By God's grace, I was able to forgive my father for the wrongs he had done against my family and me. Eventually, the Lord changed my father's heart as well and allowed me the privilege of praying with him as he trusted Christ. It was the greatest miracle I have ever witnessed. His life was changed right before my eyes. He died just fourteen months later from complications as a result of years of alcoholism, but not before the Lord used his changed life to lead more than one hundred people in our town to Christ.

I had genuinely forgiven my father for the pain he had inflicted on my life, but I didn't realize there were still deep-seated hurts that I was holding on to. And these hurts became unhealthy behavior patterns that led to more and more hurt in my life. I saw things in myself that I knew were not pleasing to God, but I had no idea what was causing them or how to deal with them.

I had developed a compulsion to try to meet people's needs. Whenever people shared their problems or struggles with me, anxiety built up within me, and I would try to solve whatever they were dealing with. I couldn't say no to anyone. As you can imagine, this was very frustrating for my wife, Dottie. Whenever people needed my time, no matter how busy I was, I would always find a way to fit them in. If they needed money, I wouldn't hesitate to give mine away. It may sound like I was a great guy to know, but there was a problem. I was always saying yes on the outside while resenting it on the inside. It got to where I would try to keep almost every conversation on a surface level, because I knew if it got too deep, the person would eventually share a need or a hurt. And I knew that if a need was shared, I would be compelled to fix it. I was controlled by other people's hurts.

A dear friend helped me to see that I struggled with the tendencies of a "rescuer," a common struggle among children of alcoholics. For years as a child and teenager, I saw my mother hurting and I desperately wanted to rescue her. Now as an adult, I still had a compulsion to rescue others. To me, love was having to say yes. As soon as I said no, I felt I was no longer being a loving person. And this pattern was killing me.

That's when I telephoned Henry Cloud and asked for his help. One of the first things he did was give me a copy of his book *Changes That Heal.* I studied it for a full month. Everything in the book was biblically based, and that gave me tremendous confidence in the principles he shared. That book along with Henry's personal counsel helped to allow the Lord's healing in my life.

Changes That Heal describes four critical decisions that can bring hope and direction into your life. It shares advice for bonding in our relationship to God and others, establishing boundaries so we are not controlled by others, resolving the good-versus-evil syndrome within us, and choosing to abandon childhood patterns for responsible adulthood. Henry calls these "the basic developmental issues that all of us must negotiate to function and grow emotionally and spiritually. If we fail to resolve these basic growth crises," he writes, "meaning, purpose, satisfaction, and fulfillment will escape us, and our lives will not function in the way God intended."[2]

Although we all struggle at different times and to different degrees with each of these issues, the part that spoke most directly to me was the section about boundaries. Henry describes boundaries as recognizing one's self as distinct from others and realizing one's own limits. He tells the story of a young pastor named Stephen who was burned out in the ministry. Stephen had a soft heart and could not allow suffering people to go without help. He responded to every crisis. In short, he was controlled by the needs of others. Because he had no sense of boundaries, Stephen could not choose what he wanted to do apart from what others wanted him to do. "He wasn't able to say no," Henry writes.[3] I saw myself in Stephen's situation. The anxiety and resentment in my life stemmed from not having a clear sense of boundaries. It is biblical and honoring to God to set limits on your life—to set boundaries on what you do, how much you help, what you get involved in.

God intends for us to have boundaries for our bodies, our feelings, our choices, our limits, our attitudes, desires, thoughts, and behaviors. We must own these things for ourselves. If I don't own my own choices, I lose control of my life, allowing others to control me. I may wind up resenting those whom I believe are controlling me, but the fault is really mine for not owning my choices.

Paul instructs us: "Each one must do just as he has purposed in his heart; not grudgingly or under compulsion, for God loves a cheerful giver" (2 Corinthians 9:7, NASB). This verse isn't just talking about money. It's talking about money, time, energy—all the different ways we can give of ourselves. The Greek word for *grudgingly* speaks of an external pressure— giving because you're afraid of what others will say or do if you don't give. That was never my problem. My problem was compulsion, an *internal* pressure to give. *Changes That Heal* helped me realize that I had been giving to people, not out of love and compassion, but out of obligation and compulsion…and that leads to resentment.

Not only did I learn to own my own choices, but I also learned that I had to allow—even insist—that others own their choices and also the consequences of their actions. I used to think that as long as I said yes to people, I was doing the loving thing. In reality, I was often doing an *unloving* thing. By jumping in and solving people's immediate problems—instead of letting them learn from their mistakes and improve their behavior—I was "loving" them to an even greater dysfunction. In fact, I was sinning against them. With the help of this book and Henry's counsel, I began to give myself permission to say no and still be a loving person.

Let me put it this way. Galatians 6:2 tells us to "bear one another's burdens" (NASB). The rescuer reads that as his or her personal "Great Commission!" But just a few verses later, Paul writes that each one is to "bear his own load" (verse 5, NASB). On the surface it may seem like a contradiction, but here's the difference. The Greek word for *load* in verse five refers to a military knapsack. When you go into battle, you have to carry your own backpack with all the supplies you need. But the Greek word for *burden* in verse two refers to a boulder, a large rock that is too heavy to carry alone. I am not to carry other people's knapsacks—the things that God has made them responsible to carry for themselves. I am not to carry somebody else's thoughts, opinions, needs, feelings, time, money, talents, attitudes, beliefs, or choices. But I am to put my strength into helping others carry their "boulder" when they need help.

Henry Cloud taught me to carry my own knapsack. He helped me become responsible for my own life before Christ—taking responsibility for my feelings, how I react to people, even the hurts of my past. And he helped me realize that it isn't loving to carry someone else's knapsack. Sometimes the most loving thing I can do is to say no.

Establishing and abiding by boundaries does not mean that we close ourselves off from the rest of the world. That might be a safe existence, but it would not be a biblical one and it would leave us falling short of love. Henry addresses this issue as well:

The biblical concept of agape love involves loving others and being willing to lay down one's life for others…. However, it is impossible to give away what we do not own, and boundaries are our way of becoming aware of the self that we can then choose to give away. We must own our lives before we can give them away. This is the essence of freedom, and there is no love without freedom. When we give before we are free and truly own ourselves, we have fallen short of bond servanthood and [have fallen] into slavery. Realize what you own, and then share yourself with others.[4]

Changes That Heal helped me to begin a healthier lifestyle, but the improvement didn't come overnight. Another principle in the book showed me that real healing would take grace, truth, and time. In Luke 13 Jesus tells the parable of a man who owned a vineyard that contained a fig tree. For three years the man found no fruit on the tree, so he instructed the caretaker to cut it down. But the caretaker entreated him to leave it alone for one more year. He said he would dig around the tree and fertilize it, and they would see if it would bear fruit the following year.

The vineyard owner had a right to expect fruit from the tree. But while he was ready to cut it down, the caretaker knew that it needed grace, truth, and time. Grace is indicated in these words: "Leave it alone. Don't cut it down." Truth is represented in the actions of digging around the tree and providing fertilizer to help it grow. And time is seen as well: "Let's give it a year and see what happens."[5]

When we struggle as believers, too often we hear people yelling, "Cut him down!" Sometimes we are yelling it about ourselves if we are not seeing the kind of progress we think we should see. But the biblical view is to give it grace, truth, and time. It takes the combination of the three to bring real healing. Contrary to popular opinion, time does not heal all wounds. We see this in the fig tree. Without special attention—without grace and truth—all the time in the world would not have enabled that tree to produce fruit. Henry put it this way: The nature of time is "God's way of bringing about the wholeness lost in Eden. It takes time to work the soil with His ingredients of grace and truth and to allow them to have their effect."[6]

And what about grace without truth? Grace alone in this context gives license to sin. It has no direction or structure and says that there is no responsibility for our actions. And truth without grace is harsh. It brings condemnation and judgment, and we react with legalism and perfectionism. Grace and truth are integral aspects of God's character, and we see them united together in the person of Christ: "And the Word became flesh, and dwelt among us, and we saw His glory, glory as of the only begotten from the Father, *full of grace and truth*" (John 1:14, NASB). It takes grace and truth, applied together in the context of time, for God to bring about restoration.

I would recommend *Changes That Heal* to almost every believer. It has given me longevity in the ministry. It kept me going when my own unhealthy behavior patterns were causing burnout, resentment, and frustration. The book has also been one of the greatest contributions to joy in my marriage, as I have gained an understanding of biblical boundaries and limits, along with the healing principles of grace, truth, and time.

The Other Side of Faith

Larry Crabb

Where God finds space, He enters.

—IAIN MATTHEW, *The Impact of God*

When I turned fifty, I realized (somewhat tongue-in-cheek) that I had not yet gone through a midlife crisis. All my middle-aged friends had gone through or were going through theirs, and I felt a little cheated. So I prayed about it, and God answered in ways that exceeded all I could imagine. My experience was not the stereotypical midlife crisis. Instead, it was a radical revision of thought, especially in my understanding of psychology.

This period of my life was the context for my encounter with the book that has stirred me and made me think more than any other: *The Impact of God,* by Iain Matthew.[1] The book is a study of the theology, thought, and ministry of St. John of the Cross, a sixteenth-century monk and mystic. In particular, *The Impact of God* has influenced the shape of my theology and the direction of my ministry, not because I agree with all that St. John taught, but because he led me to new levels of wrestling with what *I* believe.

I came to believe that the theology of the New Covenant is pivotal to every understanding of the interior world for the Christian. The essence of the New Covenant, the gospel message, is that we are not only forgiven and declared righteous positionally, but that at conversion something actually happens inside us. It is far more than merely a forensic righteousness. It is literally true that a new heart is given to us (see Ezekiel 36:26-27). There is a longing for God that is put in the heart of the person the minute he or she becomes a believer. Once I saw the ramifications of these beliefs, I revised my approach to counseling. I scrapped all focus on repairing the damage that has been done to an innocent self. I began to recognize that all this damage has been filtered through the lens of depravity. There is something inside the fallen personality that says, "I'm going to find some way to preserve myself against this pain because my number one priority is self-preservation, and if God wants to help that's great. If He doesn't, the heck with Him, I'll do it my way."

When a person becomes a believer, a whole new inclination is placed within his or her heart, which means that counseling is no longer about sorting through all the difficulties of the past to repair the damage. Counseling now becomes the process of looking at the difficulties of the past to see the miracle of Christ that has survived all that has gone wrong, and then releasing the appetite for God that, in fact, is already there. That is a *very* different approach to counseling than is traditionally held.

With those thoughts running through my mind, along with realizing that the New Covenant is a far richer theology than I had grasped before, I became open to revisiting my thinking about counseling and the models I had developed. Maybe the counseling focus on easing problems needed to shift to a concern with using problems to more radically depend on God.

I had become dissatisfied with the understandings that I had gained over my years as a psychologist and as a Christian. Some central piece was missing from this puzzle, and although I was not sure what it was, I knew it was wrapped up somehow in New Covenant theology. All of this was already stirring in me when I picked up *The Impact of God*, but the book helped crystallize my thinking and made it come alive by giving a clear picture of a man's consuming desire to know and enjoy God as the center of his being. I first began to reflect some of this thinking in my books *Connecting* and *The Safest Place on Earth*.[2]

I still hold to most of what I earlier taught about counseling but now with a clearer foundation in our hearts' desire to enjoy God.

THE CENTRALITY OF RELATIONSHIP

The apostle John, in his first epistle, describes the fellowship that believers have with the Father, with the Son, and with the Spirit (see 1 John 1:3; 4:13). His words are not just empty or symbolic "Christianese." John is saying that it is actually possible to have a relationship with each member of the Trinity, a relationship that becomes consuming in the center of your soul in a way that transcends in satisfaction and value every other relationship. One's relationship with God becomes the most valued, precious, treasured, and satisfying relationship of all. It will far exceed a relationship with the best spouse in the world, the best friend, or the best child. When the thought occurred to me that enjoying God is central to mental health, I felt liberated. Experiencing this depth of relationship with God is the main message of Iain Matthew's book. The writings of St. John of the Cross are themselves sometimes difficult. He buries his nuggets in lots of words. Iain Matthew helps us see the core message that there is a path to vital union with God that transforms every aspect of our lives.

As I read about John of the Cross, I began to see that he not only believed what the apostle John said, he centered his entire life on knowing God! That struck me as *so* different from the typical American Christian, including me. So often our relationship with God is not about knowing Him, but using Him. As a psychologist, I have felt for years that most of us in American Christianity use God to solve our problems. In contrast, John of the Cross used his problems to find God.

Let me give an example. I have a friend whose son spent a weekend with his father (my friend's ex-husband). The dad took this opportunity to "poison" the son's mind against his mother, telling him the divorce was his mother's fault. The mother said to me, "I've got to find a Christian counselor. You need to tell me whom I can talk to because I need to find out what a Christian approach to regaining my son would be. Do I bad-mouth his father? Do I just take it on the chin and say nothing? What biblical principles can I follow to get my family life back to where I want it to be? I can't bear the thought of losing my son."

What I hear happening in that story is typical of almost everybody, me included, when a problem comes up. It could be a son who is poisoned against you, a daughter who is promiscuous, a tough marriage, depression that sets in, or panic attacks. Whatever the problem might be, the most natural thing for a Christian to do is to go to the Bible and ask what biblical principle will help us straighten out our situation.

When finding a biblical principle that will solve our problems becomes our number one priority, it is far less healthy than it may seem. What it really amounts to is using God to make our life on earth more pleasant. But that's not what God has promised. Hebrews 7:19 explains that keeping the law (doing everything *right*) to make life more pleasant has been replaced by a better hope. That is to say, there is much more to the life of a Christian than making life work.

Trying to figure out a biblical approach to dealing with a problem is basically like coming to God and saying, "All right, You're the Santa Claus; You're the emergency-room physician. I don't want to know You, I just want to use Your resources." It is the prodigal son who says to his father, "I don't care about relating with you. I don't value *you* at all. Just let me have my money, and I'll go have the life that I want. A relationship with you doesn't matter at all." That's what many of us naturally do, and we call it the Christian life.

John of the Cross exemplified a very different approach to the spiritual journey. He didn't say to God, "How do I become a successful priest? How do I make my monastery work, rise in the ranks, and become influential?

How do I get books written so I'll be important, famous, and rich?" His basic thought was, "God, how do I get to know You? I'll pay any price for that!" Here was a man who lived it; he didn't just talk about it. He came to the conclusion that God can literally be experienced at a level of satisfaction that exceeds that of getting our lives straightened out. That just thrilled me, and made me think, *Can I actually know God? Could that be more important to me than using Him to make my life better?*

This type of questioning sent me off pondering the nature of my own relationship with God, as well as what I perceive going on in the greater Christian culture. I began to see that most of us are spiritual pragmatists, but we use Christian language to dress it up and make it sound like an authentic spiritual journey. A high percentage of books in the average Christian bookstore are about how to use God to fix your life—a biblical approach to effective marital communication, a better way to raise your kids, a solution to depression or any other problem you're facing. God basically becomes a vending machine. We stick in a quarter and get our treat, eat it, and walk away. However, you don't see people hugging a vending machine. We walk away from it as soon as we get the desired treat. We focus on the treat rather than on the Giver of the treat.

When God introduced the New Covenant in Ezekiel 36, He basically told the House of Israel why He was doing so. "It is not for your sake, O house of Israel, that I am going to do these things, but for the sake of my holy name, which you have profaned among the nations where you have gone" (verse 22). God introduced the gospel in order to create a race of people who would proclaim to the world that knowing Him is more valuable than anything else. Knowing God is the basis of our joy, whether He gets us out of prison or leaves us there, keeps us from having cancer or lets us die from it, or keeps our kids off drugs or allows them to become serious addicts. Those things are important, but they're secondary. Primary is knowing Him, and that's the reason for the gospel. Our joy then develops a stability. God is always available though certain blessings may not be.

Matthew's book is so important because it presents a clear illustration of a man who lived his life, by no means perfectly, but with the hunger for knowing God dominant in his mind and soul. John of the Cross's life is an example of "As the deer pants for streams of water, so my soul pants for you, O God" (Psalm 42:1), and "One thing I ask of the LORD, this is what I seek: that I may dwell in the house of the LORD all the days of my life, to gaze upon the beauty of the LORD and to seek him in his temple" (Psalm 27:4). We modern Christians have changed it to, "One thing I seek, that you would fix my life and tell me what to do so I can do it to make sure my marriage works." Perhaps we have misunderstood the Christian life and therefore read the Bible to glean only principles to make life work.

The Impact of God, by giving me an illustration of a man who lived only to know God more intimately, supplied me with the courage to follow suit. Somebody once said that if you want to get a message across, wrap it up in somebody's life and send the person. The message of the New Covenant is wrapped up in John's life for me in a way that I was ready to see and to connect with deeply.

I have concluded that because the core health of the human personality depends on relationship—not on being fixed by an expert—the most important thing I can do as a therapist is to help people navigate through to a deeper relationship with God. This has shifted me away from traditional psychotherapy to spiritual direction. Because of this I founded a school of spiritual direction. I would like to see us all follow John of the Cross's example of truly hungering after God and learn how to draw out and identify that hunger in other people. Only the Spirit can instill the hunger. But nourishing that hunger is work that belongs to the believing community, to pilgrims walking together.

The woman whose son's mind has been poisoned against her spent a couple of hours chatting with me. Toward the end of our discussion she said, "That's an entirely different approach. You're telling me that when my son is breaking my heart by blaming me for the divorce, I don't need to figure out the best way to biblically straighten him out. Instead, I can take my soul with all of its pain into the presence of God, enjoy relationship with the Father, Son, and Spirit, and energized by the wholeness that relationship brings, I can engage my son with a very different passion, goal, and wisdom. And the chances of my son changing are actually higher, even though it's no longer the goal?" She got it 100 percent.

THE LOGIC OF POETRY

Not only did St. John's message grip me, but his method reached me as well. He bridged the gap between my head and heart, and he did it through poetry. That was perhaps the first time I ever *deeply* appreciated poetry. One of his poems that influenced me most, "The Spiritual Canticle," was written when he was going through his dark night of the soul (a phrase he coined).

> Where have you hidden,
> Beloved, and left me groaning?
> You fled like a stag
> having wounded me;
> I went out in search of you, and you were gone.[3]

In another poem, "The Living Flame of Love," he gives us a glimpse of the soul's joy after coming through the dark night and into the intoxicating presence of God.

> Flame, alive, compelling,
> yet tender past all telling,
> reaching the secret center of my soul!

Burn that is for my healing!
Wound of delight past feeling!
Ah, gentle hand whose touch is a caress,
Foretaste of heaven conveying
And every debt repaying:
slaying, you give me life for death's distress.

O lamps of fire bright-burning
with splendid brilliance, turning
deep caverns of my soul to pools of light!
Once shadowed, dim, unknowing,
now their strange new-found glowing
gives warmth and radiance for my Love's delight.

Ah! Gentle and so loving
you wake within me, proving
that you are there in secret and alone;
your fragrant breathing stills me,
your grace, your glory fills me
so tenderly your love becomes my own.[4]

He did not write these poems to explain to God what was happening, as in some cerebral exercise. He did it simply to pour out his soul in free-verse poetry. As I read through these beautifully transparent lines, I was touched in a part of me that I rarely access.

The effect did not stop there, though. In those moments my eyes were opened as something I had believed in my mind for years became real in my heart. It struck me that the Holy Spirit is literally a person. The person-hood of the Spirit became a living fact, a living truth. I know what the word *person* means. I have a wife and two sons; they are persons. Finally "seeing" that the Holy Spirit is a person whom I can actually worship, listen to, and talk with opened up a whole new dimension of what communion with God means. Intimacy with God, a true relationship with my soul's Maker, became increasingly my heart's desire over my previous comfortable position of focusing primarily on the blessings of God. I am coming to see that the real blessing of God is relationship with Him. He is the present beneath the Christmas tree.

In Romans 7:6 Paul makes a contrast between the "old way" versus the "new way": "But now, by dying to what once bound us, we have been released from the law so that we serve in the new way of the Spirit, and not in the old way of the written code." John of the Cross illumined that verse for me. The "old way of the written code" is basically getting it right so life works, and living for the life of circumstantial blessings. After reading the poetry of John of the Cross, something in my soul stirred. I felt as though the violin of my heart were being played for the first time, and I experienced in a new and deeper way that intimacy with God could actually be a *joy!*

I am now starting a ministry called New Way Ministries, which is based on the truth of Romans 7:6. I believe that the new way of the Spirit fundamentally is to follow the Spirit into the presence of the Father through the grace of Christ, and to make *that* the consuming preoccupation of our life, not to get our life figured out and straightened out. The old way of the written code says, "Tell me what to do. I'll do *anything*, just fix my life." The new way of the Spirit is to come to God. Whatever life throws us, the new way is to draw near to Him with the promise that He will draw near to us.

THE TRUTH ABOUT JOY

This process of experiencing a deeper, more joyful, relationship with God made me take a step back and reflect on that elusive word *joy*. I have known many people who, when they let their hair down and get really honest, basically ask, "Where's the joy?" There is one core question that makes me suspect that few have a true understanding of joy: Do I know anybody who knows what the word *joy* means experientially apart from "this world" blessings? Sometimes, when I ask people how they are doing, they say, "I'm doing great—just filled with the joy of the Lord!" I ask for clarification by asking what they mean, to which they respond, "Oh, my kids are doing great, my ministry is going gangbusters, my books are selling, my church is growing." This statement begs the question: "Well, how about God?" Their answer is very telling: "Oh, isn't He wonderful? Look how He's blessing!"

How awful it would be if somebody were to ask me if I had joy in my marriage and my response were something like, "Man, she cooks great, we have great sex, she's fun to be with. She gives me everything I want!" I imagine that person would be curious to know what I thought of *her* as a person. What if I answered by saying, "I don't know. But she gives me everything I want, so what's the problem?" It would be a sad testament to my view of our relationship!

Yet this is exactly the way that many of us think about God. I don't know if I could easily identify ten people who would use the word *joy* where it is truly rooted in their personal intimacy with Christ. In almost every case, joy has much more to do with the blessings of life, and that makes it circumstance-dependent. When afflictions come—and we're promised afflictions—what happens to our joy?

Jesus said real life is *knowing* God (see John 17:3). The path to knowing seems to involve brokenness, repentance, abandonment to Him, confidence in Him, then release of who we truly are to Him and His purpose.

Now, I am not convinced that once we go through a dark night and emerge from it experiencing the joy of intimacy with God, our joy remains constant. I would want to ask John of the Cross: Does the joy we experience once the dark night breaks remain as a constant, or do we go through more dark nights? Is our joy deepened as we come out of each progressive cycle? My prediction, based on my own experience, is that it is cyclical, not linear.

Henri Nouwen writes about the fact that one of God's greatest gifts to us is the gift of absence.[5] What he means by this, I believe, is not the gift of *literal* absence (God will always be with us), but the gift of *felt* absence. God sometimes removes Himself from our awareness to deepen our hunger for Him. These periods will feel like we're going through a dark night all alone. This is the theme of *Shattered Dreams,* a recent book of mine, which was influenced heavily by John of the Cross.[6]

When suffering comes, there is a price to pay if we are to discover joy. That price includes discipline and the decision to rest and remain faithful, repenting of *all* demands that life be different. This simply will not happen without the Spirit's speaking through His Word to quiet our hearts. If we maintain our fast-paced, get-in-quick little devotions in the morning, and quickly run off to church on Sunday morning, the likelihood of developing a deeply spiritual relationship with the Lord is about zero. We have to find time where we can look into our heart and discover that beneath our fast pace, beneath the business deals we're closing and the money we make, beneath the good things we do, our hearts have deeper longings. And we will not do that without quietness, silence, and solitude. I am not suggesting you give up your job and go become a monk. I am suggesting that you recognize the importance of solitude by scheduling time away. Without that I have no hope for you at all.

However, if you do find that time, you will discover there is an ache in your heart to know more, to experience more than you have. When that ache and that longing become alive and you begin to realize that your deepest longing is for God and not success—even some form of "Christian" success—you will in the core of your being begin to open up to a new way of living. That which used to inhibit you will seem insignificant. You will open yourself to the enjoyment of God, and that will start to color your life. Your energy toward your business activities will not diminish, but you will not be fulfilled in the deepest part of your soul until you know God well enough to love somebody else. Knowing God that well transforms you.

THE DEPTH OF REASON AND THE BEAUTY OF SIMPLICITY

The impact of Matthew's book is part of a long journey. In weighing the influence of the various books I have read and reflecting on the few that have played the biggest role in shaping me, I began to see a theme develop. *The Impact of God,* along with Francis Schaeffer's *True Spirituality* and C. S. Lewis's *The Great Divorce,* have all awakened in me the right side of my brain, my poetic side.[7]

I read *True Spirituality* in graduate school days when I had abandoned the faith. When I got into graduate school, I told myself not to believe anything that would require me to dump my intellect. Several psychology professors told me that I could not be a good psychologist and still believe in nonsensical Christianity. So for a year or two I became a self-chosen agnostic. I wanted to start from scratch to see what is true. Lewis and Schaeffer were my two greatest mentors in those days. Schaeffer was *so* brilliant in helping me think everything through. I have been primarily a left-brained guy all my life. When I got hold of *True Spirituality,* I realized that I also had a right brain. I felt passion. I was not persuaded only by reason. Schaeffer enabled me to understand that the Christian way of living is not only true; it can be lived! Being an orthodox Christian means allowing the truth of Christianity to be absorbed into one's soul, which changes one's approach to life. I began moving toward God, wanting to relate to Him, not just to do what I was told.

The major thought that came out of *True Spirituality* is that the most difficult command to obey is to "rejoice with those who rejoice, and weep with those who weep" (Romans, 12:15, NASB). I began to realize that when somebody else had something go right for them that was not going right for me, I didn't rejoice with them—I got jealous! If somebody I didn't like had something go bad, I didn't weep. I said they deserved it. Something was wrong with my heart! I began to understand that being a Christian is not merely subscribing to doctrinal truth, but letting it change your heart so you actually weep with those who weep and rejoice with those who rejoice. *True Spirituality* set me on a path of learning how to internalize truth as opposed to just believing it. It led me in the path of taking Christianity seriously, not just holding to a variety of convictions. I was in New Covenant preschool then. Now, reading Matthew, I'm beginning second grade. C. S. Lewis had earlier introduced me to kindergarten. Strange, an Oxford don simplified profound truth into the ABC's.

Lewis's *The Great Divorce* is a story about people who take a bus ride from hell to heaven. When they get to the country outside of heaven, they are revealed as ghosts; they are insubstantial. In order to become solid people who can walk on the grass of heaven without it cutting their feet, they have to give up the one thing in their lives that is taking the place of God. An angel meets each of these people as they get off the bus and shows each of them what it is that they are clinging to—what their core idol is. Those who see it and repent go on to the joys of heaven. Those who cling to their source of joy return to hell.

My theology of sin was most influenced by *The Great Divorce.* I began to realize that sin is not just doing bad things or breaking the rules. It certainly includes that, but the evil of sin is not that you have an affair. The evil of sin is that you wanted the pleasure of the affair more than you wanted God. This idea revolutionized my theology of sin. Skipping church was no longer a core sin. *Why* I skipped church became the focus. It eliminated (or at least reduced) my legalism. Sin is not just rule breaking; it is wrongly directed passion. It's as if you looked at God and said, "Big deal, I want something else!" In *Mere Christianity,* Lewis draws the distinction between the "Animal Self" and the "Diabolical Self."[8] An example of a sin stemming from the Animal Self would be lusting after dancers at a strip joint or telling a lie. Sins of the Diabolical Self are the internal sins of pride; sins of basically saying to God, "You're not the center; something else is." *The Great Divorce* opened up this whole idea to me.

When I went into the therapy room straight out of a secular university's psychology program I assumed that the sin involved in my clients' problems was behavioral in nature. Maybe a guy was having an affair or cheating on his income taxes. When I thought about the sin of my clients, I thought of it purely as action, behavior, or transgression of obvious rules. When I looked below the surface into the interior world, I didn't think in terms of sin categories. I thought in the categories of damage, hurt, and woundedness. Had this guy been abused or neglected? Was this woman raped when she was ten? All I could think about was the damage and the pain. When you think about sin as external and pain as internal, it really affects the way you do therapy. You may legalistically exhort people to stop sinning, and then put all your therapeutic energy into dealing with the interior world of pain and damage.

Now, when I "climb inside" somebody's soul and move away from the behavioral expressions of sin, I find even worse kinds of sin in the core of the human soul. I now find sin where the person is turning to God, saying, "You're not the best thing going. There's something a whole lot better than You,"—and it's a truly good thing, such as a solid marriage or wonderful children. A person turns to God merely to have Him do things for them. I now understand that when I do deep therapy, I am dealing with sin issues, not just damage issues. That is why I changed my therapy to spiritual direction. The core issue is not damage to an innocent self (which most therapy addresses); it is idolatry in a depraved soul.

So where am I now? With Schaeffer, Lewis, and Matthew, along with many other mentors guiding my path, I see myself as a neophyte, a pilgrim walking with God seeking more of Him. I am a second grader on the spiritual journey. I have a deep, deep conviction that God can literally be enjoyed. And I have a deep frustration that I do not often experience that enjoyment of God. When somebody spiritually directs me, I want that person to direct me not toward figuring out how to be a better husband or a better dad—that is all secondary, though it is important. I will not be a better husband or a better dad until I learn to enjoy God more. Otherwise,

I would be doing it out of my own strength and in the energy of the flesh. Nothing transforms a person other than encounter with God.

I want to see a revolution in the way Christians live. If one hundred Christians read *The Impact of God* and read it thoughtfully and slowly, ninety would come away saying that John of the Cross's understanding of the spiritual journey is actually what the Bible teaches. I think there would be a hunger, a hope that intimacy with God is possible. We would become consumed with knowing God for His glory and for our satisfaction rather than using God to make our lives more pleasant. And we would longingly wait for the day when every blessing will be ours, with God at the center as our richest joy—and *that's* the abundant, soul-healthy life available to the Christian.

The Books That Shape Other Christian Leaders

A library of wisdom, then, is more precious than all wealth, and all things that are desirable cannot be compared to it. Whoever therefore claims to be zealous of truth, of happiness, of wisdom or knowledge, aye, even of the faith, must needs become a lover of books.

—RICHARD DE BURY, *The Philobiblon*

More than 130 additional Christian leaders—authors, pastors, magazine editors, business executives, professors, musicians, and ministry leaders—provided a list of the books they have found to be most influential in their lives. Some included the disclaimer that the titles they list are merely *among* the most influential. In cases where more than one publication date is indicated, the first is the original publication date and the second is a recent printing date.

Out-of-print titles (when such could be determined) are indicated by an asterisk (*). The bookstores and Web sites listed at the end of this appendix will serve as a starting point to locate any books you now want to read but can't find at the library.

RANDY ALCORN—author of *Safely Home, In Light of Eternity,* and *Pro Life Answers to Pro Choice Arguments.*

The Knowledge of the Holy, A. W. Tozer (New York: Harper & Row, 1961; reprint, San Francisco: HarperSanFrancisco, 1992). Shaped my view of God when I was a young believer; have gone back to it many times, and it always has more to offer.

The Chronicles of Narnia, C. S. Lewis (New York: HarperCollins, 1950–1956; reprint, 2002). Continuously prompts my yearning for heaven and the great story.

A tie for third:

Desiring God, John Piper (Sisters, Oreg.: Multnomah, 1995). It made me fully realize that the quest for joy is from God, and he delights in our seeking pleasure in him.

He Is There and He Is Not Silent, Francis A. Schaeffer (Wheaton, Ill.: Tyndale, 1972; reprint, 2001). When I was a young Christian, Schaeffer gave me the satisfying intellectual answers I was looking for.

DIOGENES ALLEN—Stuart Professor of Philosophy, Princeton Theological Seminary.

*Mystery and Philosophy, Michael B. Foster (Westport, Conn.: Greenwood Publishing Group, 1957; reprint, 1980). The best response to logical positivism and scientific reductionism I have ever read. Gives a clear account of the nature of mystery, which lies at the core of Christian revelation, in relation to modern philosophy.

Waiting for God, Simone Weil (New York: HarperCollins, 1951; reprint, 2000). A philosopher, political activist, and mystic who has written most profoundly on human suffering and the love of God, and especially on the centrality of the suffering of Christ on the cross.

*Philosophical Investigation, Ludwig Wittgenstein (Oxford, U.K.: Oxford University Press, 1968). His works liberate one from conventional

thinking and fashions so that one may recognize meaning and truth wherever they are to be found.

JOHN H. ARMSTRONG—author of *Reforming Pastoral Ministry* and *True Revival;* editor of *The Compromised Church* and *This We Believe.*

Here I Stand: A Life of Martin Luther, Roland Bainton (Nashville: Abingdon, 1955; reprint, New York: Penguin Putman, 1995). This biography put fortitude and resolve into my soul in my earliest days in the ministry. I still read this biography to keep my soul enlivened with the reality of true ministry.

Life Together, in volume 5 of *Dietrich Bonhoeffer Works,* Dietrich Bonhoeffer, ed. Geffrey B. Kelly (Minneapolis: Fortress, 1996). A short work that bears much good for Christians in the West as we seek to recover the theology and practice of church as community.

Knowing God, J. I. Packer (Downers Grove, Ill.: InterVarsity, 1973; reprint, 1993). Introduced me to the centrality of God and divine mystery. Every Christian teacher and minister ought to read it at least once.

STEPHEN ARTERBURN—author of more than thirty books and coauthor of *Every Man's Battle* and *Every Man, God's Man.*

Mere Christianity, C. S. Lewis (New York: Macmillan, 1960; reprint, San Francisco: HarperSanFrancisco, 2001). Showed me that most of what I had been taught about what a Christian is and is not was not true.

The Holy Spirit: The Key to Supernatural Living? Bill Bright (San Bernadino, Calif.: Campus Crusade for Christ International, Here's Life, 1980). Showed me there was a power and a presence available to me that I could call on. It changed the way I approached the challenges before me.

The Road Less Traveled, Scott Peck (New York: Simon & Schuster, 2002).
Introduced me to two life-changing concepts: responsibility and
delayed gratification.

GEORGE BARNA—author of *Boiling Point* and *Growing True Disciples.*

A Christian Manifesto, Francis Schaeffer (Wheaton, Ill.: Good News,
Crossway Books, 1981). Impressed upon me the importance of a
Christian worldview and provided the building blocks for that
perspective.

Leaders: Strategies for Taking Charge, Warren Bennis and Burt Nanus
(New York: HarperBusiness, 1997). Underscored the importance
of leadership, the difference between leadership and management,
and gave tangible clues as to how to define and refine a person's
leadership capacity.

Rich Christians in an Age of Hunger, Ronald Sider (Dallas: Word, 1990).
The compelling data and passionate argument regarding our
responsibility to bless others who have significant tangible and
spiritual needs was heartbreaking and motivating.

ROBERT N. BELLAH—professor emeritus of sociology, University of California, Berkeley; coauthor of *Habits of the Heart.*

The Courage to Be, Paul Tillich (New Haven, Conn.: Yale University
Press, 2000). In graduate school, it reconverted me to Christianity.

After Virtue, Alasdair MacIntyre (Chicago: University of Notre Dame
Press, 1984). The most convincing criticism of what is wrong with
the modern project.

WILLIAM J. BENNETT—editor/author of more than ten books, including
The Book of Virtue and *The Death of Outrage.*

The Odyssey, Homer (New York: Penguin, 1999).

The Republic, Plato (New York: Viking, 1979).

The Federalist Papers, Alexander Hamilton, James Madison, and John Jay
(New York: Penguin Putnam, 1999).

JIM NELSON BLACK—author of *When Nations Die;* coauthor of more than
thirty books; senior policy analyst, Sentinel Research Associates, Washington, D.C.

Crime and Punishment, Fyodor Dostoyevsky (New York: Bantam, 1984).
Democracy in America, Alexis de Tocqueville (New York: Knopf, 1945;
reprint, New York: Bantam, 2000).
*50 Modern American and British Poets 1920–1970, Louis Untermeyer,
ed. (2 vols.) (New York: McKay, 1973).

HENRY BLACKABY—coauthor of *Experiencing God.*

My Utmost for His Highest, Oswald Chambers (New York: Dodd, Mead
& Company, 1935; reprint, Uhrichsville, Ohio: Barbour, 2000).
*The Preacher: His Life and Work, J. H. Jowett (New York: Harper &
Brothers, 1912).
The Path of Prayer, Samuel Chadwick (Fort Washington, Pa.: Christian
Literature Crusade, 1931).

TERRI BLACKSTOCK—novelist; author of seventeen books, including *Emerald Windows.*

This Present Darkness, Frank Peretti (Wheaton, Ill.: Good News, Crossway Books, 1986). Showed me the power and possibility of Christian fiction and reminded me of the power of prayer.
As Silver Refined, Kay Arthur (Colorado Springs: WaterBrook, 1999).
Showed me how lovingly the Lord refines us to make us look
more like him.
Secrets of the Vine, Bruce Wilkinson (Sisters, Oreg.: Multnomah, 2001).
I don't think I understood the full meaning of abiding in Christ
until I read this book.

KENNETH BOA—author of numerous books; president of Reflections Ministries.

Confessions, Augustine (New York: Viking, 1979; reprint, New York: Knopf, 1998). An exquisite synthesis of heart and mind, combining authentic devotional reflection and brilliant philosophical perception.

Pensées, Blaise Pascal (1670; reprint, New York: Penguin, 1966). A prescient portrait of the dilemma of the human condition with insights on the avoidance strategies of distraction and indifference that well characterize contemporary culture.

The Brothers Karamazov, Fyodor Dostoyevsky (1880; reprint, New York: Vintage, 1991). Introduced the use of polyphonic narrative to explore the loss of harmony due to the fragmentation of sin.

JERRY BRIDGES—author of *Trusting God, The Joy of Fearing God,* and *The Discipline of Grace.*

The Apostles' Doctrine of the Atonement, George Smeaton (Carlisle, Pa.: Banner of Truth Trust, 1991). The best book on the atoning work of Christ. It greatly enriched my appreciation for the work of Christ and for the gospel message about that work.

The Sovereignty of God, A. W. Pink (Grand Rapids: Baker, 1984). Sets forth the sovereignty of God in a way no other book has done. It drove me to my knees in humility and worship.

*Sin and Temptation, John Owen (Minneapolis: Bethany, 1996). A compilation of three treatises on sin by the Puritan John Owen, restated in modern language by James Houston. These treatises taught me much about the pursuit of holiness.

BILL BRIGHT—founder of Campus Crusade for Christ.

*The Strong Name, James Stewart (Grand Rapids: Baker, 1972). Stewart was a New Testament scholar from Edinburgh. He said, "If we

could but show the world that being committed to Christ is no tame humdrum sheltered monotony, but the most exciting adventure the human spirit could ever know, those who have been standing outside the Church looking with suspicion at Christ, will come crowding in to pay allegiance, and we might well experience the greatest reviving since Pentecost." His words made a lasting impression on me.

STUART BRISCOE—Bible teacher; author; pastor of Elmbrook Church, Brookfield, Wisconsin.

The Cross of Christ, John Stott (Downers Grove, Ill.: InterVarsity, 1986). A masterly treatment of the greatest of all subjects by one of the twentieth century's great Christian leaders.

The Training of the Twelve, Alexander B. Bruce (Grand Rapids: Kregel, 1971; reprint, 2000). An old book full of eternal truth wonderfully relevant to today's church.

BROTHER ANDREW—author of *God's Smuggler.*

My Utmost for His Highest, Oswald Chambers (New York: Dodd, Mead & Company, 1935; reprint, Uhrichsville, Ohio: Barbour, 2000). Chambers's deep teaching, his practical application, and the fact that he was known as a follower of Jesus Christ (without being pious or religious) all have greatly impacted me. He remained a disciple of Jesus Christ in the midst of the military and then the Muslim world. All of his books still are a blessing to me.

*C. T. Studd: Cricketer and Pioneer, Norman P. Grubb (London: Religious Tract Society, 1933; reprint, Fort Washington, Pa.: Christian Literature Crusade, 1991). Studd's total and radical devotion still speaks to me. His choice for the mission field and the Great Commission at the expense of his family made some suffer and many rejoice. I wish we would face this squarely and be willing to pay the price.

Sukarno: An Autobiography, Sukarno (New York: Bobbs-Merrill, 1965).

Behind the Ranges: The Life-Changing Story of J. O. Fraser, Geraldine
    Taylor (London, U.K.: OMF Books, 1998). I read biographies
    because I want to know what God can do with a life fully dedi-
    cated to him, but I also want to know what the devil can do with
    a life that turns away from Christ or who has never heard of him.

STEVE BROWN—author of *Approaching God;* professor of preaching, Reformed Theological Seminary; radio host of the Key Life Network.

Most of the books of C. S. Lewis, beginning with *Mere Christianity*
    (New York: Macmillan, 1960; reprint, San Francisco: HarperSan-
    Francisco, 2001).

Celebration of Discipline, Richard Foster (San Francisco: Harper & Row,
    1978; reprint, San Francisco: HarperSanFrancisco, 2002). Enabled
    me to begin a fairly successful contemplative prayer life.

Church Dogmatics, Karl Barth (Edinburgh, U.K.: T & T Clark, 2000).
    Early in my own walk with Christ, theologically, I came to an
    orthodox/evangelical view "through" Barth's *Dogmatics,* some of
    Emil Brunner's works, Carnel, Schaeffer, and others within the
    evangelical camp.

J. BUDZISZEWSKI—author of *How to Stay Christian in College* and *What
We Can't Know: A Guide.*

The Divine Comedy, Dante Alighieri (New York: W. W. Norton, 1977).
    So compelling was Dante's great poem that, while still an atheist, I
    took to using its lines to illuminate to my students the austere
    teachings of Thomas Aquinas. I don't know whether this did them
    any good, but it did me.

FREDERICK BUECHNER—author of *Alphabet of Grace, Sacred Journey,* and
Longing for Home: Recollections and Reflections.

The Power and the Glory, Graham Greene (New York: Penguin, 2003).
Started me writing novels about saints.

The Brothers Karamazov, Fyodor Dostoyevsky (1880; reprint, New York:
Vintage, 1991). Deepened my view of holy matters.

The poems of Gerard Manley Hopkins. Had much to do with the early
formation of my literary style.

CLIVE CALVER—president of World Relief.

The Pursuit of God, A. W. Tozer (Camp Hill, Pa.: Christian Publications,
1993). When I was a young Christian, A. W. Tozer first awakened
me to what it means to seek God for who he is, and for his purpose for my life. Tozer stirred me to seek after the Lord in a way
that I had not previously understood.

In the Name of Jesus, Henri Nouwen (New York: Crossroad, 1989).
Nouwen's moving account of what it meant to live and work
among those with extreme learning difficulties—the way in which
they opened his eyes to the love that God has for all his people,
and the lessons that we can learn from one another—has had a
profound impact on my desire to serve the disadvantaged.

The Gravedigger File, Os Guinness (Downers Grove, Ill.: InterVarsity,
1983). Moved me to recognize the way in which the forces of
secularization, privatization, and pluralism impact our worldview,
and the attitudes that prevail within society.

TONY CAMPOLO—author; professor emeritus of sociology at Eastern
College.

The Brothers Karamazov, Fyodor Dostoyevsky (1880; reprint, New York:
Vintage, 1991). The "Pro and Contra" section of this book and
the responses given against Christianity by Alyosha proved to be
decisive in my understanding of how to handle "the problem of
evil" in my theology.

The Elementary Forms of Religious Life, Emile Durkheim (New York: The Free Press, 1965; reprint, New York: Oxford University Press, 2001). No book has more influenced my understanding of the religious strictures and theologies in my own society, as well as providing me with a critique of my own understanding of God.

I and Thou, Martin Buber (New York: Scribner's Sons, 1970; reprint, New York: Simon & Schuster, The Free Press, 2000). Half poetry and half philosophy, this book enables the reader to bring together the spirituality of mystical encounters from the perspective of existentialist philosophy. Essential for anyone who wants to understand the meaning of love in terms that relate to our contemporary culture.

NANCIE CARMICHAEL—author of *Raising Kids Right in a World Gone Wrong* and *Desperate for God.*

Three books that I reread and keep on my "beloved" shelf:

*A Life of Prayer, St. Teresa of Avila, James M. Houston, ed. (Portland: Multnomah, 1983).

The Imitation of Christ, Thomas à Kempis, William C. Creasy, trans. (Notre Dame, Ind.: Ave Maria Press, 1989).

The Sacred Journey, Frederick Buechner (San Francisco: HarperSanFrancisco, 1991).

BRYAN CHAPELL—president of Covenant Seminary, St. Louis, Missouri.

Mere Christianity, C. S. Lewis (New York: Macmillan, 1960; reprint, San Francisco: HarperSanFrancisco, 2001). Lewis's thoughtful and sensitive defense of Christianity resonated with the faith needs of my teen years.

Sola Scriptura: Problems and Principles in Preaching Historical Texts, Sidney Greidanus (Eugene, Oreg.: Wipf & Stock, 2001). At a time when

I was despairing that my preaching could be more than carping at people to straighten up, this unusual doctoral dissertation revealed to me the grace of God in all Scripture.

101 Famous Poems, Roy J. Cook (New York: McGraw-Hill, 1919; reprint, 1994). This sentimental book of well-known poems has been through many editions, but as it was read by my father to his children, I learned the beauty of words well crafted and spoken from a loving heart.

RODNEY CLAPP—author of *A Peculiar People* and *Families at the Crossroads.*

Church Dogmatics, Karl Barth (Edinburgh, U.K.: T & T Clark, 2000). The single greatest twentieth-century work of theology, written in great swells of prayer. At one juncture it was God's instrument to save my faith.

The Peaceable Kingdom, Stanley Hauerwas (Chicago: University of Notre Dame Press, 1983). Combines story, worship, and a radical Christian social ethic in exciting ways that continue to push me further on and deeper in the faith.

For the Life of the World, Alexander Schmemann (Crestwood, N.Y.: St. Vladimir's Seminary Press, 1973). Schmemann's rich sacramental vision (with other influences) drew me into a eucharistically centered spirituality that nurtures and challenges me to this day.

RON CLINE—former president of HCJB World Radio; radio host of *Beyond the Call.*

Games People Play, Eric Berne, M.D. (New York: Ballantine, 1996). Taught me how to work with Christians in the church.

Why Am I Afraid to Tell You Who I Am? John Powell (Niles, Ill.: Argus, 1972; reprint, Grand Rapids: Zondervan, 1999). This and other books written by the same author helped set me free in my relationships, even with my enemies.

Handbook to Happiness, Charles Solomon (Wheaton, Ill.: Tyndale, 1999). Always close at hand when I counseled Christians living defeated lives. Probably the book I loaned out the most!

ROBERT E. COLEMAN—author of *The Master Plan of Evangelism.*
Religious Affections, Jonathan Edwards (Uhrichsville, Ohio: Barbour, 1999).
John Wesley on Christian Beliefs: The Standard Sermons in Modern English, John Wesley (Nashville: Abingdon, 2002).
Pensées, Blaise Pascal (1670; reprint, New York: Penguin, 1966).

LOUISE COWAN—coeditor of *Invitation to the Classics;* founding fellow of Dallas Institute of Humanities and Culture.
The Brothers Karamazov, Fyodor Dostoyevsky (1880; reprint, New York: Vintage, 1991). Showed me the significance of suffering as the way to active love—which is the meaning of the passage from John's gospel cited as epigraph to the novel: "Except a corn of wheat fall into the ground and die, it abideth alone: but if it die, it bringeth forth much fruit." (12:24, KJV).

ROGER CROSS—president/CEO of Youth for Christ, USA.
Knowing God, J. I. Packer (Downers Grove, Ill.: InterVarsity, 1973; reprint, 1993). What you believe about God will determine how you approach life. Packer gives a wonderful foundation for all of life by helping us know the character of our Creator.
The Return of the Prodigal Son, Henri Nouwen (New York: Doubleday, 1994). Instrumental in helping me see my condition as the older brother in relationship to my heavenly Father.
The Lion, the Witch and the Wardrobe, C. S. Lewis (New York: Harper-Collins, 1950; reprint, 2002). Lewis takes deep biblical truths and helps us see them from a human perspective.

MARVA DAWN—teaching fellow in spiritual theology, Regent College.

The Lutheran Hymnal, (St. Louis: Concordia, n.d.). My theology was first shaped before I could read by singing it, and hymns that I have memorized have constantly encouraged my faith in the midst of struggles with physical handicaps. Today I am nourished by hymnals from many denominations.

Luther's Small Catechism, Martin Luther (St. Louis: Concordia, 1943; reprint, Plymouth, Minn.: Ambassador Publications, 1992). Luther wisely prepared this volume so that laypeople could learn the basics of Christian faith—the Apostle's Creed, the Lord's Prayer, the Ten Commandments, and other elements along with Luther's brilliant explanations.

The Chronicles of Narnia, C. S. Lewis (New York: HarperCollins, 1950–1956; reprint, 2002). Lewis's fantasies deepen our ability to make the biblical story our own and nourish more profound wonder and joy in the gracious truths of God's mission to reconcile the cosmos.

LYLE DORSETT—editor of *The Essential C. S. Lewis.*

A Man Called Peter, Catherine Marshall (Grand Rapids: Chosen, 2002). Inspired me to consider full-time ministry and to trust God as a personal God and Savior who is concerned about the smallest details in my life.

Mere Christianity, C. S. Lewis (New York: Macmillan, 1960; reprint, San Francisco: HarperSanFrancisco, 2001). Was instrumental in my conversion to faith in Jesus Christ as Savior and Lord.

*A Life of Trust, George Müller (Boston: Gould & Lincoln, 1861). Made it clear that I worship the same God who parted the Red Sea, fed the thousands, and healed the lame and blind. Müller showed me that our God is great—still today.

DAVE DRAVECKY—former major league pitcher; author of *Comeback* and *The Worth of a Man.*

My Utmost for His Highest, Oswald Chambers (New York: Dodd, Mead & Company, 1935; reprint, Uhrichsville, Ohio: Barbour, 2000).

Intimacy with the Almighty, Chuck Swindoll (Dallas: Word, 1996).

Roaring Lambs, Bob Briner (Grand Rapids: Zondervan, 2000).

ELISABETH ELLIOT—author of twenty-eight books, including *Through Gates of Splendor* and *Passion and Purity.*

The one whose writings have most profoundly influenced my life is Amy Carmichael of Dohnavur. I have forty of her books. She wrote beautifully, powerfully, and with profoundly spiritual depth. It is impossible for me to describe how my own life has been changed because of her.

TED W. ENGSTROM—president emeritus of World Vision.

What's So Amazing About Grace? Philip Yancey (Grand Rapids: Zondervan, 2002). One of the greatest words in the English vocabulary is *grace.* Yancey beautifully illustrates how this concept is operative in our lives as Christians.

Mere Christianity, C. S. Lewis (New York: Macmillan, 1960; reprint, San Francisco: HarperSanFrancisco, 2001). This is a basic treatise on the Christian faith, which is wonderfully profound in its simplicity.

The Taste of New Wine, Keith Miller (Waco, Tex.: Word, 1965; reprint, Orleans, Mass.: Paraclete Press, 1993). I had the privilege of editing this manuscript when it was first published years ago, and I was tremendously moved by this new Christian's concept of his newly found and formed faith.

C. STEPHEN EVANS—professor of philosophy and humanities, Baylor University; author of *Wisdom and Humanness in Psychology* and *Faith Beyond Reason: A Kierkegaardian Account.*

Philosophical Fragments, Søren Kierkegaard (Princeton, N.J.: Princeton
    University Press, 1936; reprint, 1985). Helped me see not only
    the profound differences between Christianity, which is grounded
    in God's transcendent revelation in Christ, and every form of
    philosophical immanence, but also that liberal Christian theology
    is just a disguised form of that immanence. There is an essential
    difference between Christ as the Son of God and every human
    teacher, even a teacher as profound as Socrates.

GABRIEL FACKRE—Abbot Professor of Christian Theology Emeritus, An-
dover Newton Theological School; former president of The American Theological Society.

The Nature and Destiny of Man, Vols. 1 and 2, Reinhold Niebuhr
    (1941(vol. 1), 1943 (vol. 2); reprint New York: Scribner's Sons,
    1964). Read during my years at the University of Chicago Divinity
    School, Niebuhr's retrieval of the classical Christian tradition
    exposed me to a compelling alternative to the divinity school's reg-
    nant "neonaturalism," an alternative that conjoined a generous
    orthodoxy to a concern for social change.

*God Was in Christ, Donald Baillie (New York: Scribner's Sons, 1948;
    reprint, Paramus, N.J.: Prentice-Hall, 1980). Hearing Baillie
    give excerpts of the manuscript at a conference in 1948
    introduced me to an early version of "narrative theology" and
    made this book a staple in Christology courses I taught at two
    seminaries.

Institutes of the Christian Religion, John Calvin (1536; reprint, Louisville,
    Ky.: Westminster John Knox Press, 1960). The sourcebook of my
    Reformed faith, one read, however, with the eyes of two subse-
    quent streams of interpretation, the nineteenth century's Mercers-
    burg theology (John Williamson Nevin and Phillip Schaff) and
    the twentieth century's Karl Barth.

GORDON D. FEE—professor of New Testament studies, Regent College; coauthor of *How to Read the Bible for All It's Worth.*

*C. T. Studd: Cricketer and Pioneer, Norman P. Grubb (London: Religious Tract Society, 1933; reprint, Fort Washington, Pa.: Christian Literature Crusade, 1991). Helped to ignite the fire within; I can still quote line after line from his letters.

Mere Christianity, C. S. Lewis (New York: Macmillan, 1960; reprint, San Francisco: HarperSanFrancisco, 2001). Helped me realize that a burning heart did not necessarily mean one had to have a pumpkin for a head (despite Studd!).

AJITH FERNANDO—national director of Youth for Christ in Sri Lanka; author of ten books, including *Sharing the Truth in Love: How to Relate to People of Other Faiths.*

The Master Plan of Evangelism, Robert E. Coleman (Grand Rapids: Revell, 1963; reprint, 1992). Helped define the priorities of my life.

The Preacher's Portrait, John Stott (Grand Rapids: Eerdmans, 1964; reprint, 1988). I read this while I was a university student. It thrilled me about the glory of the ministry.

Methodical Bible Study, Robert A. Traina (1952; reprint, Grand Rapids: Zondervan, 1985). Introduced me to inductive Bible study, which I use daily when reading the Bible.

CHERI FULLER—speaker; author of *When Mothers Pray* and *Quiet Whispers from God's Heart for Women.*

*The Edge of Adventure, Keith Miller (Waco, Tex.: Word, 1974; reprint, Grand Rapids: Revell, 1991). My husband and I read this book when we'd just recommitted our lives to God's purposes. We led a study group with the tapes and book, and through it God showed us how to seek his will in very practical ways. Our life became an

adventure, as I quit teaching and started my first book, and my husband left the retail business and went into home building.

Hinds' Feet on High Places, Hannah Hurnard (Wheaton, Ill.: Tyndale, 1995; reprint, Uhrichsville, Ohio: Barbour, 2000). I read this when God was calling me out of my comfort zone. I was being asked to do public speaking. How I could identify with the main character, Much Afraid. The book helped me surrender more and more to God's call on my life.

What Is a Family? Edith Schaeffer (Grand Rapids: Baker, 1997). I was in college when the feminist movement was gaining steam. After teaching two years I started graduate school and was directing a lot of my efforts outside the home, although we had two sons under the age of four. God used *What Is a Family?* to redirect my priorities and to give me a picture of the impact of a godly family.

GEORGE GALLUP JR.—pollster; author of *Growing Up Scared in America.*

Mere Christianity, C. S. Lewis (New York: Macmillan, 1960; reprint, San Francisco: HarperSanFrancisco, 2001). Brought me a heart-stopping awareness, when I was a student at Princeton, that Christianity is a religion of the head as well as the heart, and that our hope is not in finding ourselves, but in losing ourselves—in God.

The Practice of the Presence of God, Brother Lawrence (Grand Rapids: Revell, 1999; reprint, Gainesville, Fla.: Bridge-Logos, 2000). Reminds me that we must turn to God at all times and in all situations, and that what really matters is not our position in the world, but the kind of person we are in response to God's will for us.

My Utmost for His Highest, Oswald Chambers (New York: Dodd, Mead & Company, 1935; reprint, Uhrichsville, Ohio: Barbour, 2000). Daily readings that call us back to our utter dependence on God in Christ and remind us that we need to trust God as well as believe in him.

NORMAN L. GEISLER—president of Southern Evangelical Seminary; author of some fifty books, including *Christian Apologetics, Creating God in the Image of Man?* and *Baker's Encyclopedia of Christian Apologetics.*

Summa Theologica, Thomas Aquinas (New York: Benziger Brothers, 1947–1948; reprint, Allen, Tex.: Christian Classics, 1998). The most comprehensive treatment ever done on systematic theology, comprising sixty volumes in the Latin-English edition, yet the most concise, logical, and penetrating production on the topic by perhaps the greatest Christian mind of all time. Molded my thinking about God and his relation to his creation more than any other book.

GRAEME L. GOLDSWORTHY—lecturer in Old Testament and biblical theology, Moore Theological College, Sydney, Australia; author of *The Goldsworthy Trilogy: Gospel and Kingdom, Gospel and Wisdom,* and *The Gospel in Revelation.*

Kingdom of God, John Bright (Nashville: Abingdon, 1955; reprint, 1980). My first real introduction to biblical theology as an overview of the story line of the whole Bible.

Heirs of the Reformation, Jacques de Senarclens (London: SCM Press, 1963). Established for me the first question about any position or system as concerning presuppositions or the "starting point." Compares Catholicism, liberal Protestantism, and Reformed theologies from this point of view.

For Such a Time As This, J. S. Halsey (Phillipsburg, N.J.: Presbyterian and Reformed Publishing, 1976). A readable introduction to Cornelius Van Til's position on a consistently Calvinistic approach to apologetics and epistemology. Once again, the question of a starting point and presuppositions is in view.

ALICE GRAY—speaker; editor of Stories for the Heart books.

Knowing God, J. I. Packer (Downers Grove, Ill.: InterVarsity, 1973;

reprint, 1993). Lifted doubts and fears and helped me fully trust the God I love and serve.

Behold Your God, Myrna Alexander (Grand Rapids: Zondervan, 1978). A favorite over twenty years ago, and it still is. Each time I return to it, I grow deeper in faith.

STANLEY J. GRENZ—Pioneer McDonald Professor, Carey Theological College and Regent College; author of *Revisioning Evangelical Theology* and *Renewing the Center.*

Escape from Reason, Francis Schaeffer (Downers Grove, Ill.: InterVarsity, 1968). I read this as a university student. I was anticipating a career as a nuclear physicist; Schaeffer sparked my interest in issues of faith and philosophy and was instrumental in my sense of divine call to the ordained ministry and to theology as a vocational pursuit.

Changed into His Likeness, Watchman Nee (Wheaton, Ill.: Tyndale, 1978; reprint, Fort Washington, Pa.: Christian Literature Crusade, 1992). Nee shaped my understanding of Christian spirituality and has sparked an ongoing desire to grow in conformity to Christ.

Habits of the Heart, Robert Bellah, Richard Maken, William Sullivan, Ann Swidler, and Steve Tipton (Berkeley, Calif.: University of California Press, 1985; reprint, 1996). Bellah's work was the most important among several that shook me out of my individualistic approach to the faith and led me to see the focus on relationships or community that lies at the heart of the gospel.

DOUGLAS GROOTHUIS—associate professor of philosophy, Denver Seminary; author of *Truth Decay.*

The God Who Is There, Francis Schaeffer (Downers Grove, Ill.: InterVarsity, 1968; reprint, 1998). I first read it my sophomore year in college—just a few months after my conversion. It revolutionized my

view of Christian faith and endeavor. I had spent the first few
troubled months of the Christian life not knowing how to think
about the great intellectual issues I had been introduced to at college. But Schaeffer wasn't afraid of the great ideas. He argued that
the Christian worldview is objectively true, rational, and that it
offers unique hope and meaning to a post-Christian culture awash
in despair and confusion. Schaeffer did not answer all my questions, and I have come to question a few of his judgments (particularly his reading of a few philosophers), but *The God Who Is
There* helped spark a grand view of ministry that has never
dimmed. We must love the lost, take culture seriously, and out-
think the world for Christ!

Pensées, Blaise Pascal (1670; reprint, New York: Penguin, 1966). The volume consists of more than nine hundred fragments of a book Pascal never completed, which would have been an apologetic for the
Christian faith. Nevertheless, many of the fragments were so brilliant that Pascal's family published them after his death. Pascal, a
celebrated scientist and mathematician, understood that the gospel
was the only key that could unlock the meaning of the human
condition. His reflections on the greatness and misery of humanity are unparalleled in their wisdom and apologetic power. We are
great because we are made in God's image and likeness, but we are
miserable because we are fallen. We are deposed royalty in need of
the Mediator, Jesus Christ.

Purity of Heart Is to Will One Thing, Søren Kierkegaard (New York:
Harper, 1956). Kierkegaard aimed to reform the dry and dead
Lutheran orthodoxy of his day by stimulating his readers to redis-
cover the Christianity of the New Testament and to stand naked
as individuals before God. This book summons readers to consider their lives before the "audit of eternity" and to order all their
affairs so as to "will the good in the truth," without excuse and

without wavering and against the crowd, if need be. Through reading it, I discovered that God was calling me to engage the life of the mind as a lifelong pursuit.

VERNON GROUNDS—chancellor of Denver Seminary.
These are only three of the most influential:
Training in Christianity, Søren Kierkegaard (Oxford, U.K.: Oxford University Press, 1967).
Markings, Dag Hammarskjöld (New York: Knopf, 1964; reprint, New York: Ballantine, 1985).
Confessions, Augustine (New York: Viking, 1979; reprint, New York: Knopf, 1998).

WAYNE GRUDEM—research professor of theology and Bible, Phoenix Seminary; former president of The Evangelical Theological Society.
Institutes of the Christian Religion, John Calvin (1536; reprint, Louisville, Ky.: Westminster John Knox Press, 1960).
Christianity and Liberalism, J. Gresham Machen (Grand Rapids: Eerdmans, 1946).
Hidden Life of Prayer, David MacIntyre (Minneapolis: Bethany, 1993).

JOHN GUEST—pastor of Christ Church at Grove Farm; cofounder of Trinity Episcopal School of Ministry.
Fundamentalism and the Word of God, J. I. Packer (Grand Rapids: Eerdmans, 1958). I read this soon after I was ordained to the ministry in the Anglican Church. While I believed the Bible was God's Word, Packer clarified the issues concerning the authority of the Bible and set me free to preach it with authority and without hesitation.
Mere Christianity, C. S. Lewis (New York: Macmillan, 1960; reprint, San Francisco: HarperSanFrancisco, 2001). Lewis's clear thinking about the relativism he saw advancing, and his giftedness at making

relativism look "silly," helped me challenge such silliness—and thereby make the gospel all the more relevant.

George Whitefield's Journals, George Whitefield (Carlisle, Pa.: Banner of Truth Trust, 1978; reprint, 1998). The chronicling of the Great Awakening in Whitefield's personal journal gave me a grasp of the Holy Spirit's power to change society in a single generation. When Whitefield began his ministry, there was deadness in the church with the Bishop in London saying, "He did not expect Christianity to survive that generation." Not only was Great Britain radically transformed, but so were the American Colonies—and all through the preaching of the Word of God. It gave me the dream of seeing the same thing in our lifetime.

GARY R. HABERMAS—Distinguished Professor of Apologetics and Philosophy, Liberty University.

The Cost of Discipleship, Dietrich Bonhoeffer (New York: Macmillan, 1959; reprint, New York: Simon & Schuster, 1995). In the area of total commitment to Christ, where few truly penetrating books seem to be written, this one shook me to my soul. As Bonhoeffer declares, "When Christ calls a man, he bids him come and die" (p. 99).

Telling Yourself the Truth, William Backus and Marie Chapian (Minneapolis: Bethany, 1981). Taught me the revolutionary idea that hurtful things that happen to us are not what cause us the most harm; the more crucial question concerns what we *tell* ourselves about what happens to us. Applying this truth can free us to live above our circumstances.

Heaven: The Heart's Deepest Longing, Peter J. Kreeft (New York: Harper & Row, 1980; expanded edition, San Francisco: Ignatius Press, 1989). Kreeft argues convincingly that "the hope of heaven fulfills the heart's deepest quest for joy" (p. 1), showing how heaven provides an answer that satisfies humankind's deepest longings at the theoretical level, as well as in everyday life.

SCOTT J. HAFEMANN—Gerald F. Hawthorne Professor of New Testament Greek and Exegesis, Wheaton College; author of *The God of Promise and the Life of Faith.*

Desiring God, John Piper (Sisters, Oreg.: Multnomah, 1995). Showed me from Scripture that God's pursuit of his own glory and my desire to be happy were not in conflict, since the demonstration and enjoyment of God's glory is the good of his people. Piper uncovers the biblical motivation for living by faith.

*Christ and Time, Oscar Cullman (Louisville, Ky.: Westminster John Knox Press, 1950; reprint, New York: Gordon Press, 1977). Makes clear the central framework for understanding how the history of Israel and the life of Christ fit together.

The Unity of the Bible, Daniel Fuller (Grand Rapids: Zondervan, 1992). Uncovered for me the inextricable link between faith and obedience so that I could overcome the age-old "law-gospel" contrast that wrongly divides the Bible into two different ways of relating to God. Fuller explains why every act of obedience is an act of faith and why every act of disobedience is disbelief gone public.

MARK O. HATFIELD—former U.S. senator.

The Jesus I Never Knew, Philip Yancey (Grand Rapids: Zondervan, 2002).

The Art of Dodging Repentance, D. R. Davies (London: Canterbury, 1952).

Silence, Shusaku Endo (New York: Taplinger, 1980).

STANLEY M. HAUERWAS—Gilbert T. Rowe Professor of Theological Ethics, Duke University Divinity School; author of *Resident Aliens, The Peaceable Kingdom,* and *A Community of Character.*

Church Dogmatics (any volume), Karl Barth (Edinburgh, U.K.: T & T
Clark, 2000). Revolutionized modern theology by reclaiming the
integrity of theological speech to do work for the forming of our
lives as Christians.

*Philosophical Investigations, Ludwig Wittgenstein (Oxford, U.K.: Oxford
University Press, 1968). Necessary training to free anyone from
the myths of modernity. Through careful philosophical analysis,
Wittgenstein presents the world as he found it, but the world as
he found it turns out to be magical.

After Virtue, Alasdair MacIntyre (Chicago: University of Notre Dame
Press, 1984). Revolutionized how we think about ethics by
reclaiming the significance of Aristotle.

JACK HAYFORD—founding pastor of The Church on the Way; chancellor
of King's College and Seminary; author of more than forty books; com-
poser of more than four hundred gospel songs.

Power Through Prayer, E. M. Bounds (Grand Rapids: Baker, 1992).
Teaches how one's prayer life can become intimate and influential.

In the Day of Thy Power, Arthur Wallis (1956; reprint, Columbia,
Mo.: Cityhill, 1997). Demonstrates that the pursuit of God
will result in a heart for evangelism and revival by the power of
the Spirit.

My Utmost for His Highest, Oswald Chambers (New York: Dodd, Mead &
Company, 1935; reprint, Uhrichsville, Ohio: Barbour, 2000).
A book to draw one into the circle of God's love.

CYNTHIA HEALD—speaker; author of *Becoming a Woman of Excellence* and
A Woman's Journey to the Heart of God.

My Utmost for His Highest, Oswald Chambers (New York: Dodd, Mead
& Company, 1935; reprint, Uhrichsville, Ohio: Barbour, 2000).
Chambers's thoughts have kept me focused on the centrality of the

Cross, God's purposes, the priority of abiding, and the necessity of surrender and obedience.

If, Amy Carmichael (Fort Washington, Pa.: Christian Literature Crusade, 1992). Her insightful and concise sentences on the impact of Calvary's love continue to challenge and humble me.

HOWARD G. HENDRICKS—distinguished professor, Dallas Theological Seminary; chairman of Center for Christian Leadership.

He That Is Spiritual, Lewis Sperry Chafer (Grand Rapids: Zondervan, 1983).

The Training of the Twelve, Alexander B. Bruce (Grand Rapids: Kregel, 1971; reprint, 2000).

Spiritual Leadership, J. Oswald Sanders (revised edition, Chicago: Moody, 1999).

CARL F. H. HENRY—founding editor of *Christianity Today* magazine; author of *Remaking the Modern Mind, Aspects of Christian Social Ethics,* and the six-volume *God, Revelation, and Authority.*

The Christian View of God and the World, James Orr (Grand Rapids: Kregel, 1989).

Institutes of the Christian Religion, John Calvin (1536; reprint, Louisville, Ky.: Westminster John Knox Press, 1960).

MICHAEL HORTON—president of Alliance of Confessing Evangelicals; author of *A Better Way* and *Where in the World Is the Church?*

Institutes of the Christian Religion, John Calvin (1536; reprint, Louisville, Ky.: Westminster John Knox Press, 1960). This running commentary on the Apostles' Creed is actually quite devotional.

The Bondage of the Will, Martin Luther (Grand Rapids: Revell, 1989). Part of a lively debate with the great Renaissance figure Erasmus, Luther's treatise is a marvelous defense of God's grace and glory.

The Heidelberg Catechism (New York: G. & R. Waite, 1805; reprint, Temecula, Calif.: Reprint Services, 1992). This summary of the Christian faith remains the most relevant teaching for new and mature Christians alike.

R. KENT HUGHES—pastor; editor of Preaching the Word Series; author of *Disciplines of a Godly Man* and *Liberating Ministry from the Success Syndrome.*

*Shadow of the Almighty, Elisabeth Elliot (San Francisco: HarperSanFrancisco, 1979). Reading this when I was fifteen, the story of Jim Elliot's death as he was taking the gospel to the Auca Indians helped set the course of my life. Especially powerful is Jim Elliot's phrase "he is no fool who gives what he cannot keep to gain what he cannot lose."

The Pursuit of God, A. W. Tozer (Camp Hill, Pa.: Christian Publications, 1993). The first and best of the books to challenge me toward deeper devotion.

The Sermon on the Mount, D. Martyn Lloyd-Jones (Grand Rapids: Eerdmans, 1984). This incisive exposition of the Beatitudes has had more theological influence in my life than any other book.

ANGELA ELWELL HUNT—novelist; author of *The Immortal, The Note,* and *The Tale of Three Trees.*

*The Nun's Story, Kathryn Hulme (Boston: Little, Brown & Company, 1956; reprint, New York: Simon & Schuster, Pocket Books, 1977). What appeals to me most is the incredible spiritual discipline that the nuns had to adopt—the disciplines of silence, humility, and especially obedience. Sister Luke, the protagonist, struggled constantly with complete obedience, and that's a struggle I see mirrored in my own life.

BILL HYBELS—pastor of Willow Creek Community Church; author of *Too Busy Not to Pray.*

The Practice of the Presence of God, Brother Lawrence (Grand Rapids: Revell, 1999; reprint, Gainesville, Fla.: Bridge-Logos, 2000).

The Spirit of the Disciplines, Dallas Willard (San Francisco: HarperSan-Francisco, 1999).

The Divine Conspiracy, Dallas Willard (San Francisco: HarperSan-Francisco, 1999).

WALTER C. KAISER JR.—president of Gordon-Conwell Theological Seminary.

The Prophets and the Promise, Willis J. Beecher (1905; reprint, Eugene, Oreg.: Wipf & Stock, 2002). The most influential book in my life.

PHIL KEAGGY—musician, songwriter, and recording artist of more than forty albums.

After the Bible, these books have been the most influential:

My Utmost for His Highest, Oswald Chambers (New York: Dodd, Mead & Company, 1935; reprint, Uhrichsville, Ohio: Barbour, 2000). This devotional refocuses my attention on the work of Christ, my relationship to God and my fellow man. I'm encouraged to see Jesus in a practical application to my daily walk—to focus on his goodness and holiness and not my successful or failed efforts. God initiates and completes my desire to serve his will in my life. Chambers teaches me to look unto Jesus, the Author and Finisher of my faith, and to take suffering in stride; to realize that hardships as well as blessings shape and mold us into his image—all to the glory of God. This devotional also helps me desire to take a closer look into my Bible and delve deeper into the truths of the gospel.

The Jesus I Never Knew, Philip Yancey (Grand Rapids: Zondervan, 2002).
I found that many of us Western believers and nonbelievers miss
out on the historical person of Jesus—who he really was, what
shaped him to be the person he is, and the cultural context of his
life on earth. I gained a bigger picture of our most loving, gracious, and merciful Savior—how he is the true Son of God sent to
all of us, whoever we are and wherever we're from. He's the Friend
to the friendless—the loving and compassionate One to the
"unlovely." Yet he is the great Victor, the Triumphant One, who
overcame death by the giving of his life. Yancey has helped us see
more of the true glory of God "in the face of Christ."

*The Continual Burnt Offering, H. A. Ironside (Neptune, N.J.: Loizeaux
Brothers, 1981). A treasure to me and a source of musical inspiration as I've written several songs with the use of the poetry and
words contained therein. Ironside's book of devotions has provided me with fellowship and encouragement in my travels.

Not a Tame Lion, Terry Glaspey (Nashville: Cumberland House, 1996). A
look into the life and convictions of C. S. Lewis, who has inspired
me as a believer and a musician. Glaspey reveals the heart of this
fine writer on the topics of morality, the arts, prayer, pride, and
humility. Lewis had an imagination and a love for the Redeemer
of our fallen world to such an extent that he wanted to reveal his
love for everyone—men, women, boys, and girls of all walks of
life. Good news indeed!

PETER KREEFT—professor of philosophy, Boston College; author of *Christianity for Modern Pagans (Pascal's Pensées), Back to Virtue,* and *The Journey.*

The Measure of Man, Joseph Wood Krutch (New York: Bobbs-Merrill,
1954; reprint, Magnolia, Mass.: PeterSmith, 1990). I read this critique of materialism by this old-fashionedly honest humanist when
I was in high school and promptly fell in love with philosophy. Its

"Grand Strategy" chapter remains the best critique I know of Freud, Darwin, and Marx, the three thinkers most responsible for our world's deepest disease: moral relativism.

Fire Within, Thomas Dubay (San Francisco: Ignatius Press, 1989). The best book I've read on Christian mysticism. It shows how utterly biblical the Christian mystics are, and how clearly different they are from all others. It also proves that contemplation is God's will for all his children.

Mere Christianity, C. S. Lewis (New York: Macmillan, 1960; reprint, San Francisco: HarperSanFrancisco, 2001). This book accomplishes two things in my life. First, every time I am tempted to either doubts or confusions about Christian fundamentals, it acts as a benchmark or touchstone. Second, it puts everything into right perspective, relative to Christ, the center. The reader emerges with not only knowledge, but wisdom.

WOODROW KROLL—president and senior Bible teacher of Back to the Bible.

Mere Christianity, C. S. Lewis (New York: Macmillan, 1960; reprint, San Francisco: HarperSanFrancisco, 2001). Lewis makes sense when he states the case for Christianity. It was compelling the first time I read it; it remains compelling today. Every Christian needs a basement without cracked walls upon which to build his or her house. *Mere Christianity* is mine.

No Place for Truth, David F. Wells (Grand Rapids: Eerdmans, 1993). It was reading this penetrating appraisal of the state of religion in America that first burdened my heart about Bible illiteracy. Wells dares to see that the church has caved in to the postmodern world and has taken much of Christian influence with it. The hope that Wells has for the reform and recovery of evangelicalism is heartening.

Boiling Point, George Barna and Mark Hatch (Ventura, Calif.: Regal Books, Gospel Light Publications, 2001). No Christian can read this book and still be able to look the Lord in the eye if he or she does nothing about the spiritual decline in America. Much more than a wake-up call, this book is a call to arms to all who will be influenced by it.

KEVIN LEMAN—author of *Sex Begins in the Kitchen* and *The New Birth Order Book.*

Mere Christianity, C. S. Lewis (New York: Macmillan, 1960; reprint, San Francisco: HarperSanFrancisco, 2001). After reading this book, I realized what God's grace means: He loves us despite our stupidity, despite our many flaws and blemishes. That insight, more than anything, has helped me grow. It's something that each of us battles every day because the carnal self is so easily accessible for all of us.

DUANE LITFIN—president of Wheaton College, Wheaton, Illinois. Most influential have been the writings, particularly the essays, of C. S. Lewis. Along with the Scriptures, Lewis's writings are the only literature I have returned to repeatedly. Also instrumental in shaping my faith have been:

Escape from Reason, Francis Schaeffer (Downers Grove, Ill.: InterVarsity, 1968).

The Pursuit of God, A. W. Tozer (Camp Hill, Pa.: Christian Publications, 1982).

De Doctrina Christiana (On Christian Doctrine), St. Augustine (Paramus, N.J.: Prentice-Hall, 1958).

SAMUEL TALBOT LOGAN JR.—president of Westminster Theological Seminary.

The Brothers Karamazov, Fyodor Dostoyevsky (1880; reprint, New York: Vintage, 1991). Does a magnificent job of "incarnating" many of the issues surrounding the question of the existence of God and embodies, in Alyosha, a powerful symbol of what it means to be a "Christ-ian" in a broken and sinful world.

*Treatise on Religious Affections, Jonathan Edwards (Grand Rapids: Baker, 1982). I know of no other source outside the Bible that provides as powerfully convicting and reassuring an answer to the question, "What makes a person a Christian?" Edwards asserts, "No light in the understanding is good which does not produce holy affection in the heart." This work surely does produce "holy affection in the heart."

TREMPER LONGMAN III—author; professor of biblical studies, Westmont College.

Defense of the Faith, Cornelius Van Til (Phillipsburg, N.J.: Presbyterian and Reformed Publishing, 1967). Van Til's apologetic was critical to my survival as a graduate student at Yale. He was well before his time as he discussed the role of presuppositions and worldview in our thinking and in our appropriation of evidence.

2 Chronicles, Raymond B. Dillard (Nashville: Nelson, Nelson Reference, 1988). Of inestimable value to me, not so much for its perceptive understanding of Chronicles as much for its illuminating understanding of Old Testament narrative. It also provided me with a wonderful model for writing a commentary that serves both scholars and the church.

The Healing Path, Dan Allender (Colorado Springs: WaterBrook, 2000). My longstanding relationship with Allender has had a huge impact on how I read the Bible, culture, people, and life generally. This book is illustrative of his insight.

ERWIN W. LUTZER—pastor of Moody Church; author of *One Minute After You Die* and *Cries from the Cross*.

The Bondage of the Will, Martin Luther (Grand Rapids: Revell, 1989). Convinced me of how the lost are both deceived and spiritually dead, and the need for total dependence on God in the proclamation of the gospel.

Jonathan Edwards: A New Biography, Iain Murray (Carlisle, Pa.: Banner of Truth Trust, 1992). Reminded me of the struggles of the ministry, the need for precise theology, and that we as Christian ministers must find our happiness in God alone.

JOHN MACARTHUR—pastor; author of *The Gospel According to Jesus* and *Our Sufficiency in Christ*.

The Existence and Attributes of God, Stephen Charnock (Grand Rapids: Baker, 1996). He comes as close as anyone could to expressing in human language the inexpressible majesty of God.

Preaching and Preachers, D. Martyn Lloyd-Jones (Grand Rapids: Zondervan, 1972). Lloyd-Jones bares his heart on a subject he was eminently qualified to speak about. This book elevated my appreciation for the role of preaching in church life.

Jonathan Edwards: A New Biography, Iain Murray (Carlisle, Pa.: Banner of Truth Trust, 1992). Murray made Edwards come alive.

PAUL MAIER—Russell H. Seibert Professor of Ancient History, Western Michigan University; author of *In the Fullness of Time: A Historian Looks at Christmas, Easter, and the Early Church* and *A Skeleton in God's Closet*.

Jewish Antiquities, Flavius Josephus (Cambridge, Mass.: Harvard University Press, 1930; reprint, 1998).

The Jewish War, Flavius Josephus (New York: Viking Penguin, 1984).

The History of the Church, Eusebius (New York: Viking Penguin, 1965; reprint, 1990).

I was always interested in trying to learn more about biblical personalities and events, and Josephus, of course, is our main source of extrabiblical information. In the case of Eusebius, who continues where Josephus leaves off, we have another treasury of information on the apostles and earliest Christianity.

BRENNAN MANNING—author of *The Ragamuffin Gospel* and *Ruthless Trust.*
On Being a Christian, Hans Küng (New York: Doubleday, Image, 1984).
   A powerful presentation of the Jesus of history. Combines exhaustive scholarship with passionate conviction that Jesus Christ is the center of human existence.
Jesus Before Christianity, Albert Nolan (Maryknoll, N.Y.: Orbis Books, 2001). If you have time to read only one book on Jesus, let this gem be the one. Nolan's portrait of Jesus is lucid, persuasive, challenging, and decidedly different.
*Jesus Means Freedom, Ernst Käsemann (Philadelphia: Fortress, 1969; reprint, Mifflintown, Pa.: Sigler Press, 1972). Helped me understand why the apostle Paul preached only Jesus Christ crucified.

GEORGE MARSDEN—Francis A. McAnaney Professor of History, University of Notre Dame.
The City of God, St. Augustine (New York: Modern Library, 2000). This book has been basic for me in thinking about how Christians might live in the world while keeping their higher allegiances preeminent. The City of God is united by love to God. The cities of the world are always divided by their competition for created things.
The Works of Jonathan Edwards, Jonathan Edwards (Peabody, Mass.: Hendrickson, 1998) or *Selections from His Works,* Jonathan Edwards (Prospect Heights, Ill.: Waveland, 1992). I have long been helped by Edwards's emphasis on God as constantly active in communicating his love and beauty to his creatures. Edwards illuminates all

of creation as the language of God. Christian experience is the affective response that comes from being given the eyes to see this "Divine and Supernatural Light."

The Irony of American History, Reinhold Niebuhr (New York: Scribner's Sons, 1952; reprint, Farmington Mills, Mich.: Gale Group, 1982). Niebuhr makes the point that human failings, including those of Christians, often involve the irony of turning our virtues into vices. I have found this a valuable principle in personal reflection and in historical interpretation.

MARTIN E. MARTY—Fairfax M. Cone Distinguished Service Professor Emeritus, the University of Chicago; author of *Education, Religion, and the Common Good.*

Confessions, Augustine (New York: Viking, 1979; reprint, New York: Knopf, 1998). A template for Christian experience for so many.

Luther's Large Catechism, Martin Luther (St. Louis, Mo.: Concordia, 1988). A condensation of pretty much all of the theology I know and an angle on the faith I hold, or that holds me.

Letters and Papers from Prison, Dietrich Bonhoeffer (London: SCM Press, 1953; reprint, Old Tappan, N.J.: Macmillan, 1981). Combined and updated what Augustine and Luther did for me: experience plus theology manifest.

BILL MCCARTNEY—founder of Promise Keepers.

This We Believe, John Akers, John Armstrong, and John Woodbridge, eds. (Grand Rapids: Zondervan, 2000). A comprehensive presentation that helped me more fully understand what I believe and why.

Under Cover, John Bevere (Nashville: Nelson, 2001). Freed me from the rebellion and lawlessness that I embraced because I didn't fully understand authority.

ALISTER MCGRATH—professor of historical theology, Oxford University; author of *Knowing Christ* and *Evangelicalism and the Future of Christianity*.

Mere Christianity, C. S. Lewis (New York: Macmillan, 1960; reprint, San Francisco: HarperSanFrancisco, 2001).

Creed or Chaos? Dorothy L. Sayers (Manchester, N.H.: Sophia Institute Press, 1949; reprint, 1996).

The Mind of the Maker, Dorothy L. Sayers (San Francisco: HarperSanFrancisco, 1987).

DAVID MCKENNA—president emeritus, Asbury Theological Seminary; author of *How to Read a Christian Book*.

Confessions, Augustine (New York: Viking, 1979; reprint, New York: Knopf, 1998). Stands alone among psychological literature for its in-depth understanding of the human personality, especially as it relates to spiritual crisis, conversion, and development.

Surprised by Joy, C. S. Lewis (New York: Harcourt Brace, 1955; reprint, 1995). I identify with the author's journey of search and discovery for the gift of joy that comes when Christ becomes our "overwhelming First." I sign my letters "With his joy," words that reflect the tone of life that God has given me as his gift.

In the Name of Jesus, Henri Nouwen (New York: Crossroad, 1989). All other books on Christian leadership pale before the pungent truth and servant spirit of Nouwen's writing.

MARK MITTELBERG—author of *Building a Contagious Church;* coauthor of *Becoming a Contagious Christian*.

Knowing God, J. I. Packer (Downers Grove, Ill.: InterVarsity, 1973; reprint, 1993). I have never gotten over Packer's point about how privileged we are to not only be forgiven of our sins—God could have left us in that state as merely forgiven slaves—but to also be adopted as his sons and daughters. And even beyond that, we've been commissioned as ambassadors who can actually speak to others for him. Amazing!

Systematic Theology of the Christian Religion, J. Oliver Buswell (Grand Rapids: Zondervan, 1969). A powerful biblical and logical defense of the evangelical Christian faith. Buswell's clear teaching concerning the substitutionary nature of the atonement of Christ helped me understand the logic of the gospel message.

Foxe's Book of Martyrs, John Foxe (Nashville: Nelson, 2000). I picked up this book soon after making a commitment to Christ. At first I was just shocked by the lithographs of Christians suffering and dying for their faith. But soon I was drawn into the accounts of how these ordinary men and women—no different from you or me—could face every kind of opposition rather than deny their Lord. Reading their stories marked me and helped me resolve to follow Christ no matter the cost.

R. ALBERT MOHLER JR.—president of Southern Baptist Theological Seminary.

The Pilgrim's Progress, John Bunyan (1678; reprint, New York: Penguin, NAL, 2002).

The Bondage of the Will, Martin Luther (Grand Rapids: Revell, 1989).

The City of God, Augustine (New York: Modern Library, 2000).

J. P. MORELAND—professor of philosophy, Talbot School of Theology; author of *Christian Perspectives on Being Human* and *Love Your God with All Your Mind.*

The Divine Conspiracy, Dallas Willard (San Francisco: HarperSanFrancisco, 1999).

Celebration of Discipline, Richard Foster (New York: Harper & Row, 1978; reprint, San Francisco: HarperSanFrancisco, 2002).

The Evolution of the Soul, Richard Swinburne (New York: Oxford
University Press, 1987; reprint, 1997).

PATRICK MORLEY—author of *Man in the Mirror.*
The Making of a Leader, J. Robert Clinton (Colorado Springs: NavPress,
1988). Identifies six stages of leadership development. Helped me
see what God is doing through all the trials and tribulations.
The Problem of Pain, C. S. Lewis (New York: Macmillan, 1962; reprint,
San Francisco: HarperSanFrancisco, 2001). Helped me resolve a
number of key questions. "The fact that life is short...might be
regarded as a Divine mercy" (p. 124).
*The Life of Dwight L. Moody, William R. Moody (Grand Rapids: Revell,
1900; reprint, Uhrichsville, Ohio: Barbour, 1985). No book has
so enflamed my imagination for what God will do, as the book
says, "with and for and through and in and by the man who is
fully and wholly consecrated to Him" (p. 134).

RICHARD MOUW—president of Fuller Theological Seminary; author of
Consulting the Faithful and *The Smell of Sawdust.*
Lectures on Calvinism, Abraham Kuyper (Grand Rapids: Eerdmans, 1943).
Kuyper founded the Free University of Amsterdam, edited newspapers, started a new denomination, led a political party, and
served a term as prime minister of the Netherlands. This book—
lectures he delivered at Princeton Seminary in 1898—is his summary of what he sees as Calvinism's profound "world and life view."
The Republic, Plato (New York: Viking, 1979). The key images—
philosopher-king, eternal Forms, ideal society, the prisoners in
the Cave—are indelibly impressed on my consciousness.
The Hiding Place, Corrie Ten Boom (Grand Rapids: Chosen, 1971;
reprint, Uhrichsville, Ohio: Barbour, 2000). Serves as a model for
me of what it means to follow Jesus without counting the cost.

KEN MYERS—founder of Mars Hill Audio; author of *All God's Children and Blue Suede Shoes.*

These have haunted me the most over the past fifteen years:

The Cultural Contradictions of Capitalism, Daniel Bell (New York:
    Perseus, Basic Books, 1976; reprint, 2000). Helped me under-
    stand how many of the social and economic forces of nineteenth-
    and twentieth-century Western culture have encouraged contem-
    porary cultural attitudes, by which forms of moral authority are
    rejected and the Self becomes God.

What Are People For? Wendell Berry (San Francisco: North Point Press,
    1990). Demonstrates how radical individualism is encouraged
    by our loss of commitment to local culture and by a widespread
    indifference to how we position ourselves in relationship to the
    rest of creation.

Sacralizing the Secular: The Renaissance Origins of Modernity, Stephen A.
    McKnight (Baton Rouge: Louisiana State University Press, 1989).
    McKnight's study examines certain seminal thinkers in the fif-
    teenth and sixteenth centuries and shows how they influence the
    modern assumptions that knowledge (as power) will "redeem" us,
    that creation is simply a batch of raw material waiting for the ren-
    dering of our desires, and that human nature is defined solely by
    the attribute of choice. If scientism and faith in technology are
    recognized as significant modern problems, McKnight gives
    important clues about how old that problem is.

TED NOBLE—president of Greater Europe Mission.

My Utmost for His Highest, Oswald Chambers (New York: Dodd, Mead
    & Company, 1935; reprint, Uhrichsville, Ohio: Barbour, 2000).
    The challenge to focus more carefully on Jesus has encouraged
    me to keep Christ at the center of my thoughts, decisions, and
    relationships.

Devotional Classics, Richard Foster (San Francisco: HarperSanFrancisco, 1993). Reading how Jesus has been the center of godly lives through the ages has been driving me to put Christ first in everything.

The Spirit of the Disciplines, Dallas Willard (San Francisco: HarperSanFrancisco, 1999). Helped me strengthen my relationship with Christ with godly disciplines I had only heard about, but did not understand. As the song of old says, "Trust and obey. There is no other way to be happy in Jesus, but to trust and obey." The book helped me strengthen "obeying."

DAVID A. NOEBEL—founder and president of Summit Ministries.

The Christian View of God and the World, James Orr (Grand Rapids: Kregel, 1989). Orr sets forth some of the stepping stones of a Christian worldview that I expanded on in my work *Understanding the Times.*

God, Revelation and Authority (6 vols.), Carl F. H. Henry (Wheaton, Ill.: Good News, Crossway Books, 1999). Henry clearly understands the importance of developing a total Christian perspective of life.

The Road of Science and the Ways to God, Stanley L. Jaki (Chicago: University of Chicago Press, 1980). Provided me with a clear understanding of the Christian influence on modern science. Besides, Jaki is a very engaging writer and thinker, even though I believe he misses the boat on biological evolution.

MARK A. NOLL—McManis Chair of Christian Thought, Wheaton College; author of *The Scandal of the Evangelical Mind.*

I am not able to say what books have been most "influential" in my life, but I am able to specify books that left a major impression when I read them and that I continue to look back to with great fondness:

The New England Mind, Perry Miller (Cambridge, Mass.: Harvard University Press, Belknap Press, 1983). Rescued the Puritans' Augustinian perspective from obloquy and modeled a very high level of authorial engagement with a powerful subject.

Fundamentalism and American Culture, George Marsden (New York: Oxford University Press, 1982). Showed how to write persuasively and with integrity about a history regularly neglected, lampooned, or caricatured.

Here I Stand: A Life of Martin Luther, Roland Bainton (Nashville: Abingdon, 1955; reprint, New York: Penguin Putnam, 1995). Limpid prose to describe a complex person at an extraordinary time in the history of the Western church.

THOMAS C. ODEN—Henry Anson Buttz Professor of Theology, Theological School of Drew University.

*In Defense of His Flight to Pontus, and His Return, After His Ordination to the Priesthood, with an Exposition of the Character of the Priestly Office, (Oration 2) as found in Gregory Nazianzen, *A Select Library of the Nicene and Post-Nicene Fathers of the Christian Church,* eds. P. Schaff et al. (1887–1894; reprint, Grand Rapids: Eerdmans, 1971–1979). A powerful narrative of the struggle for honesty in ministry.

St. Gregory the Great: Pastoral Care, St. Gregory (Mahwah, N.J.: Paulist Press, 1994). The one great book historically on pastoral ministry.

The Life of Anthony, Athanasius (Mahwah, N.J.: Paulist Press, 1950); *On the Incarnation,* Athanasius (Crestwood, N.Y.: St. Vladimir, 1993). Both are life-transforming works that made waves for many centuries, including our own.

JANETTE OKE—author of *Women of the West* and the Love Comes Softly series.

The following books by Phillip Keller: **A Gardener Looks at the Fruits of* *the Spirit* (Waco, Tex.: Word, 1979); *A Shepherd Looks at Psalm 23* (Grand Rapids: Zondervan, 1970; reprint, 2000); **A Layman Looks at the Love of God* (Minneapolis: Bethany, 1984). Valuable lessons on practical Christian living and a glimpse into the heart of a loving God.

My Utmost for His Highest, Oswald Chambers (New York: Dodd, Mead & Company, 1935; reprint, Uhrichsville, Ohio: Barbour, 2000). Many biblical truths are available in these daily readings. It is a catalyst to Christian growth.

Christy, Catherine Marshall (Grand Rapids: Revell, 1995; reprint, Grand Rapids: Zondervan, 2001). The story is well told, intriguing, and inspiring. I felt I walked the mountain paths with Christy and the folks she came to love.

MARVIN OLASKY—editor of *World* magazine.

The American Puritans: Their Prose and Poetry, Perry Miller, ed. (New York: Doubleday, 1956; reprint, New York: Columbia University Press, 1982). As I was becoming a Christian, Puritan sermons helped me see that Christianity could be tough-minded as well as warm-hearted.

*Witness, Whittaker Chambers (New York: Random House, 1952). Chambers showed me how to face a past and transcend it, through God's grace.

Institutes of the Christian Religion, John Calvin (1536; reprint, Louisville, Ky.: Westminster John Knox Press, 1960). When I was trying to think through issues of God's sovereignty and providence, Calvin was an enormous help.

STEPHEN F. OLFORD—founder and senior lecturer, The Stephen Olford Center for Biblical Preaching.

The Problem of Pain, C. S. Lewis (New York: Macmillan, 1962; reprint,

San Francisco: HarperSanFrancisco, 2001). Written in light of
World War II, Lewis's classic treatment of the mystery of suffering
revolutionized my thinking on this whole subject.

The Cross of Christ, John Stott (Downers Grove, Ill.: InterVarsity, 1986). I
know no other book that is so comprehensive and challenging on
the cross of Christ. It is expository rather than topical; devotional
and practical, as well as theological. Must-reading for preacher and
layman alike.

Memoir and Remains of the Rev. Robert Murray McCheyne (Philadelphia:
Presbyterian Board of Publication, 1844; reprint, Carlisle, Pa.:
Banner of Truth, 1978), including *His Letters and Messages,*
Andrew Bonar (Carlisle, Pa.: Banner of Truth Trust, 1996).
McCheyne's preaching, his prayers, his poetry, and his life of
purity have led me to pray daily, "O God, make me as holy as a
saved sinner can be."

ROGER E. OLSON—professor of theology, George W. Truett Theological
Seminary, Baylor University.

*The Christian Doctrine of God: Dogmatics, Vol. 1, Emil Brunner (London: Lutterworth, 1949; Louisville, Ky.: Westminster John Knox
Press, 1980). Revolutionized my thinking about theology and
about God; it presents Brunner's "biblical personalism" approach
to both.

*An Interpretation of Christian Ethics, Reinhold Niebuhr (New York:
Seabury, 1979; reprint, San Francisco: HarperSanFrancisco,
1986). Changed my way of thinking about biblical and Christian
ethics; it presents Niebuhr's "Christian realism" approach.

The Crucified God, Jürgen Moltmann (New York: Harper & Row, 1974;
reprint, Minneapolis: Fortress, 1993). Challenged my thinking
about God and Christian living; it presents God as suffering in the
cross of Christ and calls for a cruciform discipleship.

STORMIE OMARTIAN—speaker; author of *The Power of a Praying Wife.*

My Utmost for His Highest, Oswald Chambers (New York: Dodd, Mead
& Company, 1935; reprint, Uhrichsville, Ohio: Barbour, 2000).
For years, every morning after I read the Bible, I read in this book.
It gave me strength and guidance to live each day successfully.

Living at His Place, Jim May (Lakewood, Colo.: Building on the Rock,
1996). One of the best books on moving from a self-centered to a
Christ-centered life. It gave me the right perspective on living for
the Lord.

The Cost of Discipleship, Dietrich Bonhoeffer (New York: Macmillan,
1959; reprint, New York: Simon & Schuster, 1995). Taught me
that walking with God required surrendering everything to him
and making him the center of my life.

JOHN ORTBERG—author of *The Life You've Always Wanted, Love Beyond
Reason,* and *If You Want to Walk on Water, You've Got to Get out of the Boat.*

The Spirit of the Disciplines, Dallas Willard (San Francisco: HarperSan-
Francisco, 1999). The clearest explanation of how spiritual formation actually takes place. It gave me hope that change is possible.

Thomas Wingfold, Curate, George MacDonald (Eureka, Calif.: Sunrise,
1989). It's not great fiction, but it contains amazingly powerful
ideas about God and faith.

FERNANDO ORTEGA—storyteller, songwriter, musician, recording artist, and
worship leader.

East of Eden, John Steinbeck (New York: Penguin, 1952; reprint, 2002).
When I became a Christian at age fifteen, I stopped reading, thinking it was a worldly waste of time. When I finally came to my
senses, *East of Eden* was one of the first things I read. I was deeply
moved by Steinbeck's ability to craft a great story and by the economy of his writing. It renewed my appreciation for the power of

words and made me hunger to read more good literature. I would not be writing songs today if I hadn't begun to read again.

The Habit of Being: Letters of Flannery O'Connor, Sally Fitzgerald, ed. (New York: Farrar, Straus & Giroux, 1988). O'Connor's short stories and novels are among my favorites in contemporary American literature. Her keen, clear-eyed observations about the moving of the Holy Spirit in a fallen world are brilliant, funny, and often disturbing. This collection of her letters reveals much about her theology and how it played itself out in her everyday life. *The Habit of Being* is best read after an immersion into her fiction.

The Subversion of Christianity, Jacques Ellul (Grand Rapids: Eerdmans, 1986). Takes a hard look at the practices and teachings of the modern church, contrasting them with traditional and historical Christian thought.

RAYMOND C. ORTLUND—president of Renewal Ministries.

The Practice of the Presence of God, Brother Lawrence (Grand Rapids: Revell, 1999; reprint, Gainesville, Fla.: Bridge-Logos, 2000). Opened me and Anne, my wife, to seek constant intimacy with God.

Holiness, J. C. Ryle (Moscow, Idaho: Charles Nolan, 2001). A treasure. I've given or recommended this to younger, serious Christians to help them get biblical theological clarity.

LES PARROTT III—cofounder of Center for Relationship Development at Seattle Pacific University; author of *When Bad Things Happen to Good Marriages* and coauthor of *Saving Your Marriage Before It Starts.*

The Road Less Traveled, Scott Peck (New York: Simon & Schuster, 2002). It inspired me in my quest to integrate psychology and theology at a practical level. It also inspired me to be vulnerable in my own writing.

Desiring God, John Piper (Sisters, Oreg.: Multnomah, 1995). Taught me
never to settle for short-lived "pitiful pleasures" but instead to
glory in God—to delight myself in him. It caused me to carefully
examine my motivations in my walk with Christ; to do the right
things for the right reasons. And it taught me that the pursuit of
joy in God is not an option.

The Jesus I Never Knew, Philip Yancey (Grand Rapids: Zondervan, 2002).
I was brought closer to Christ through this book than I've ever
been and was challenged anew to live the life he modeled.

LESLIE PARROTT—cofounder of Center for Relationship Development at
Seattle Pacific University; coauthor of *Becoming Soul Mates* and *Proverbs for
Couples.*

Phantastes, George MacDonald (1858; reprint, Grand Rapids: Eerdmans,
1981). In the same vein as the classic *Pilgrim's Progress,* MacDonald's
book captures the journey of a soul in unforgettable clarity.

The Waste Land and Other Poems, T. S. Eliot (New York: Viking Penguin,
1998). Eliot's narrative poetry revealed to me the artistry of written words. Its visual impact of biblical imagery opened my mind
to the depth of meaning that can be conveyed in the economy of
language. Second only to Scripture, I have committed more of its
pages to memory than any other book.

*Catherine Booth, Catherine Bramwell-Booth (London: Hodder &
Stoughton, 1970; reprint, Grand Rapids: Baker, 1996). This biography of the cofounder of the Salvation Army gave me a vision for
how marriage, motherhood, and ministry could be lived out with
full-throttle passion.

PAIGE PATTERSON—president of Southeastern Baptist Theological Seminary.

The Suffering Savior, F. W. Krummacher (Grand Rapids: Kregel, 1992;
reprint, Eugene, Oreg.: Wipf & Stock, 2002).

The Reformers and Their Stepchildren, Leonard Verduin (Grand Rapids: Eerdmans, 1964).

FRANK PERETTI—author of *The Visitation* and *The Wounded Spirit*.

How Should We Then Live? Francis Schaeffer (Wheaton, Ill.: Good News, Crossway Books, 1983). It was a massive cultural illumination for me, setting the course of much of my ministry in regard to the Christian worldview.

Amusing Ourselves to Death, Neil Postman (New York: Penguin, 1986). The book's message continues to haunt me as I see all around me a culture that, as Ravi Zacharias puts it, "hears with its eyes and thinks with its feelings."[1]

*The Cult Explosion, Dave Hunt (Eugene, Oreg.: Harvest House, 1980). This was the first definitive "primer" on the core lies of every cult or occult movement, and it became an ingredient in my first major novel, *This Present Darkness*.

JOHN PIPER—pastor; author of numerous books, including *Desiring God*.

The End for Which God Created the World, Jonathan Edwards (1754) in *The Works of Jonathan Edwards: Vol. 1*, (Peabody, Mass: Hendrickson, 1998).

The Freedom of the Will, Jonathan Edwards (Morgan, Pa.: Soli Deo Gloria Publications, 1996).

The Weight of Glory, C. S. Lewis (Grand Rapids: Eerdmans, 1965; reprint, San Francisco: HarperSanFrancisco, 2001) and lots of other books by Lewis.

REBECCA MANLEY PIPPERT—author of *Out of the Salt Shaker*, *Hope Has Its Reasons*, and *A Heart Like His*.

Mere Christianity, C. S. Lewis (New York: Macmillan, 1960; reprint, San Francisco: HarperSanFrancisco, 2001). I wasn't raised in an evangelical Christian home. Like most young adults I had lots of doubts and questions. I feared rationality and faith were mutually exclusive. Then it occurred to me that I had never read the Bible. Looking through my parents' library, I stumbled across a clearly unread book called *Mere Christianity* that someone had given my mother. In Lewis I found myself face-to-face with an intellect so disciplined, so lucid, so relentlessly logical, that all my intellectual pride at not being a "mindless believer" was quickly squelched. Lewis made the Christian faith comprehensible. Second, he made me realize that I hadn't known what biblical Christianity really was. Third, he sparked my interest to read the Bible.

The Fall, Albert Camus (New York: Knopf, Vintage, 1991). I read *The Fall* when I was a freshman in college. I had a newfound faith in Christ and this book changed my life. What had initially drawn me from agnosticism to faith was the firm conviction that the Christian faith was true. However, it was through reading *The Fall* that God brought a profound conviction of personal sin. Camus's ruthless, scathing analysis of human nature forced me to take a deeper, more honest look at my own humanity.

The Seven Deadly Sins, Rabbi Solomon Schimmel (New York: Oxford University Press, 1997). With Schimmel, a rabbi and a psychologist, there is no "psychology-lite." His analysis of the inadequacy of contemporary psychology to deal with the problem of sin is worth the price of the book alone. He examines sin through the moral wisdom mediated through Jewish, Christian, and classical reflections on human nature.

ALVIN PLANTINGA—John A. O'Brien Professor of Philosophy, University of Notre Dame.

Treatise on Religious Affections, Jonathan Edwards (Grand Rapids: Baker,

1982). A wonderfully subtle exploration of the interplay between heart and mind in Christian spirituality.

Institutes of the Christian Religion, John Calvin (1536; reprint, Louisville, Ky.: Westminster John Knox Press, 1960). I like especially Calvin's warm spirituality, spiritual realism, and terrific ideas for epistemology.

CORNELIUS PLANTINGA JR.—president of Calvin Theological Seminary.

Mere Christianity, C. S. Lewis (New York: Macmillan, 1960; reprint, San Francisco: HarperSanFrancisco, 2001). Lewis's book got me in the heart at a vulnerable time. Who else so wonderfully combines sharp thinking, soaring theological imagination, and noble simplicity? Like Jesus, Lewis seems to say: Give up your life and you shall find it.

God and Other Minds, Alvin Plantinga (Ithaca, N.Y.: Cornell University Press, 1990). My brother wrote this book when he was thirty-two and I nineteen. "Faith seeking understanding" can be a spiritual and intellectual adventure, and Al shows us how.

SIR JOHN POLKINGHORNE—former president of Queen's College, Cambridge University; author of *Science and Christian Belief* and *Faith, Science, and Understanding.*

The Crucified God, Jürgen Moltmann (San Francisco: HarperSanFrancisco, 1974; reprint, Minneapolis: Fortress, 1993). A deep and moving exposition of the cross of Christ, understood in Trinitarian terms as the divine participation in the suffering travail of Creation. Truly a book of theology "after Auschwitz."

Love's Endeavour, Love's Expense, W. H. Vanstone (London: Darton, Longman, and Todd, 1977). A meditative reflection on the value and necessary precariousness of creativity by Love, strikingly consonant with scientific insight into evolutionary process when considered as God's continuing act of creation.

What Happens in Holy Communion? Michael Welker (Grand Rapids: Eerdmans, 2000). A remarkable, ecumenically based Eucharistic theology, written by a leading German reformed theologian. The book is helpful to Christians of all traditions as they seek to "do this in remembrance" of Christ.

BILL POLLARD—CEO of ServiceMaster.

The Mind of the Maker, Dorothy L. Sayers (San Francisco: HarperSan-Francisco, 1987).

Management Challenges for the 21st Century, Peter F. Drucker (New York: HarperBusiness, 2001).

Living Faith, Jimmy Carter (New York: Crown, 1998).

DENNIS RAINEY—executive director of FamilyLife.

Humility: The Beauty of Holiness, Andrew Murray (Fort Washington, Pa.: Christian Literature Crusade, 1993). A compelling biblical explanation for why we need to practice humility and not give pride any kind of opportunity in our lives. It changed the course of my relationship with Christ and also anchored me in a proper biblical understanding of who I am in Christ.

HUGH ROSS—founder and president of Reasons to Believe.

These three mark turning points in my life:

Intelligent Life in the Universe, Iosef Shklovskii and Carl Sagan (Boca Raton, Fla.: Holden-Day, 1966). Though I strongly disagreed with the atheist authors' conclusions, they did alert me to the fact that powerful philosophical and theological conclusions could be drawn from astronomical data. They also were the first

to stimulate me to consider what kind of design of the solar
system is necessary to explain life on Earth.

The Kingdom of the Cults, Walter Martin (Minneapolis: Bethany,
1968; reprint, 2002). Martin's book challenged me to read
through the entire Bible rapidly, systematically, and repeatedly
with a particular theme in mind as a way to gain a grasp of that
theme. His book transformed the way I prepare myself and
others for reaching out to nonbelievers with the truth claims of
Jesus Christ.

*Information Theory and Molecular Biology, Hubert P. Yockey (New York:
Cambridge University Press, 1992). I marvel at how rigorously
and thoroughly this agnostic scholar demonstrates the impossibility of a naturalistic explanation for life's origin. Throughout the
book I have found valuable tips on how to persuade resistant
scholars to let go of their failed models.

LELAND RYKEN—editor of *The Christian Imagination;* author of *How to
Read the Bible as Literature* and *Worldly Saints.*

Mere Christianity, C. S. Lewis (New York: Macmillan, 1960; reprint, San
Francisco: HarperSanFrancisco, 2001). Helped to codify my
thinking about Christian belief and practice during my college
years.

Fundamentalism and the Word of God, J. I. Packer (Grand Rapids: Eerdmans, 1958). Made the case for the authority of the Bible in such
a way as to provide an orientation for my thinking that has never
left me.

The Complete Poems, John Milton (New York: Penguin, 1999). Baptized
my literary imagination during my first year in graduate school by
showing me what the Christian faith looks like when transmuted
into poetry of the highest order.

PHILIP GRAHAM RYKEN—senior minister, Tenth Presbyterian Church, Philadelphia.

The Chronicles of Narnia, C. S. Lewis (New York: HarperCollins, 1950–1956; reprint, 2002). In addition to stimulating my imagination, these stories taught me about courage, loyalty, friendship, honor, and the ultimate triumph of good over evil.

Inspiration and Authority of the Bible, B. B. Warfield (Philadelphia: Presbyterian and Reformed Publishing, 1948). Warfield's essays on Scripture helped confirm my conviction that the evangelical doctrine of inerrancy is biblically correct and logically defensible.

Human Nature in Its Fourfold State, Thomas Boston (Carlisle, Pa.: Banner of Truth Trust, 1997). My doctoral research on this book taught me how to preach biblical theology in a pastoral way and underscored the centrality of union with Christ as the source of spiritual vitality.

CHARLES C. RYRIE—distinguished professor and former president of Philadelphia Biblical University.

Hudson Taylor's Spiritual Secret, Howard and Geraldine Taylor (Chicago: Moody, 1932; reprint, 1989); *He That Is Spiritual,* Lewis Sperry Chafer (Grand Rapids: Zondervan, 1983). Two books that greatly influenced me as a young believer.

The Knowledge of the Holy, A. W. Tozer (New York: Harper & Row, 1961; reprint, San Francisco: HarperSanFrancisco, 1992). One of a number of books that have influenced me throughout the years.

DAVID SANFORD—adjunct professor of journalism, Western Baptist College; coauthor of *God Is Relevant* and *Calling America and the Nations to Christ.*

Spiritual Leadership, J. Oswald Sanders (revised edition, Chicago: Moody, 1999). Provides hundreds of timeless insights for every Christian leader.

Lectures on the Revival of Religion, Charles Finney (currently in print as
    Lectures on Revival, Minneapolis: Bethany, 1989). Finney's call to
    holy boldness is electric.

Daws, Betty Lee Skinner (Grand Rapids: Zondervan, 1974; Colorado
    Springs: NavPress, 1994). The inspiring story of Dawson
    Trotman, founder of The Navigators. Provides hundreds of
    real-life lessons on Christian leadership and living on fire for
    Jesus Christ.

RON SIDER—president of Evangelicals for Social Action; author of *Rich
Christians in an Age of Hunger.*

Miracles, C. S. Lewis (1947; reprint, San Francisco: HarperSanFrancisco,
    2001). Clarified for me the great debate between theists and natu-
    ralists that has raged since the Enlightenment. Lewis has helped
    me see that the very widespread view in modern intellectual circles
    that science makes belief in miracles more and more irrational and
    irresponsible is confused and wrong.

Freedom of a Christian, Martin Luther (in *Three Treatises,* 1520; reprint,
    Minneapolis: Augsburg, 1988). Growing up as an Anabaptist who
    was called to follow Jesus and a Wesleyan who was supposed to be
    sanctified, I discovered Luther's clear description of justification by
    faith alone liberating.

The Cost of Discipleship, Dietrich Bonhoeffer (1937 in German;
    New York: Macmillan, 1949). Perhaps I especially liked this
    book because I never felt that Luther managed the right
    balance between justification by faith alone and the sweeping
    sanctification that the New Testament promises through the
    power of the Holy Spirit. Bonhoeffer articulates a radical call
    to costly obedience without abandoning the wonderful truth
    of justification.

MOISES SILVA—author of *Foundations of Contemporary Interpretation* and *God, Language, and Scripture.*

Inspiration and Authority of the Bible, B. B. Warfield (Philadelphia: Presbyterian and Reformed Publishing, 1948). His erudition and clear thinking placed at the service of biblical knowledge was a tremendous influence on me during college.

The Origin of Paul's Religion, J. Gresham Machen (1925; reprint, Eugene, Oreg.: Wipf & Stock, 2002). His powers of analysis seemed remarkable to me when I was a college student, especially as he courteously but thoroughly demolished the arguments of those who tried to explain Paul by denying the supernatural character of his gospel.

The Epistle of St. Paul to the Galatians, J. B. Lightfoot (Grand Rapids: Zondervan, 1957) (including the appendix on *St. Paul and the Three*). A clear and profound commentary on Galatians.

JAMES W. SIRE—author of *The Universe Next Door* and *Habits of the Mind.* Here are three of the hundreds of books that have influenced my life:

The Cost of Discipleship, Dietrich Bonhoeffer (New York: Macmillan, 1959; reprint, New York: Simon & Schuster, 1995). Transformed the way I view the relationship between belief and behavior. He who does not obey does not believe.

The Seventeenth Century Background: Studies in the Thought of the Age in Relation to Poetry and Religion, Basil Willey (New York: Columbia University Press, 1942). Helped me learn the relationship between intellectual culture and literature, sparking as well an early understanding of the nature of worldviews.

The Spirit of the Disciplines, Dallas Willard (San Francisco: HarperSanFrancisco, 1999). Gave intellectual credibility to the practice of the classical spiritual disciplines, which in turn prompted a significant change in my life.

GERALD L. SITTSER—professor of religion, Whitworth College.

Confessions, Augustine (New York: Viking, 1979; reprint, New York: Knopf, 1998). His deeply reflective and insightful story of his own spiritual journey has helped me to think of my life story from a redemptive perspective, seeing the hand of God in everything that has happened in my life.

The Pilgrim's Progress, John Bunyan (1678; reprint, New York: Penguin, NAL, 2002). Bunyan has helped me see that the Christian life is a pilgrimage, and that the periods of blessing and the periods of difficulty are both parts of the journey. An easy life is not the point; it is the direction in which we are headed that matters.

The Sacrament of the Present Moment, Jean-Pierre de Caussade (San Francisco: HarperSanFrancisco, 1989). In this work, de Caussade shows that the best and only time in which to know and follow God is right now, however exciting or mundane. He has enabled me to hallow every moment as a gift from God.

CHUCK SMITH—pastor of Calvary Chapel of Costa Mesa; author of *Living Water* and *Charisma vs. Charismania.*

*The Apostle John, W. Griffith Thomas (Grand Rapids: Eerdmans, 1948; reprint, 1984). Inspired me to expositional teaching as I followed his chapter of outline studies in 1 John.

Romans Verse by Verse, William Newell (1948; reprint, Grand Rapids: Kregel, 1994). This book led me into an understanding of the grace of God and thus brought me into a whole new relationship with God. I no longer seek to relate to God on the basis of my goodness and my work for him, but on the basis of his goodness and his work for me.

Halley's Bible Handbook, Henry H. Halley (1927; reprint, Grand Rapids: Zondervan, 2000). Halley suggests that every church should have a congregational plan of reading through the Bible, and that the pastor's sermon should come from the reading of that week. I began following this suggestion in 1958 and have continued ever since.

HOWARD A. SNYDER—author of *Earth Currents: The Struggle for the World's Soul* and *Models of the Kingdom.*

The Journal of John Wesley, John Wesley (Nashville: Abingdon, n.d.). Puts me in touch with the life, heart, and ministry of perhaps the greatest scholar-evangelist-reformer since the apostle Paul.

The Technological Society, Jacques Ellul (New York: Knopf, 1954). Showed me that technology creates its own morality—a morality of means, not ends.

The Promise of Trinitarian Theology, Colin Gunton (Edinburgh, U.K.: T & T Clark, 1997). Opened up the practical relevance of the doctrine of the Trinity and why its implications aren't taken more seriously in the West.

WESLEY K. STAFFORD—president of Compassion International.

Through Gates of Splendor, Elisabeth Elliot (Wheaton, Ill.: Tyndale, 1986; reprint, Durham, N.C.: Duke University Press, 1997). This was integral to my calling.

Margin, Richard Swenson (Colorado Springs: NavPress, 1994). Helped me maintain under the pressures of leadership and the totality of my life.

Built to Last, James C. Collins and Jerry I. Porras (New York: Harper-Business, 2002). Helped me as I have guided and led the ministry of Compassion International, setting standards to help make it topnotch in every way.

GLENN T. STANTON—manager of research, legislative, and cultural affairs, Focus on the Family.

Decisive Issues Facing Christians Today, John Stott (1984; reprint, Grand

Rapids: Revell, 1998). Stott explains that a fuller view of God, humanity, Christ, salvation, and the church compels us to apply our faith to all areas of life and not just those we associate as being "spiritual." It helped me see God as the God of Creation rather than merely the God of religious, church life.

A Christian Manifesto, Francis Schaeffer (Wheaton, Ill.: Good News, Crossway, 1981). I have not had the same view of God, spirituality, and all reality since the day I picked up *A Christian Manifesto.* Schaeffer showed me that all of life is spiritual: We are not to shut up our spiritual lives into certain compartments, but to see Christ as Lord over all of Creation. The book led me into the larger body of Schaeffer's works, which helped me see God as so much bigger than the manageable gods we try to construct.

Ancient-Future Faith, Robert Webber (Grand Rapids: Baker, 1999). Helped me at a time when I questioned whether evangelicalism has what it takes to answer the important questions. Webber shared many of the same concerns, but he had much more thoughtful explanations for these concerns. If all he did was let me know there was someone else in the room with me, that would have been great. But he also offered an answer: that the future of the evangelical church runs through the past. He urges Christians to reacquaint themselves with the early Christian fathers. They forged the church in a syncretistic culture much like we have in postmodernity, and the faith they had was much more well thought out. It was also truer to ultimate reality and answered, rather than accommodated, the Gnostic/platonic view that the material world is something to be overcome rather than enjoyed as God's Creation, that he will redeem, just as he redeems each one of us. It helps draw a larger picture of God and a deeper view of church history and experience.

Charles Swindoll—pastor; author; chancellor of Dallas Theological Seminary.

The Pilgrim's Progress, John Bunyan (1678; reprint, New York: Penguin, NAL, 2002).

The Pursuit of God, A. W. Tozer (Camp Hill, Pa.: Christian Publications, 1993).

Knowing God, J. I. Packer (Downers Grove, Ill.: InterVarsity, 1973; reprint, 1993).

John Michael Talbot—musician; author; founder and general minister of The Brothers and Sisters of Charity.

The patristic (or church father) tradition and the Franciscan/monastic heritage have much to teach us about the church from which the Scriptures came. Furthermore, there is a wealth of mystical and contemplative traditions in these sources that people hunger for.

The Writings of St. Francis of Assisi (Chicago: Franciscan Herald Press, 1976).

St. Francis of Assisi: First and Second Life of St. Francis with Selections from "Treatise on the Miracles of Blessed Francis," Thomas of Celano (Chicago: Franciscan Herald Press, 1963).

The Little Flowers of St. Francis of Assisi, St. Bonaventure (Springfield, Ill.: Templegate, 1988).

The Sayings and Lives of the Desert Fathers (Kalamazoo, Mich.: Cistercian Publications, 1987).

Added to these, I would recommend the writings of St. John of the Cross and St. Theresa of Avila.

Major W. Ian Thomas—founder of Torchbearers of the Capernwray Missionary Fellowship; author of *The Saving Life of Christ.*

The only book I have ever really needed in order to know the truth as to who the Lord Jesus is, what he did and why, and what he wants to be in us

now and forever, has been the Bible. Other books that have been very helpful in confirming the truth are:

My Utmost for His Highest, Oswald Chambers (New York: Dodd, Mead
& Company, 1935; reprint, Uhrichsville, Ohio: Barbour, 2000).

*The New Man and *The New Boy,* Capt Reginald Wallis (New York:
Bible Truth Press, 1931; London: Religious Tract Society, 1921).

Anything by Andrew Murray, F. B. Meyer, or A. W. Tozer.

In each case, the focus of the author is upon the person of the Lord
Jesus and his role in the life of the believer.

MARY STEWART VAN LEEUWEN—professor of psychology and philosophy,
Eastern University; author of *Gender and Grace.*

Anne of Green Gables, Lucy Maud Montgomery (New York: Random
House, 2002). As a youngster (and periodically as an adult) I have
reread the story of an eleven-year-old girl who is adopted by an
unmarried brother and sister who run a farm on Prince Edward
Island in the late nineteenth century. It shows, in an indirect way,
how wide God's covenant is, and how little it depends on blood ties.
I also liked it because it was about an intelligent young woman who
transcended the limitations of her rural community without ever
losing her love for it and for her adoptive family and friends there.

The Gospel in a Pluralist Society, Lesslie Newbigin (Grand Rapids:
Eerdmans, 1989). The author shows a remarkable grasp of the
significance of worldviews for the conduct of science and an appreciation of cultural pluralism while maintaining his confession of
Christ as the only way to God, and the One in whom all things
hold together.

DAVE VEERMAN—author of more than forty books, including *Tough Parenting for Tough Times;* editor of the *Life Application Bible.*

*Faith That Makes Sense, J. Edwin Orr (Valley Forge, Pa.: Judson, 1960).

Made a profound impact on me in college as I struggled with
doubts and intellectual issues.

The Great Divorce, C. S. Lewis (New York: Macmillan, 1946; reprint,
San Francisco: HarperSanFrancisco, 2001). Combines fiction and
apologetics as Lewis answers a vexing question with profound
creativity.

The Taste of New Wine, Keith Miller (Waco, Tex.: Word, 1965; reprint,
Orleans, Mass.: Paraclete Press, 1993). Pushed me to a vulnerable,
open, and honest faith.

C. PETER WAGNER—president of Global Harvest Ministries; chancellor of
Wagner Leadership Institute.

For me, doing is more important than being. In fact, being is so unimpor-
tant that I have always been willing to give my life if that is what it takes
to do what God has called me to do. These books helped me more than
others in accomplishing the ministry assignments that God has given me:

Understanding Church Growth, Donald A. McGavran (Grand Rapids:
Eerdmans, 1970; reprint, 1990). After spending sixteen frustrating years as a field missionary to Bolivia, I was totally renewed
by coming into contact with McGavran, a man who was able
to explain where the missionary enterprise had gotten off
God's track and how to reposition missions to fulfill the Great
Commission.

Power Evangelism, John Wimber (North Pomfret, Vt.: Trafalgar Square,
2000). McGavran helped me establish a new paradigm for the
human side of completing the Great Commission, and later on,
Wimber helped me enter into the supernatural dimensions of the
task.

Prophets and Personal Prophecy, Bill Hamon (Shippensburg, Pa.: Destiny
Image, 1987; reprint, New Kensington, Pa.: Whitaker House,
2001). Wimber helped bring me to the place where I believed that

God continues to speak to people today, but because of my cessationist background, I had a hard time making sense of what I was hearing about the gift of prophecy and contemporary prophets. Hamon's book broke the barriers and helped set my mind in order so that I could integrate prophecy into my worldview.

SHEILA WALSH—speaker for Women of Faith conferences; recording artist; author of *A Love So Big, Living Fearlessly,* and *Unexpected Grace.*

The Prisoner in the Third Cell, Gene Edwards (Wheaton, Ill.: Tyndale, 1992). A book about John the Baptist, who lived his life preparing the way for the Lamb of God but died before the death and resurrection of that Lamb. The question of the text is this, "Will you love a God who does not live up to your expectations?"

The Brothers Karamazov, Fyodor Dostoyevsky (1880; reprint, New York: Vintage, 1991). This book has deeply challenged and comforted me. It reveals the struggle between shadow and light that exists in all of us.

ROBERT E. WEBBER—William R. and Geraldyne B. Myers Professor of Ministry, Northern Baptist Theological Seminary; author of *Worship Is a Verb, Worship Old and New,* and *The Complete Library of Christian Worship.*

Early Christian Doctrines, J. N. D. Kelly (New York: Harper & Row, 1960; reprint, New York: Continuum International, 2000). By far the best one-volume introduction to the times and thought of the early church fathers. Kelly approaches the fathers' thought by organizing their theology according to themes.

Byzantine Theology, John Meyendorff (Bronx: Fordham University Press, 1974; reprint, 1987). Meyendorff introduced me to Eastern Christian thought, a kind of theological thinking that is more pertinent to the postmodern world than that of the Western tradition. The Eastern emphasis integrated Creation, Incarnation, and

re-creation in a more holistic way than the West. Salvation is not
only for people but for the whole cosmos.

Christus Victor, Gustav Aulen (New York: Macmillan, 1969). The Christus Victor view of salvation is much fuller than the sacrificial view.
It points out that because of Christ's sacrifice, a victory has been
achieved over the powers of evil. This view is pertinent to a postmodern faith because it speaks forcibly to the presence of the
powers as well as to the victory of Christ over them.

JERRY E. WHITE—president of The Navigators.

Words to Winners of Souls, Horatio Bonar (Grand Rapids: Baker, 1979;
reprint, Phillipsburg, N.J.: Presbyterian and Reformed Publishing,
1995). Written in 1866, this book succinctly and powerfully
speaks of the need for a life that reflects Christ and reaches out to
those who are without him.

The Pursuit of God, A. W. Tozer (Camp Hill, Pa.: Christian Publications,
1993). Tozer incisively puts his finger on the major issues of the
heart as he describes a life lived in pursuit of God. This is one of
the books that stirred me deeply as a young believer and continues to bring me back to the fundamental issues of living life in
Christ.

Reaching for the Invisible God, Philip Yancey (Grand Rapids: Zondervan,
2002). Yancey raises the questions that bother everyone. This book
is a boon to the critics and skeptics who are honestly seeking truth.

LUDER WHITLOCK—president emeritus, Reformed Theological Seminary.

*By Oath Consigned, Meredith G. Kline (Grand Rapids: Eerdmans,
1968). This volume and several others of Kline's works radically
revised my approach to historical-grammatical exegesis. I began to
discover new information that forced me to consider biblical and
theological material in a different way.

The Noise of Solemn Assemblies, Peter L. Berger (New York: Doubleday, 1961). Opened the way for me to realize the substantial contribution sociology could make to an analysis of the church in the world. As I read this and later volumes, such as *Homeless Mind* (New York: Knopf, Vintage, 1974), I was led to see our world in a new way.

Connections, James Burke (New York: Little, Brown & Company, 1978; reprint, 1995). Upon becoming acquainted with *Connections,* I reacted by thinking this is the way more history should be written, because life is a fabric. Burke's presentation of understanding the relationship of people, events, and innovations makes perception and comprehension of history fuller and far easier to grasp and interpret.

DONALD S. WHITNEY—associate professor of spiritual formation, Midwestern Baptist Theological Seminary; author of *Spiritual Disciplines for the Christian Life.*

The Life of D. Martyn Lloyd-Jones: The Fight of Faith 1939–1981, Iain Murray (Carlisle, Pa.: Banner of Truth Trust, 1990). Lloyd-Jones's absolute confidence in the power of the Word of God, and yet his eager dependence on the unction of the Holy Spirit, impressed me in powerful ways with the need for both.

Jonathan Edwards: A New Biography, Iain Murray (Carlisle, Pa.: Banner of Truth Trust, 1992). Showed me the fruitfulness of a minister's life lived in balance of head and heart, light and heat, life and doctrine, as taught in 1 Timothy 4:16.

George Müller: Delighted in God, Roger Steer (Colorado Springs: WaterBrook, Shaw Books, 2000). Deepened not only my prayer life but also my faith in God.

ROD J. K. WILSON—president of Regent College.

My Utmost for His Highest, Oswald Chambers (New York: Dodd, Mead & Company, 1935; reprint, Uhrichsville, Ohio: Barbour, 2000).

The emphasis on spirituality and being rather than on service and doing has impacted me deeply.

The Creative Word: Canon as a Model for Biblical Education, Walter Brueggemann (Philadelphia: Fortress, 1982). I have had a lifelong interest in the interface of Scripture and education. This book unpacks Scripture and the process of education by exposing the latter through an understanding of the former.

Let Your Life Speak: Listening for the Voice of Vocation, Parker J. Palmer (Hoboken, N.J.: John Wiley & Sons, 1999). Palmer's ability to speak to the heart of issues, in simple language, elicits worship in me and a desire to live from a sense of center.

JOHN WILSON—editor of *Books & Culture.*

The Underground Man or *Notes from Underground,* Fyodor Dostoyevsky (1864; reprint, New York: Knopf, 1994). In the summer of 1961, when I turned thirteen, I read *The Underground Man,* and for the first time I began to grasp the twistiness of the human mind, of my own mind. Words I'd heard for as long as I could remember— words like *sin* and *salvation*—took on new meaning.

BEN WITHERINGTON III—professor of New Testament, Asbury Theological Seminary; author of *The Jesus Quest.*

The Prophets, Abraham Heschel (New York: HarperCollins, 1975; reprint, 2001). Heschel was important in helping me understand the character of God, especially God's pathos.

The Screwtape Letters, C. S. Lewis (New York: Macmillan, 1954; reprint, San Francisco: HarperSanFrancisco, 2001). I read Lewis when in high school, and this book helped me begin to think about supernatural evil as well as supernatural good.

Knowing God, J. I. Packer (Downers Grove, Ill.: InterVarsity, 1973; reprint, 1993). Packer's classic book was something my wife and I read through together early in our marriage. It helped us better understand our relationship with God.

ROBERT WOLGEMUTH—founder of Wolgemuth & Associates, author of *She Calls Me Daddy.*

*The Holiness of God, R. C. Sproul (Wheaton, Ill.: Tyndale, 1998). I had spent most of my Christian life focused on my walk, my talk, my habits, my conduct. This book began a journey that resulted in a radical adjustment to my theology. This wasn't about me; it was about the living God. My wife and I changed our parenting goals from arbiting rules to giving our children an idea of what it's like literally to be in the presence of a holy God.

The Taste of New Wine, Keith Miller (Waco, Tex.: Word, 1965; reprint, Orleans, Mass.: Paraclete Press, 1993). During my college years, the airlines promoted "Student Standby Fares." In exchange for being the last to fill empty seats, tickets were half-price. I was on my way to visit my girlfriend's family and had to spend the night at O'Hare waiting for my empty seat. A serviceman asked me to watch his gear while he slept, so I stayed awake all night and read this book. The story of Miller's conversion gripped me and gave me a fresh new outlook on my life in Christ.

What's So Amazing About Grace? Philip Yancey (Grand Rapids: Zondervan, 1997). Yancey's brilliantly composed text gripped me unlike any other book ever had regarding God's amazing grace in its manifold expressions.

N. T. WRIGHT—Canon theologian, Westminster Abbey; has taught New Testament studies at Cambridge, Oxford, and McGill Universities.

Miracles, C. S. Lewis (1947; reprint, San Francisco: HarperSanFrancisco, 2001).

The Language and Imagery of the Bible, George B. Caird (Grand Rapids: Eerdmans, 1997).

The Aims of Jesus, B. F. Meyer (London: SCM Press, 1979; reprint, San Jose, Calif.: Pickwick, 2002).

VINITA HAMPTON WRIGHT—novelist; author of *Velma Still Cooks in Leeway* and *Grace at Bender Springs.*

Decision Making and the Will of God, Garry Frieson and Robin Maxson (Sisters, Oreg.: Multnomah, 1980; reprint, 2000).

Women at the Crossroads: A Path Beyond Feminism and Traditionalism, Kari Torjesen Malcolm (Downers Grove, Ill.: InterVarsity, 1982).

EDWIN YAMAUCHI—professor of history, Miami University, Ohio.
The three books that influenced me the most soon after my conversion in high school were:

St. Paul's Epistle to the Philippians, J. B. Lightfoot (Grand Rapids: Zondervan, 1968; reprint, Wheaton, Ill.: Crossway, 1994). It got me to learn Greek on my own in order to read the New Testament in its original language.

The Life of Christ, F. W. Farrar (New York: E. P. Dutton, 1877; reprint, Salt Lake City: Deseret, 1994); and *The Life and Letters of St. Paul,* F. W. Farrar (New York: E. P. Dutton, 1880). I learned of these through Wilbur Smith's column in *Moody Monthly.* They introduced me to the wealth of historical background that could illuminate the New Testament books.

ZIG ZIGLAR—founder of Ziglar Training Systems; author of *Zig, See You at the Top,* and *Confessions of a Happy Christian.*

The Light and the Glory, Peter Marshall and David Manuel (Grand Rapids: Revell, 1987).

The Power of Positive Thinking, Norman Vincent Peale (Paramus, N.J.:
    Prentice-Hall, 1952; reprint, New York: Ballantine, 1996).
The Magic of Thinking Big, David Schwartz (Old Tappan, N.J.: Prentice
    Hall, 1990).

SOURCES FOR OUT-OF-PRINT BOOKS

Abooksearch.com, *www.abooksearch.com*
Alibris, *www.alibris.com*
Amazon zShops, *www.amazon.com*
Anybook International, 916-313-3405, *www.anybook.com*
Baker Book House, *www.bakerbooks.com*
BestBookDeal.com, *www.bestbookdeal.com*
Book Look, 800-223-0540
Book Search, 651-292-1842, *www.booksearch.com*
Christian Book Distributors, *www.christianbook.com*
East Bay Book Co., 800-899-5544, *www.eastbaybooks.com*
Half.com, *www.half.ebay.com*
Hay-on-Wye, *www.booktown.co.uk*
InterVarsity Press, *www.gospelcom.net/ivpress/info/op.php*
Kregel Used Books, 616-459-9444, *usedbooks@kregel.com*
Rare Christian Books, 573-336-7316,
    www.abebooks.com/home/RARECHRISTIANBOOK
Steel's Used Christian Books, 816-300-2665, Steels@mwis.net,
    www.fathersbusiness.com/steels
Used Book Central, *www.usedbookcentral.com*

APPENDIX TWO

Author Profiles

DONALD G. BLOESCH is professor emeritus of theology at the University of Dubuque Theological Seminary in Dubuque, Iowa. He is a minister in the United Church of Christ and also a past president of the American Theological Society (Midwest division). He is the author of hundreds of articles and more than thirty books, including the two-volume systematic theological work *Essentials of Evangelical Theology* (San Francisco: Harper & Row, 1978–79) and the nearly completed seven-volume Christian Foundations Series (Downers Grove, Ill.: InterVarsity Press, vol. 7 forthcoming). He lives in Dubuque, Iowa, with his wife, Brenda.

JILL BRISCOE is an internationally known speaker and author who co-founded with her husband, Stuart, Telling the Truth media ministries. For years the Briscoes have given presentations at conferences and mission organizations around the globe. Jill is the executive editor of *Just Between Us,* a magazine for women in ministry and leadership. She is the author of more than forty books, including *Prayer That Works* and *Faith Enough to Finish.* A native of Liverpool, England, Jill resides with Stuart in suburban Milwaukee.

MICHAEL CARD is a widely recognized and highly regarded songwriter and musician. Over the years he has won several Dove Awards, and his song "El Shaddai" was recognized by the Recording Industry Association of America and the National Endowment for the Arts as one of the 365 Songs of the Century. Michael has recorded twenty-two albums, including *The Life, The Promise, Joy in the Journey,* and *Soul Anchor.* He has authored ten books, including *A Violent Grace* and *Scribbling in the Sand.* Michael is married to Susan, and they live with their four children in the Nashville area.

GARY R. COLLINS, a native of Canada, is a licensed clinical psychologist who received his Ph.D. in clinical psychology from Purdue University. He has taught psychology at Bethel College in St. Paul, Minnesota, and at Trinity International University, serving as department chair at the latter institution for most of his tenure. He was executive director and president of the American Association of Christian Counselors during the years of the organization's rapid growth and founded the official AACC magazine, *Christian Counseling Today.* He was general editor for the thirty-volume *Resources for Christian Counseling* and is the author of more than fifty books, including *Christian Counseling: A Comprehensive Guide* and his most recent book, *Christian Coaching: Helping Others Turn Potential into Reality.* Now the chairman of the Bridge Institute, devoted to building emerging vision-ary leaders through coaching, Dr. Collins also heads the International Christian Counseling Alliance and travels frequently to present seminars internationally. He and his wife, Julie, live in northern Illinois.

CHARLES COLSON, the one-time "hatchet man" for President Richard Nixon, has been for three decades a champion for ministering to prisoners and their families. He is the founder and chairman of Prison Fellowship Ministries, which reaches prisoners with the gospel in ninety-three coun-tries and also provides for their families' material needs. In 1983 Colson founded Justice Fellowship, which seeks to reform the criminal justice sys-tem. He is the author of eighteen books, including *Loving God, The Body,* and *How Now Shall We Live?* In 1993 he received the prestigious Templeton Prize for Progress in Religion. He is also the host of *BreakPoint,* a nationally syndicated daily radio broadcast.

LARRY CRABB has, over the past thirty years, sought the ways of God as a licensed psychologist. After teaching psychology at secular universities, he spent ten years in private practice. He then reentered academia, but this time in the Christian arena—first at Grace Theological Seminary and then at Colorado Christian University, as chairman and professor. In 1996, while remaining a professor, he left the chair to become the Distinguished Scholar in Residence. He is the founder and president of New Way Ministries, which focuses on bringing healing to the church through encounter, transformation, and community. Crabb has written twenty books, including *The Pressure's Off, Shattered Dreams,* and *Inside Out.* He and his wife, Rachael, have two grown sons and two grandchildren. They live in Colorado.

LIZ CURTIS HIGGS spent ten years as a radio personality before she left broadcasting in 1986 to begin her public speaking career. She is the author of twenty books for both adults and children, including her best-selling titles *Bad Girls of the Bible, Really Bad Girls of the Bible,* and *Mad Mary: A Bad Girl from Magdala Transformed at His Appearing.* Her award-winning children's titles include *The Pumpkin Patch Parable* and *The Parable of the Lily.* Liz and her husband, Bill, live with their two teenagers in Kentucky.

PHILLIP E. JOHNSON is emeritus professor of law at the University of California, Berkeley, where he taught for more than twenty-five years. Prior to this he served as law clerk for Chief Justice Roger Traynor of the California Supreme Court and for Chief Justice Earl Warren of the United States Supreme Court. A widely respected critic of the theory of evolution, Johnson often lectures and participates in discussions around the country and is a leading spokesman for the Intelligent Design movement. He has authored six books, most notably *Darwin on Trial, Reason in the Balance,* and *Wedge of Truth.* He and his wife, Kathie, have three children between them and live in Berkeley, California.

DR. D. JAMES KENNEDY is senior minister of the nearly ten-thousand-member Coral Ridge Presbyterian Church in Fort Lauderdale, Florida. He is founder and president of Evangelism Explosion International, which is the first ministry to be established in every nation on earth. He is chancellor of Knox Theological Seminary and founder of The Center for Christian Statesmanship in Washington, D.C., which endeavors to bring the gospel of Christ to those who hold the reins of power in our government. He is founder of The Center for Reclaiming America, which seeks to equip men and women to work in their communities to transform our culture. He is the author of more than fifty-five books.

Dr. Kennedy's messages are broadcast by television and radio to more than forty thousand cities and towns in the United States and in more than two hundred foreign countries, making him the most listened to Presbyterian minister in the world. Dr. Kennedy is a *summa cum laude* graduate and holds nine degrees, including a Ph.D. He is listed in several dozen registries, including 2000 Outstanding Intellectuals of the 20th Century and International Man of the Year 1999–2000 by the International Biographical Centre in Cambridge, England, and the 1000 Leaders of World Influence by the American Biographical Institute.

JAY KESLER is a former president of Taylor University in Upland, Indiana. During his tenure the school was listed twelve times in the *U.S. News and World Report* survey as one of America's best colleges. He currently serves the university as chancellor. Prior to this he served as president of Youth for Christ, having been with the organization for thirty years. The Council for Christian Colleges and Universities honored Kesler as a Distinguished Senior Fellow in 2000, joining Dr. Richard Halverson, former Chaplain of the United States Senate, and Charles Colson as its only other recipients. Among Kesler's twenty-three books are *Emotionally Healthy Teenagers, Challenges for the College Bound,* and *Being Holy, Being Human.* He and his wife, Jane, live in Indiana and are parents to three children and grandparents to nine grandchildren.

SCOTT LARSEN, general editor of *Indelible Ink,* is a native of the Jersey Shore. He received both his B.A. and M.A. in clinical psychology from Wheaton College in Wheaton, Illinois, where his love for books and reading was ingrained. He currently works in the financial services industry and does some writing and editing work on the side. He has enjoyed coteaching his adult Sunday-school class for the past several years. He now lives in the western suburbs of Chicago with his wife, Mary, and their two sons, Andrew and Tyler.

JOSH MCDOWELL began his speaking ministry in 1964 when he joined Campus Crusade for Christ International. He continues to minister through speaking, a radio ministry, overseas mission and humanitarian efforts, and campaigns such as Beyond Belief to Convictions, which is designed to assist families and churches in equipping youth to stand strong in the face of today's culture. McDowell has spoken on the campuses of more than seven hundred colleges and universities in eighty-four countries to more than seven million young people. He is the author or coauthor of more than seventy-five books, including *Evidence That Demands a Verdict, More Than a Carpenter,* and *Beyond Belief to Convictions.* He and his wife, Dottie, have four children and live in Dallas.

CALVIN MILLER, a native of Oklahoma, has spent his adult life in ministry. He was a pastor for thirty years and is a former professor at Southwestern Baptist Theological Seminary. He currently holds the post of professor of preaching and ministry studies at Beeson Divinity School, Sanford

University, in Birmingham, Alabama. Miller is the award-winning author of fifty books, including *The Singer Trilogy; Spirit, Word, and Story;* and *Into the Depths of God.* He is a much sought after preacher and guest lecturer. He and his wife, Barbara, have two adult children.

J. I. PACKER was born in Twyning, Gloucestershire, England, and attended Oxford University. Upon his ordination in 1952, he was assistant minister at St. John's Church of England in Harborne, Birmingham. For twenty-seven years he preached and taught in the United Kingdom before he moved to Regent College in Vancouver, British Columbia, to become professor of systematic and historical theology. In 1989 he was made Sangwoo Youtong Chee Professor of Theology, and since 1996 has been the Board of Governors' Professor of Theology. He is a senior editor of *Christianity Today* magazine. Among the books he has written are *Truth and Power, Fundamentalism and the Word of God, Knowing and Doing the Will of God,* and the modern-day classic *Knowing God.* He and his wife, Kit, have three grown children and live in Vancouver.

LUIS PALAU, originally from Buenos Aires, Argentina, has long had a passion for evangelism. In 1961 he joined Overseas Crusades (now OC International) to minister to Spanish-speaking people, and in 1966 he held his first evangelistic campaign in Bogotá, Colombia. The Luis Palau Evangelistic Association became a separate ministry in 1978. Palau has organized hundreds of evangelistic crusades and festivals around the world. He is the author of nearly fifty books in both English and Spanish, including *It's a God Thing, God Is Relevant,* and *Say Yes! How to Renew Your Spiritual Passion.* He and his wife, Patricia, live in Oregon and have four grown sons and nine grandchildren.

EDITH SCHAEFFER, the child of missionaries with the China Inland Mission, attended Beaver College in Germantown, Pennsylvania, where she met her future husband, Francis A. Schaeffer. They were married in 1935 and after more schooling and ministry work were sent in 1948 to Switzerland by the Independent Board for Presbyterian Foreign Missions. In 1955 they began L'Abri, a community that welcomed people who were seeking answers to questions about God and the meaning of life. Edith is the author of seventeen books, including *L'Abri, What Is a Family?* and *Christianity Is Jewish.* Widowed since Francis's death in 1984, she lives near two of her children in Switzerland.

LUCI N. SHAW is a renowned poet, essayist, and teacher. Along with her husband, Harold Shaw, she founded Harold Shaw Publishers and served as vice president until Harold's death in 1986, when she became president. She is now Writer in Residence at Regent College, Vancouver, British Columbia, and poetry editor of *Radix Magazine.* In addition to her many writings included in various anthologies, she has written twenty-five books, including *God in the Dark, The Green Earth,* and *The Angles of Light.* In 1991 she remarried and now lives in Bellingham, Washington, with her husband, John Hoyte. She is the mother of five children and has five grandchildren.

JOHN R. W. STOTT was ordained in 1945 and served in various capacities at All Souls Church in Langham Place, London, where he continues to minister. He has been Rector Emeritus since 1975. He was appointed Chaplain to the Queen from 1959 to 1991, and an Extra Chaplain in 1991. As a lifelong leader among evangelicals around the world, he was the principal framer of the Lausanne Covenant (1974), which called for "justice and reconciliation throughout human society." Since 1970 Stott has focused much energy traveling and speaking in the Third World and has established The Evangelical Literature Program and the Langham Partnership International to provide books and scholarships to students and pastors in the developing world. He is the founder and honorary president of the London Institute for Contemporary Christianity. He is the author of fifty books. Some of his most notable titles are *Basic Christianity, The Contemporary Christian, The Cross of Christ,* and *Commentary on Romans.*

JONI EARECKSON TADA is the founder and president of Joni and Friends, an organization focused on ministering to people with disabilities. She received a presidential appointment to the National Council on Disability, on which she served for three and a half years. Her daily radio broadcast, *Joni and Friends,* can be heard on more than 850 stations. She is in high demand for conferences and speaking engagements around the world. Joni has received numerous honors, including being named the Churchwoman of the Year in 1993 by the Religious Heritage Foundation. She has written more than thirty books, including *All God's Children; A Quiet Place in a Crazy World; Heaven, Your Real Home;* and her best-selling autobiography, *Joni.* She and her husband, Ken, live in Calabasas, California.

KENNETH N. TAYLOR is best known for writing *The Living Bible* paraphrase and founding Tyndale House Publishers. Prior to this he was editor for *His* magazine and at InterVarsity Press before becoming director of Moody Press. It was on the train to and from his Chicago office that he began writing the paraphrase that became *The Living Bible.* He is now chairman of the board at Tyndale House Publishers. Dr. Taylor is the author of twenty-six books for both children and adults, including *Stories for the Children's Hour* and *The Bible in Pictures for Little Eyes.* He and his wife, Margaret, are the parents of ten children and live in the Chicago area. They have a growing family of twenty-eight grandchildren and fifteen great-grandchildren.

WALTER WANGERIN, JR. is a prolific writer and storyteller. For fourteen years, beginning in 1974, he served as pastor of Grace Church in Evansville, Indiana. In 1991 he became a professor and occupant of the Emil and Elfriede Jochum Chair at Valparaiso University in Valparaiso, Indiana. He often is asked to speak at conferences and to lecture at universities. He has written thirty-four books for both children and adults, fiction and nonfiction, including *The Book of the Dun Cow, Ragman and Other Cries of Faith, Reliving the Passion,* and *The Book of God.* He lives with his wife, Thanne, on a farm near Valparaiso, Indiana. They are the parents of four children and grandparents to four grandchildren.

DALLAS WILLARD has been professor of philosophy at the University of Southern California since 1965. Between 1982 and 1985, he was director of the School of Philosophy. Among his primary areas of focus are epistemology, the philosophy of mind and logic, and spiritual formation. He is the author of six books, including *The Spirit of the Disciplines, The Divine Conspiracy,* and most recently, *Renovation of the Heart.* He and his wife, Jane, live in Southern California. They have two children and one grandchild.

RAVI ZACHARIAS, a native of India, is well known for his lectures at leading universities around the world—he has spoken in more than fifty countries. For three and a half years he held the chair of evangelism and contemporary thought at Alliance Theological Seminary. *Let My People Think,* his weekly radio broadcast, is heard on more than one thousand stations worldwide, and he also can be heard on *A Slice of Infinity,* his daily radio program. He is president of Ravi Zacharias International Ministries, which has offices in several cities around the world. He has written ten books, including *Can Man Live Without God, Deliver Us from Evil, The Lotus and the Cross,* and *Light in the Shadow of Jihad.* Ravi lives in the Atlanta area with his wife, Margaret. They have three grown children.

NOTES

Foreword

1. Franz Kafka, in a letter to Oskar Pollak dated 27 January 1904. In *Letters to Friends, Family and Editors,* trans. Richard and Clara Winston (New York: Schocken, 1977), 16.

2. See Philip Yancey, *Soul Survivor: How My Faith Survived the Church* (New York: Doubleday, 2001).

3. Alberto Manguel's *A History of Reading* (New York: Viking, 1996) includes a wonderful section about the tradition of readers in Cuban cigar factories of the nineteenth century. The workers would chip in to hire a *lector* who for hours at a time would read aloud while the workers rolled their cigars in silence. So affected were they by Dumas's novel that they wrote the novelist shortly before his death in 1870 and asked if they could name a cigar Monte Cristo. You can still buy Monte Cristo cigars today—in every country except the United States, which bans Cuban imports.

4. See Søren Kierkegaard, *Søren Kierkegaard's Journals and Papers,* vol. 5, Autobiographical Part One 1829–1848, ed. and trans. Howard V. Hong and Edna H. Hong, (Bloomington, Ind.: Indiana University Press, 1978), 335-6.

5. See W. H. Auden, "Thanksgiving for a Habitat," in *Collected Poems,* ed. Edward Mendelson (New York: Vintage Books, 1991), 696.

6. See Richard John Neuhaus, "The Public Square," *First Things,* no. 117 (November 2001): 65-84.

7. Thomas Merton, *Thoughts in Solitude* (New York: Farrar, Straus & Cudahy, 1958), 62.

Introduction

1. Scott Hafemann, "The Argument of Second Peter," presented on 25-27 February 2000 at the 2000 College Church Men's Conference, "Last Things First," Wheaton, Illinois.

2. This statement is quoted often and is consistently attributed to F. W. Boreham, though the original published source cannot be identified.

3. A. W. Tozer, quoted in "Books of the Century," *Christianity Today* (24 April 2000): 92.

4. See also Ephesians 4:22-24; Colossians 3:2; Philippians 4:8; 1 Corinthians 14:20.

5. T. S. Eliot, "Religion and Literature," in *The Christian Imagination: The Practice of Faith in Literature and Writing*, ed. Leland Ryken (Colorado Springs: WaterBrook, Shaw, 2002), 201-2.

6. Philip Yancey, ed. *Reality and the Vision: 18 Contemporary Writers Tell Who They Read and Why* (Dallas: Word, 1990), x.

7. Michele Rapkin, quoted in Steve Rabey, "No Longer Left Behind," *Christianity Today* (22 April 2002): 33.

8. On the benefits of reading good, old books, see C. S. Lewis, "On the Reading of Old Books," in *God in the Dock* (Grand Rapids: Eerdmans, 1970).

Chapter 1

1. Psalm 46:10.

2. Loraine Boettner, *The Reformed Doctrine of Predestination* (Phillipsburg, N.J.: Presbyterian and Reformed Publishing, 1932).

3. Luke 22:31.

4. Jonathan Edwards, quoted in John H. Gerstner, *The Rational Biblical Theology of Jonathan Edwards,* vol. 3 (Powhatan, Va.: Berea Publications, Ligonier Ministries, 1993), 585-6.

Chapter 2

1. Charles Colson, *Born Again* (Old Tappan, N. J.: Chosen Books, 1976), 121, 125.

2. C. S. Lewis, *Mere Christianity* (New York: Simon & Schuster, 1996), 56.

3. In *Thus Spake Zarathustra* (1883–1885; English trans., 1954), Nietzsche's most celebrated book, he introduced in "eloquent poetic prose the con-

cepts of the death of God, the superman, and the will to power. Vigor-
ously attacking Christianity and democracy as moralities for the 'weak
herd,' he argued for the 'natural aristocracy' of the superman who, driven
by the 'will to power,' celebrates life on earth rather than sanctifying it for
some heavenly reward. Such a heroic man of merit has the courage to 'live
dangerously' and thus rise above the masses, developing his natural capacity for the creative use of passion." See Thomas E. Wren, from the essay
"Nietzsche, Friedrich Wilhelm," in *New Grolier Multimedia Encyclopedia,*
version 6.03 (New Haven, Conn.: Grolier, 1993).

4. See C. S. Lewis, *The Abolition of Man* (New York: Simon & Schuster,
    1972).

5. Augustine, *The City of God* (New York: Modern Library, 2000).

6. Augustine, *Confessions,* trans. John Kenneth Ryan (New York: Doubleday,
    1988).

7. Francis A. Schaeffer, *How Should We Then Live?* (Old Tappan, N.J.: Revell,
    1976).

8. Abraham Kuyper, *Lectures on Calvinism* (Grand Rapids: Eerdmans, 1943).

9. Francis A. Schaeffer, *A Christian Manifesto* (Wheaton, Ill.: Good News,
    Crossway, 1981); *The God Who Is There* (Downers Grove, Ill.: InterVarsity,
    1968); *He Is There and He Is Not Silent* (Wheaton, Ill.: Tyndale, 1972).

10. Fyodor Dostoyevsky, *Crime and Punishment* (New York: Random House,
    1945); *The Brothers Karamazov* (Broomal, Pa.: Chelsea House, 2000).

11. Leo Tolstoy, *War and Peace* (New York: Viking, 1982); *Anna Karenina*
    (New York: Modern Library, 2000).

12. Aleksandr Solzhenitsyn, *The Gulag Archipelago* (New York: Harper & Row,
    1973).

13. Aleksandr Solzhenitsyn, *Cancer Ward* (New York: Noonday Press, 1991);
    One Day in the Life of Ivan Denisovich (New York: Penguin Books, 1963).

14. John Pollock, *Wilberforce* (Colorado Springs: Chariot Victor, Lion, 1986);
    Arnold Dallimore, *George Whitefield: The Life and Times of the Great Evan-
    gelist of the Eighteenth Century* (Carlisle, Pa.: Banner of Truth Trust, 1998).

15. John Wesley, *Journals* (Nashville: Abingdon, 1993); John Calvin, *Institutes of the Christian Religion* (Grand Rapids: Eerdmans, 1995); Dietrich Bonhoeffer, *The Cost of Discipleship* (New York: Macmillan, 1959).

16. Theodore Roosevelt, quoted in William J. Bennett and Edwin J. Delattre, "Character, the Old-Fashioned Way," *The Weekly Standard,* vol. 6, no. 46 (20-27 August 2001): 16.

Chapter 3

1. Jacques Ellul, *The Presence of the Kingdom* (1948; reprint, New York: Seabury Press, 1967).

2. George Ladd, Herman Ridderbos, John Howard Yoder, Francis Schaeffer, Tom Skinner, Bill Pannell, Richard Halverson, Tom Oden, Nicholas Woltersdorff, and Stephen Carter, to name only a few, have done much to further the maturation of the evangelical movement in America.

Chapter 4

1. William Shakespeare, *The Life of Henry the Fifth,* in *The Norton Shakespeare,* ed. Stephen Greenblatt (New York: W. W. Norton, 1997), 1.1.1.

2. *King Lear,* in *The Riverside Shakespeare,* ed. G. Blakemore Evans (Boston: Houghton Mifflin, 1974), 1.4.288.

3. William Shakespeare, *Sonnet 29,* in *The Riverside Shakespeare,* ed. G. Blakemore Evans (Boston: Houghton Mifflin, 1974), 1.

4. *Julius Caesar,* in *The Riverside Shakespeare,* ed. G. Blakemore Evans (Boston: Houghton Mifflin, 1974), 4.3.218.

5. *A Midsummer Night's Dream,* in *The Riverside Shakespeare,* ed. G. Blakemore Evans (Boston: Houghton Mifflin, 1974), 3.2.114.

6. *King Henry IV,* in *The Riverside Shakespeare,* ed. G. Blakemore Evans (Boston: Houghton Mifflin, 1974), 1.3.1.57.

7. *Hamlet,* in *The Complete Works of William Shakespeare,* ed. W. J. Craig (New York: Oxford University Press, 1928), 3.2.1.

8. William Shakespeare, *Sonnet 116*, in *The Riverside Shakespeare*, ed. G. Blakemore Evans (Boston: Houghton Mifflin, 1974), 1.

9. T. S. Eliot, "The Love Song of J. Alfred Prufrock," in *Collected Poems 1909–1962* (New York: Harcourt, Brace & World, 1970), 7.

10. Sara Teasdale, "There Will Come Soft Rains," in *Collected Poems of Sara Teasdale* (New York: Macmillan, 1966), 143.

11. T. S. Eliot, "The Hollow Men," in *Collected Poems 1909–1962* (New York: Harcourt, Brace & World, Inc., 1970), 1.11.

12. T. S. Eliot, "Choruses from 'The Rock,'" *Collected Poems 1909–1962* (New York: Harcourt, Brace & World, 1970), 17.

13. T. S. Eliot, "Little Gidding," *Four Quartets*, in *Collected Poems 1909–1962* (New York: Harcourt, Brace & World, 1970), 4.1.

14. T. S. Eliot, "Murder in the Cathedral," in *The Complete Plays of T. S. Eliot* (New York: Harcourt, Brace & World, 1967), 29.

15. T. S. Eliot, "Journey of the Magi," in *Collected Poems 1909–1962* (New York: Harcourt, Brace & World, 1970), 100.

16. Victor Hugo, *Les Miserables* (New York: Barnes & Noble Books, 1996).

17. Elisabeth Elliot, *Through Gates of Splendor* (Wheaton, Ill.: Tyndale, 1981); Helen Roseveare, *He Gave Us a Valley* (Downers Grove, Ill.: InterVarsity, 1977).

18. Major W. Ian Thomas, *The Saving Life of Christ* (Grand Rapids: Zondervan, 1961); Julian of Norwich, *Showings*, trans. Edmund Colledge and James Walsh (1343; reprint, New York: Paulist Press, 1978).

19. Richard Foster, *Celebration of Discipline* (San Francisco: Harper & Row, 1978); Dallas Willard, *The Spirit of the Disciplines* (San Francisco: Harper & Row, 1988).

20. Eugene Peterson, *Run with the Horses* (Downers Grove, Ill.: InterVarsity, 1983).

21. Shusaku Endo, *Silence* (New York: Taplinger, 1979).

Chapter 5

1. Alexandre Dumas, *The Count of Monte Cristo* (New York: Penguin, Signet Classics, 1988).
2. André Maurois, *Alexandre Dumas* (New York: Knopf, 1971), 3.
3. Maurois, *Alexandre Dumas,* 3.

Chapter 6

1. James Gilchrist Lawson, *Deeper Experiences of Famous Christians* (1911; reprint, Uhrichsville, Ohio: Barbour, 2000). Lawson's fine book was first published by The Warner Press of Anderson, Indiana.
2. Lawson, *Deeper Experiences,* 133.
3. See Matthew 6:33.
4. See, for instance, Philippians 3:7-15; Colossians 3:1-17; and 2 Peter 1:2-11.
5. See 2 Corinthians 4:7.
6. Thomas à Kempis, *The Imitation of Christ* (Chicago: Moody, 1984); John Wesley, *The Journal of John Wesley,* ed. Percy L. Parker (Chicago: Moody, 1974); John Wesley, *Sermons* (Nashville: Abingdon, 1991); William Law, *A Serious Call to a Devout and Holy Life* (Wilton, Conn.: Morehouse-Barlow, 1982); Jeremy Taylor, *Holy Living and Holy Dying* (Harrisburg, Pa.: Morehouse, 1982); Charles Finney, *Autobiography* (Minneapolis: Bethany, 1977); Charles Finney, *Revival Lectures* (Old Tappan, N.J.: Revell, 1970).
7. See Jeremiah 29:13.

Chapter 7

1. C. S. Lewis, *The Problem of Pain* (New York: Macmillan, 1962), 118.
2. See C. S. Lewis, *The Great Divorce* (San Francisco: HarperSanFrancisco, 1946).
3. C. S. Lewis, *The Weight of Glory* (San Francisco: HarperSanFrancisco, 1976), 43.
4. C. S. Lewis, *Mere Christianity* (New York: Simon & Schuster, 1980), 121.
5. C. S. Lewis, *The Screwtape Letters* (New York: Macmillan, 1961).

6. Lewis, *The Screwtape Letters,* 11.

7. Lewis, *Mere Christianity,* 170.

8. C. S. Lewis, *The Lion, the Witch and the Wardrobe* (New York: Harper-Collins, 1950).

9. Lewis, *The Weight of Glory,* 45-6.

10. C. S. Lewis, *The Four Loves* (New York: Harcourt Brace, 1988).

Chapter 8

1. Fulton Oursler, *The Greatest Story Ever Told* (Garden City, N.Y.: Doubleday, 1949).

2. Oursler, *The Greatest Story,* vii.

3. Lew Wallace, *Ben-Hur* (New York: Dodd, Mead & Company, 1953).

4. Fulton Oursler, *The Greatest Book Ever Written* (Garden City, N.Y.: Doubleday, 1951); Fulton Oursler and April Oursler Armstrong, *The Greatest Faith Ever Known* (New York: Doubleday, Image Books, 1990).

5. John Calvin, *Institutes of the Christian Religion* (Grand Rapids: Eerdmans, 1995); Augustine, *Confessions,* trans. John Kenneth Ryan (New York: Doubleday, 1988).

6. Fanny J. Crosby (words), John R. Sweney (music), "Tell Me the Story of Jesus," *The Hymnal for Worship and Celebration* (Waco, Tex.: Word Music, 1986), 172.

7. D. James Kennedy, foreword to *The Greatest Story Ever Told* by Fulton Oursler, special edition (Fort Lauderdale: Coral Ridge Ministries, 1981).

Chapter 9

1. John Calvin, *Institutes of the Christian Religion: A New Translation by Henry Beveridge* (London: James Clarke, 1949).

2. D. Martyn Lloyd-Jones, from his dust-jacket assessment of *Institutes of the Christian Religion: A New Translation by Henry Beveridge.*

3. William Cunningham, *The Reformers and the Theology of the Reformation* (London: Banner of Truth, 1967), 295.

4. John Calvin, *Institutes of the Christian Religion,* ed. John T. McNeill, trans. Ford Lewis Battles, Library of Christian Classics (Philadelphia: Westminster, 1960).

5. Alister McGrath, *J. I. Packer: A Biography* (Grand Rapids: Baker, 1997); Alister McGrath, *To Know and Serve God: A Life of James I. Packer* (London: Hodder and Stoughton, 1997).

6. W. Ward Gasque, "Theologian for the Evangelical Everyman: The Life Work of J. I. Packer," *Evangelical Studies Bulletin,* vol. 15, no. 4 (Winter 1998): 1-4.

7. See the foreword to Bruce Milne, *Know the Truth* (Downers Grove, Ill.: InterVarsity, 1982).

8. J. I. Packer, "Fan Mail to Calvin," *Christianity Today,* vol. 35, no. 1, (14 January 1991): 11. Reprinted by permission of the author.

Chapter 10

1. C. S. Lewis, *Mere Christianity* (New York: Simon & Schuster, 1980), 5.

2. Lewis, *Mere Christianity,* 6.

3. Lewis, *Mere Christianity,* 7.

4. Lewis, *Mere Christianity,* 8-9.

5. Lewis, *Mere Christianity,* 21.

6. Lewis, *Mere Christianity,* 28.

7. Lewis, *Mere Christianity,* 34.

8. Lewis, *Mere Christianity,* 35.

9. C. S. Lewis, *The Lion, the Witch and the Wardrobe* (New York: HarperCollins, 1950), 86.

10. Lewis, *Mere Christianity,* 38.

11. Lewis, *Mere Christianity,* 50.

12. Lewis, *Mere Christianity,* 53.

13. Lewis, *Mere Christianity,* 169.

14. Lewis, *Mere Christianity,* 144.

15. Lewis, *Mere Christianity*, 183.

16. Lewis, *Mere Christianity*, 117.

17. Lewis, *Mere Christianity*, 75.

18. Lewis, *Mere Christianity*, 106.

19. Lewis, *Mere Christianity*, 59.

20. Lewis, *Mere Christianity*, 175.

21. Lewis, *Mere Christianity*, 191.

22. Lewis, *Mere Christianity*, 66.

23. Lewis, *Mere Christianity*, 183.

24. Lewis, *Mere Christianity*, 190.

25. Lewis, *Mere Christianity*, 6.

Chapter 11

1. Søren Kierkegaard, *Philosophical Fragments* (1936; reprint, Princeton: Princeton University Press, 1958); Anders Nygren, *Agape and Eros* (1938–1939; reprint, Philadelphia: Westminster Press, 1953); Friedrich Heiler, *Prayer*, trans. and ed. Samuel McComb (New York: Oxford University Press, 1958).

2. Other books that have played a formative role in my theological maturation are John Calvin, *Institutes of the Christian Religion* (1536; reprint, Louisville, Ky.: Westminster John Knox Press, 1960); Martin Luther, *Lectures on Romans* (St. Louis: Concordia, 1972); John Bunyan, *The Pilgrim's Progress* (1678; reprint, New York: Penguin, NAL, 2002); P. T. Forsyth, *The Soul of Prayer* (Bellingham, Wash.: Regent College, 1993); Karl Barth, *Church Dogmatics* (Edinburg, U.K.: T & T Clark, 2000); Emil Brunner, *The Divine-Human Encounter* (Westport, Conn.: Greenwood Publishing Group, 1980), and the *Elmhurst Hymnal*.

3. "Heidelberg Disputation," 28. See Nygren, *Agape and Eros*, 725. I prefer this paraphrase to Nygren's translation.

4. Nygren, *Agape and Eros*, 732.

5. While Kierkegaard emphasized the subjectivity of faith, he was quick to affirm that faith rests on an objective foundation—God's self-revelation in the Jesus Christ of history.

6. Richard Collier, *The General Next to God* (New York: Dutton, 1965), 209.

Chapter 12

1. Mrs. Howard Taylor, *Borden of Yale* (Minneapolis: Bethany, 1988). The 1988 edition is a reprint of the original *Borden of Yale '09*.

2. In using the term "millions of dollars," I have updated the amount into equivalent present-day figures.

3. At age twenty-one, Borden became a trustee of Moody Bible Institute in Chicago. Three years later Dr. James Gray, the institute's president, asked Borden to draft a doctrinal basis for the school.

4. Taylor, *Borden of Yale*, 12.

5. Mrs. Howard Taylor, *Borden of Yale '09* (Philadelphia: China Inland Mission, 1926), 4.

6. Taylor, *Borden of Yale '09*, 5.

7. Taylor, *Borden of Yale*, 38.

8. Taylor, *Borden of Yale '09*, 53.

9. Taylor, *Borden of Yale '09*, 54.

10. Taylor, *Borden of Yale*, 132.

11. Again, I have updated the amount into equivalent present-day figures.

Chapter 13

1. Henri J. M. Nouwen, *The Genesee Diary* (New York: Doubleday, 1981).

2. Henri J. M. Nouwen, *¡Gracias! A Latin American Journal* (New York: HarperSanFrancisco, 1983); Henri J. M. Nouwen, *Clowning in Rome: Reflections on Solitude, Celibacy, Prayer, and Contemplation* (Garden City, N.Y.: Doubleday, Image Books, 1979).

3. Nouwen, *Clowning in Rome*, 2-3.

4. Rick Warren, *The Purpose-Driven Church* (Grand Rapids: Zondervan, 1995); Andy Stanley, *Visioneering* (Sisters, Oreg.: Multnomah, 1999); Henry and Richard Blackaby, *Spiritual Leadership* (Nashville: Broadman and Holman, 2001).

5. Trina Paulus, *Hope for the Flowers* (New York: Paulist Press, 1972).

6. Paulus, *Hope for the Flowers,* 21.

7. Paulus, *Hope for the Flowers,* 147.

8. Paulus, *Hope for the Flowers,* 75.

9. A. W. Tozer, *The Knowledge of the Holy* (New York: Harper & Row, 1961).

10. Tozer, *The Knowledge of the Holy,* 7, 10.

11. J. B. Phillips, *Your God Is Too Small* (New York: Macmillan, 1961).

12. Richard Foster, *Celebration of Discipline: The Path to Spiritual Growth* (New York: Harper & Row, 1978).

13. Foster, *Celebration of Discipline,* 1.

14. Elton Trueblood, *The Company of the Committed* (New York: Harper & Row, 1961); Elton Trueblood, *The Incendiary Fellowship* (New York: Harper & Row, 1967).

Chapter 14

1. Acts 9:3.

2. C. S. Lewis, *The Pilgrim's Regress* (London: Geoffrey Bles, 1933), 7.

3. C. S. Lewis, *The Problem of Pain* (London: Geoffrey Bles, 1940), 133-4.

4. Lewis, *The Pilgrim's Regress,* 146.

5. C. S. Lewis, in a letter to Dom Bede Griffiths, 5 November 1959, cited in *Letters of C. S. Lewis,* ed. W. H. Lewis (London: Geoffrey Bles, 1966), 289.

6. Annie Dillard, *Holy the Firm* (New York: Harper & Row, 1977).

7. Dillard, *Holy the Firm,* 49.

8. Dillard, *Holy the Firm,* 48.

9. Annie Dillard, "The Meaning of Life," *Life* (December 1988): 76.

10. Luci Shaw, *The Angles of Light* (Colorado Springs: WaterBrook, Shaw Books, 2000), 32.

11. Dillard, *Holy the Firm*, 17.

12. Dillard, *Holy the Firm*, 11.

13. See Annie Dillard, *The Living* (New York: HarperCollins, 1992), 3.

14. Dillard, *Holy the Firm*, 35.

15. Dillard, *Holy the Firm*, 35-6.

16. Dillard, *Holy the Firm*, 43.

17. Dillard, *Holy the Firm*, 43.

18. Dillard, *Holy the Firm*, 36.

19. Dillard, *Holy the Firm*, 36.

20. Dillard, *Holy the Firm*, 45.

21. Dillard, *Holy the Firm*, 68.

22. Dillard, *Holy the Firm*, 76.

23. Dillard, *Holy the Firm*, 68, 69.

24. Dillard, *Holy the Firm*, 71.

25. Dillard, *Holy the Firm*, 64-5.

26. Luci Shaw, *The Sighting* (Wheaton, Ill.: Harold Shaw, 1981), 85.

27. Dillard, *Holy the Firm*, 70.

28. Dillard, *Holy the Firm*, 66.

Chapter 15

1. Father Damascene Christensen, *Not of This World: The Life and Teaching of Fr. Seraphim Rose* (Forestville, Calif.: Fr. Seraphim Rose Foundation, 1993). A new edition is scheduled for release with a new title: *Father Seraphim Rose: His Life and Works* (Platina, Calif.: St. Herman of Alaska Brotherhood, 2003).

2. C. S. Lewis, *That Hideous Strength* (New York: Simon & Schuster, 1996).

3. Robert T. Pennock, *Tower of Babel* (Cambridge: The MIT Press, 1999).

4. J. R. R. Tolkien, *The Lord of the Rings* (New York: Ballantine, 1990).

5. I am paraphrasing Disraeli, based on memory.

Chapter 16

1. Major W. Ian Thomas, *The Saving Life of Christ* (Grand Rapids: Zondervan, 1961).

2. Thomas, *The Saving Life of Christ*, 62.

3. Thomas, *The Saving Life of Christ*, 62.

4. See Philippians 2:13.

5. Thomas, *The Saving Life of Christ*, 63.

Chapter 17

1. J. C. Ryle, *Holiness* (1879; reprint, Moscow, Idaho: Charles Nolan, 2001).

2. J. C. Ryle, *Knots Untied* (1877; reprint, London: William Hunt, 1883); J. C. Ryle, *Principles for Churchmen*, 4th ed. (London: Charles J. Thynne, 1900).

3. J. C. Ryle, *Light from Old Times* (1890; reprint, London: Charles J. Thynne, 1898); J. C. Ryle, *The Christian Leaders of England in the 18th Century* (1868; reprint, London: Charles J. Thynne, 1902).

4. Ryle, *Holiness*, 25.

5. Ryle, *Holiness*, 45.

6. Ryle, *Holiness*, 57-8.

7. Ryle, *Holiness*, 82-3.

8. Ryle, *Holiness*, 355.

Chapter 18

1. Dr. and Mrs. Howard Taylor, *Hudson Taylor and the China Inland Mission: The Growth of a Work of God* (Philadelphia: Morgan & Scott; China Inland Mission, 1918).

2. When I speak of the influence of Hudson Taylor's story, I need to include appreciation for Mrs. Howard Taylor for spending seven years writing her book, and for her husband, who patiently sat by her side as she consulted him during her writing. Truly, her books have influenced our lives, and they continue to do so.

Chapter 19

1. Fyodor Dostoyevsky, *Crime and Punishment* (New York: Bantam Books, 1981); Fyodor Dostoyevsky, *The Brothers Karamazov* (New York: Penguin Books, 1993).

2. This is a paraphrase.

3. Søren Kierkegaard, *Fear and Trembling* (Princeton: Princeton University Press, 1968).

4. St. John of the Cross, *The Dark Night of the Soul* (New York: Doubleday, Image Books, 1959).

5. Thomas Aquinas was much lauded for his reliance on reason to defend Christian orthodoxy.

6. Walter Wangerin, Jr., *The Book of the Dun Cow* (New York: Harper & Row, 1989).

7. See Exodus 33:22-23.

8. Walter Wangerin, Jr., *The Orphean Passages* (Grand Rapids: Zondervan, 1986).

9. See 1 Kings 19:12.

Chapter 20

1. Leonard Ravenhill, *Why Revival Tarries* (Minneapolis: Bethany, 1959).

2. Ravenhill, *Why Revival Tarries,* 19.

3. G. K. Chesterton, *Orthodoxy: The Romance of Faith* (New York: Doubleday, Image Books, 1990).

4. Albert Camus, "The Myth of Sisyphus" in *The Myth of Sisyphus and Other Essays* (New York: Vintage International, 1991), 3.

5. Albert Camus, *The Stranger* (New York: Vintage Books, 1954); Jean-Paul Sartre, *Nausea* (New York: New Directions, 1969); Jean-Paul Sartre, *No Exit* (New York: Vintage Books, 1955).

6. See Matthew 18:7 and Philippians 2:12 for further examples of paradox in Scripture.

7. Chesterton, *Orthodoxy,* 58, 61.

8. Jacques Ellul, *The Humiliation of the Word* (Grand Rapids: Eerdmans, 1985).

9. F. W. Boreham, *A Bunch of Everlastings,* or *Texts That Made History* (New York: Abingdon, 1920). The other four volumes in the Great Text Series are *A Casket of Cameos, A Handful of Stars, A Faggot of Torches,* and *A Temple of Topaz.*

10. Habakkuk 2:4, KJV.

11. Boreham, *A Bunch of Everlastings,* 162.

12. F. W. Boreham, "Please Shut This Gate," in *The Silver Shadow* (New York: Abingdon, 1919), 118-9.

13. Wrote Paul in 2 Timothy 4:13: "When you come bring…the books, especially the parchments" (NASB).

Chapter 21

1. Henry Cloud, *Changes That Heal* (Grand Rapids: Zondervan, 1992). Previously titled *When Your World Makes No Sense.*

2. Henry Cloud, *When Your World Makes No Sense* (Nashville: Nelson, 1990), 15-6. All page numbers reference the book's original edition.

3. Cloud, *When Your World Makes No Sense,* 19.

4. Cloud, *When Your World Makes No Sense,* 182.

5. See Luke 13:6-9.

6. Cloud, *When Your World Makes No Sense,* 42-3.

Chapter 22

1. Iain Matthew, *The Impact of God* (London: Hodder & Stoughton, 1955).

2. Larry Crabb, *Connecting* (Nashville: Word, 1997); Larry Crabb, *The Safest Place on Earth* (Nashville: Word, 1999).

3. St. John of the Cross, "The Spiritual Canticle," *Centred on Love,* trans. Marjorie Flower (Varroville, Australia: The Carmelite Nuns, 1983), quoted in Iain Matthew, *The Impact of God,* 10, 23-4.

4. St. John of the Cross, "The Living Flame of Love," *Centred on Love,* trans. Marjorie Flower (Varroville, Australia: The Carmelite Nuns, 1983), quoted in Iain Matthew, *The Impact of God,* 10, 23-4.

5. Henri J. M. Nouwen, *Reaching Out* (Garden City, N.Y.: Doubleday, 1975), 90-3.

6. Larry Crabb, *Shattered Dreams* (Colorado Springs: WaterBrook, 2001).

7. Francis Schaeffer, *True Spirituality* (Wheaton, Ill.: Tyndale, 1971); C. S. Lewis, *The Great Divorce* (New York: Macmillan, 1946).

8. C. S. Lewis, *Mere Christianity* (New York: Simon & Schuster, 1980), 95.

Appendix 1

1. Ravi Zacharias, *An Ancient Message, Through Modern Means, to a Postmodern Mind,* in *Telling the Truth: Evangelizing Postmoderns,* ed. D. A. Carson (Grand Rapids: Zondervan, 2000), 26.

CREDITS AND PERMISSIONS

Murder in the Cathedral by T. S. Eliot, copyright © 1935 by Harcourt, Inc., and renewed in 1963 by T. S. Eliot. Reprinted by permission of Harcourt, Inc.

"The Spiritual Canticle" and "The Living Flame of Love" by St. John of the Cross, translated by Marjorie Flower, copyright © 1983 by The Carmelite Nuns, Varroville, NSW Australia. Reprinted by permission.

For a bonus appendix and other interesting features, including a place to post your most influential books, visit:

www.indelink.com

To learn more about WaterBrook Press and view our catalog of products, log on to our Web site:
www.waterbrookpress.com

WATERBROOK
PRESS